The Essence
of Womanhood

re-awakening the authentic feminine

Susie Heath

The Essence of Womanhood - re-awakening the authentic feminine

First published in 2008 by;

Ecademy Press

6, Woodland Rise, Penryn, Cornwall, UK. TR10 8QD

info@ecademy-press.com

www.ecademy-press.com

Cover - Original painting by Cliff Warner with permission by the artist
Cover Design and Typesetting by Charlotte Mouncey in Times 11pt on 16pt

Printed and Bound by; Lightning Source in the UK and USA
Printed on acid-free paper from managed forests.
This book is printed on demand, so no copies will be remaindered or pulped.

ISBN 978-1-905823-36-9

This book is dedicated to a very special lady, my mother Nancy who brought me into this world.

To my beautiful, precious, amazingly talented daughter Georgina who taught me how to love unconditionally.

To my four wonderful nieces Joanna, Charlotte, Zoë and Rowan who have such a special place in my heart.

To the gorgeous Katie, fiancée of my son Julian, and to the lovely Aliesha - partner to my son Chris - who gave birth to my first adorable grandchild, Ashton, as this book went to print.

Praise for The Essence of Womanhood

What a truly beautiful, thought provoking book. I feel Susie has truly captured what feminism is really about; it's not about us being in competition with men, I really feel that in order to make the most out of our lives, we need to 'find' ourselves again so we feel truly fulfilled as wives, mothers, lovers etc and that the men in our lives feel completely valued instead of being under threat! Thank you Susie for pulling together this book, sharing your wisdom with us and for giving permission to women to re-awaken our authentic feminine!

Louise Heasman - The Athena Network

Hallelujah! Finally, permission to stop trying to outstrip men and be women - and still fabulous! This is a great book for any women caught in the rat race, trying to do it all, be it all and wondering why men simply don't measure up. It's not about being stuck in the dark ages; far from it - it's about being women and letting men be men so we all do what we do best and what makes us happy and balanced. What a revelation!

Lesley Morrissey - Professional Speechwriter and Commercial Copywriter

---

In a corporate world that can make women masculine and when so many women play the role of dad as well as mum, Susie shows women how they can re-awaken their authentic feminine qualities. Susie has poured her heart and soul into this nurturing book and I resonate with her views on emotional release, a natural approach to birth and mothering, connecting with the elements and so many more treasures that show women how to value and express themselves. Susie has come a long way in her own personal healing and growth journey through courageous soul searching and shares her insight and wisdom in this generous book.

Diane Priestley - Journalist and Counsellor

This book is a sympathetic but powerful look at the art of being happy from a female and distinctly feminine perspective. It is packed with practical activities, many based around movement and dance, to help women take a break from striving and achieving in a masculine world and to re-connect with their feminine essence. Susie astutely recognises that masculine and feminine have different and distinct strengths that complement each other. Although I read the book from a man's perspective (being one myself), I appreciate the value in a book that brings harmony and love to relationships. Actually, this is a book men should read; by understanding the feminine, we can come to be comfortable being masculine.

Dr Simon King - Chiropractor and Consultant Kinesiologist

Acknowledgements

Grateful thanks to Dr Tony Quinn from Educo™ whose incredible Mind Mastery system has revealed to me the secrets of the mind, the vitality, joy and effortlessness of self-expression and the essence of who I really am. Thanks to Trond Bjornstad, creator of the Moxi™ Foundation, who gave me the task to bring this book into the world. His words to me were: "Man has done his best to destroy the planet. Only woman can save it now. It is up to you! You have the power." His healing and energy work are quite extraordinary.

For Patricia Martello, my professor of the Biodanza™ system whose love, support and inspirational teaching of dance has enabled me to let go of limitations and to express the real me in the way I move and dance and teach. For Rolando Toro, an extraordinary psychologist and anthropologist from Chile, creator of the Biodanza™ system. It has been a great honour to have been trained by him and through his system, and inspired by so many other wonderful teachers worldwide.

For Tony and Nicki Vee, whose Happy House in Austria and wonderful relationship seminars have nourished and encouraged my feminine essence to come out and play. To Anthony Robbins whose Life Mastery University I completed in 2003, and his lovely wife Sage with whom I had the pleasure of spending some private girly chat time. To Diana Cooper with whom I spent many full moons; to Shakti Gawain, Laura Berman-Fortgang, Deepak Chopra, Wayne Dyer, Dr. John DeMartini and all the other teachers I have studied with who have supported me on my journey.

For my magical friends, especially Kate Mottershead, Karen Kennaby and Maggie Lawrie, and my special coaching buddies who insisted that I get this work out.

For author Allegra Taylor who encouraged my writing from my first tentative steps many years ago. For Mindy Gibbins-Klein who was mid-wife to this book, Nicola Cooper-Abs, my editor, Jane Bidder, my proof-reader, and Charlotte Mouncey who so beautifully and sympathetically did the type-setting and layout of the book for me. For Cliff Warner who generously gave me permission to use his beautiful picture on the cover of this book, and to Richard at The Drawing Room in Chesham amongst whose Aladdin's cave of wonderful original pictures and prints I discovered this gem.

For my wonderful sons Julian and Christopher who have been an incredible joy in my life and who have stretched me in more directions than I ever thought possible.

And last but not least, such tender gratitude for the very special man, who revealed my capacity for loving within a relationship and brought out a radiance in me. You held the peaceful loving space for me to write in nature both in the lushness of an English garden and in the beauty and depth of my beloved second homeland of Greece. And even though we are no longer together and you may never read this book, you always remain in my heart.

Table of Contents

Foreword

This book was conceived some five years ago on a freezing cold, sparkly, frosty February morning while I was clambering onto my roof trying to find the source of a leak. Once again, I found myself juggling the arduous tasks of single motherhood while the female in me was crying out to be heard.

I'd had enough of cutting hedges, dealing with broken lawnmowers, mending fences, endeavouring to be both mother and father to my teenage boys, all the while striving to make some sort of a living and keep my head above water financially.

I'd had enough of fighting my own dragons while men looked on, watching my extraordinary gutsiness and capability to turn my hand to virtually anything; of trying to prove that I was no pathetic, incompetent, needy female, but one capable of holding my own in a man's world. But what sort of female role model was I being for my children? I knew something needed to change.

Many books have been written extolling the virtues of singledom, advocating that life without men is not only possible but **desirable**, that men are expendable, that women are in fact the superior of the species, and we can do everything just as well, if not even better than men in the workplace. So we have watched society dictate that women should dress like men, take on all the roles that men traditionally have held, and prove themselves on and off the battle-field. Yet at what cost? And has it really made us any happier?

Back on the roof, I found where my problem lay – there in the top of my overflow pipe under a wire-mesh, was a silvery-green ball. I put my hand in cautiously and pulled out an iridescent shiny object. T'was a TOAD! The most exquisite-looking creature with not a single blemish on its back. Ah! That I could have kissed him and turned him into a prince! I know they say you have to kiss a lot of frogs, but this was going a bit too far! Heaven only knows how he got there, or maybe he was sent to show me a different ending to the fairy tale.

Balancing precariously on the roof, unwilling to clamber down the ladder with toad in hand, all I could do was lie on the roof and drop him onto a pile of long grass. I watched as my prince loped happily away, and with it my fairytale ending.

Then it suddenly dawned on me:

The answers to all my problems lay within me.

I realised that, for everything that had happened to me, all the upsets, all the trauma, all the excitement, all the joys, all the disasters, there was one common denominator - me. Which meant that rather than things happening TO me, they must have happened BECAUSE of me; that somehow I was involved in the creation of all of these events, otherwise they would be happening to other people and not to me! Somehow I had attracted them into my life. So what was I doing wrong when I experienced the bad bits? How could I do things differently?

Along with many women, I know we tend to over-compensate and over-do things for ourselves, defiantly saying to men, "Look what I can do!" hoping for a response of admiration. Instead what we often receive is a look of bewilderment accompanied by, "Well, you don't need me then!" from the men who now feel they are redundant. We complain that men have ruled the world their way too long with their testosterone-fuelled ways. But what have we been doing? We have joined them and collaborated with them by trying to become pseudo-men – AND IT IS NOT WORKING!

As a child, I was lulled into a false sense of security by fairy tales and myths from exotic lands, where the heroine was always rescued at the last minute by her powerful, strong, lusty hero. Later, I was seduced by fast-paced raunchy black and white cowboy films on TV on rainy Sunday afternoons, and by the romance of Georgette Heyer novels in night-time retreats beneath my teenage blankets. So in adulthood I was waiting and praying that my knight in shining armour would hear this desperate cry from deep inside me, take me powerfully yet gently in his arms, kiss the dirt from my face and take over, so that I could return once again to being a warm, loving, sexy, desirable feminine woman.

Meditating on my toad made me realise that my need and that of many other women, is to reclaim our WOMANHOOD in all our glory and power and magnificence and juicy femininity, by connecting once again with our natural innate feminine instincts.

Before you throw up your hands in horror, thinking I'm advocating that we get back to the kitchen sink, pink and fluffy, once again at the beck and call of our men-folk, Stepford Wives fashion, hold on! Trust me, I am not suggesting a step backwards into drudgery; instead I am inviting us all to accept an enthralling, adventurous challenge and take a giant leap forward into a future which so far we have only dreamed of.

By now you may be wondering if this is yet another personal development book. Fear not. It's actually a **personal UN-development book**. This is not a book about learning more skills and how to become **MORE**, because, guess what, **you are already enough!** In case you didn't read that correctly I will say it again –

YOU ARE ALREADY ENOUGH!

Over the years we have been taught by society, our parents, our religious institutions, our politicians and our educators that we are not good enough. But that's not true. In order to compensate for our 'imperfections' we have striven to be more, do more, have more and become more at the expense of humanity, and in so doing have veered away from our true essence.

This book is about taking away what is **NOT** you, to reveal what **IS** you! It's about stripping away all the beliefs, ideas, thoughts, behaviours, habits and limitations that prevent you from being **who you really are** in essence, which deep down you already know, but have forgotten. We're going to collect together the parts of ourselves that are scattered all over the place, and put them back together –

to RE-MEMBER.

The essence of who you are is encoded in the blueprint of your DNA, and in your ancestral heritage.

Here is an opportunity for us as women to re-awaken, to re-parent ourselves, to reveal who we truly are by being mid-wives to our deep feminine; literally giving birth to our authentic feminine self, to feel like real women again. If you have had years battling your way up the ladder in the corporate market, or years being chauffeur, builder, decorator and general skivvy as you bring up your children, you know what I mean, and you need this book.

This book is divided into seven chapters – like the birth process itself, each involves different challenges, different mind-sets, different ways of working through. In the chapter on Pre-conception, I invite you to remove all the pre-conceived ideas you have which are holding you back from being your true self. Conception deals with a new way of thinking, of choosing what it is you really want for yourself and those you love. Gestation reminds you how to look after and tend the beautiful person that you are and want to be. Labour of Love gives you the opportunity to connect deeply with your body through movement. Transition is that moment of decision – where you choose to go forward or not. Giving Birth to Yourself teaches you how to keep your femininity intact on a day to day basis, while Cutting the Cord takes you forward into a life you may so far only have dreamed of.

We move from the pragmatic gently through to that connection with the innermost part of yourself, your very essence. You will find the book heavily laden with content at the beginning, and as it moves through, becomes lighter and lighter; as you progress and RE-MEMBER your true self, you need less guidance. This is not a book to dip in and out of. Ideally it needs 'doing' from the beginning – it is a process. Throughout your journey you will find stories and anecdotes from my own life and from clients who have generously allowed me to include them to illustrate some points.

Years of working as a personal success coach and a dance and movement therapist, have taught me to explore in great depth what it is like to **feel** totally within my feminine potency. It is this knowingness which I bring to my seminars and one-to-one coaching, and endeavour to impart in this book.

Dance and movement play a key role in rediscovering your feminine self. The Celt in me refuses to be tamed, and little did I know that in the ecstasy of music and the beauty of movement, I would be reborn. Dance is my passion and my joy; without it my life would lack its lustre and sensuality. Yet what I share is neither choreographed nor totally free dance. It is letting my spirit fly in its search for wisdom and understanding deep within the knowingness of my body, while the music permeates my very existence, unlocking an unstoppable energy and power. Here in this book, alongside other exercises, you will have the opportunity to experience some of this for yourself.

I urge you not only to read this book again and again, but also to do the exercises and follow the recipes. So often in a self-help book, we skim through the exercises and say, "Yeah! Yeah! Done that before!" or "I'll do it later!" Trust me, you won't! Other less consequential things have a tendency to get in the way. Unless you take charge of your life, something or someone else will!

On my website www.essenceofwomanhood.com you will find the opportunity to purchase a special relaxation CD designed to accompany this book, and to help you tap into your extraordinary feminine wisdom, so that it once again becomes part of who you are.

This is a work in progress for your life – use the information well. This knowledge, shared with me by some of the greatest minds in the world, is among the most advanced and transformative on the planet. Take the opportunity to live it, and your life and the lives of those around you will change beyond your wildest dreams. If you do not use it, it will just stay as something interesting you once read.

Come with me now on this magical journey of re-creation, where we are remade in the image that Source / Life / God / the Universe / the Great Incandescent Soul herself intended us to be (or whatever you want to call that force which keeps the planets spinning in their orbits). See the miraculous delights to your health, your body, your relationships, your family, your work, your creativity, your well-being, your vitality and your world. See what potential you have for transforming the way we as women are living, along with a fullness of soul.

Are you willing to take this journey with me? I promise you that **life will never be the same again.**

The Journey Begins

Every journey begins with the first step, and so a new life, a new beginning also has a starting point and a destination. For women here and now, this is to reclaim our birthright as powerful, beautiful, compassionate, wonderful loving beings living on purpose, rather than by default.

Buried deep inside many women lies a restless, unsettled feeling as though we have been snatched away from our true course, a hollow anxiety that we dare not express out loud, an underlying urgency that propels us into fear and stress. It permeates our memories, penetrates our dreams and disturbs our waking hours. We know there is something we are failing to do, failing to heed, failing to be.

Pulled and swayed by the ebb and flow of the oceans, by the waxing and waning of the moon, by the rise of the sap in springtime and by the demands of our fluctuating hormones, we have learned to go out into the world and take a stand, immersed in the busyness of human 'doing' rather than human 'being,' while hiding, denying, disowning and dishonouring the depths of who we really are in essence.

There is a weariness and tension which knows no bounds as we fail to listen to what our hearts and bodies are actually telling us. In truth we have lost touch with our instincts and intuition; we have disconnected from our own innate wisdom, our own knowingness.

We continue day in, day out, toiling in the frantic pace of modern life, hoping that things will get better; that if we work hard enough and put enough effort in, then eventually we will be able to rest, to come home to who we really are. Yet life in the 21st century is

1

relentlessly speeding up while we crave peace, harmony, wholeness and balance within our creativity.

Even the extraordinary revolutions of the sixties and seventies did not live up to their promises, while the New Age world of the last decades has failed to give us that deep and lasting feeling of completeness, of beingness. In our urgency and need to transform the way we were, we put our hopes into feminism which brought incredible changes to improve the lot and the awareness of women. But feminism kills the spirit of femininity; for many it has gone too far and we have veered away from our true course.

Through the turmoil of the last century, at least in the Western world, women have won the battle of recognition, acceptance and toleration, and been allowed input into politics and the running of society. But what we have failed to recognise is the cost to us as feminine beings. The tide has swept us away into becoming imitation men, and it has been so insidious that we have failed to notice it happening.

For too long we have been hiding who we really are beneath layers of armour of our own making, as we have set out to conquer the injustices and unfairnesses in the world around us – an armour consisting of us emulating men, dressing like them, using their aggressive language and working their professions to try and prove that we are not only as good as them, but in many cases better.

We have fought with them in courts, in board rooms, on building sites and in war zones to ensure that we have been seen, heard and acknowledged for the courage, strength and endurance which our bodies have not been designed for. This battling however has taken its toll in such a subtle way, creeping up on us in ways which are unimaginable. As we deprive our man of his male function, he feels less needed and therefore less masculine; as we women assume masculine burdens we take on male characteristics to fit the job. Thus deprived of femininity and gentleness as our new male responsibility adds stress, strain and worry to our lives, our serenity vanishes and eventually our families suffer. Does any of this sound familiar?

As a consequence, many of us are living a life of painful self-enforced singledom, or as single parents, lying to ourselves and to others that we are fulfilled, when what we desire above all is to live in our authenticity with those who love us, protect us, cherish us, encourage us, respect us and contribute to our wholeness! We are not supposed to be living in isolation and solitude; it goes against the laws of nature. And perhaps now is the time to admit it. It is time for us to grow up spiritually. As women we have the power to change the world in ways we have not even thought of yet.

Women all over the world are now changing shape, voices are deepening and hormone levels are fluctuating to such a degree that many are finding it difficult to conceive. Marriages seem doomed to fail almost before they start with a divorce rate in England rising to 52%. Men no longer know what their position in society is, or even what it feels like to be in the power of their masculinity, while male sperm count has dropped dramatically for a whole host of reasons.

Obesity is now so prevalent that 1 in 4 people in Western society is clinically obese, while fashion dictates that women look like stick insects. And we are all living with such enormous levels of adrenalin that we are dying from stress-related diseases in our thousands, or existing with dis-ease wracked bodies until medical science comes up with the next body-numbing pill, which takes us even further away from our connection with our natural instincts. We need to come back to who we really are, before the science-fiction stories of mechanical humanoids which feed our fertile imaginations start to become science fact.

Our feminine mystique is being shattered into smithereens by the media as our most personal, intimate bodily functions and methods to rectify them are splattered over cinema and television screens and journals, destroying any mystery or romantic illusions men had about women. This throw-away society has taught us superficiality even in our intimate moments as we have moved from making love to having meaningless sex.

Young women are leaving it so late to have babies as their desire for financial gain and career status have overtaken the wisdom of the body, and many now are simply too frightened of the idea of pain during labour. According to latest statistics, the number of women having natural births has fallen below 50% for the first time.

Caesarean section has risen to a new high, and in certain parts of London is as high as one in three, a sevenfold increase since the 1950's. Many women are opting for 'designer babies' and caesarean section rather than following their natural ancestral energy and instinct in giving birth. And frequently if we do choose the route of motherhood, we are still even in this enlightened age, harnessed into straps supine on our backs to push our babies against the force of gravity, making it a long and arduous labour instead of following nature's exquisite design. Yet our bodies are designed to give birth perfectly!

We are bleeding our female energy into the earth, instead of healing it. It is time for a re-birthing; it is time for us to re-parent ourselves. It is a time to conceive again, to engender, to connect with the fullness of who we really are, to grow, nourish, give birth to and nurture a new way of being, a new way of womanhood that is dynamic and progressive, taking this beautiful planet and us to where we want to be. Women as the givers of life are the ones to do it. We have to show the way.

How we view ourselves and how we view others, dictates the way the world runs. All the earth is craving femininity - we have lived with such intense male energy for many centuries, and the earth is now crying out. We see it in the wars, the bloodshed, the deforestation, the poverty, the lack of respect for nature, the decisions taken at government level all over the world with scant regard for the consequences for future generations and the well-being of the planet; even in our architecture. Technology has soared off into the stratosphere with no thought as to its potentially devastating consequences … and so it goes on.

We have become so fearful and mistrusting of others because we cannot trust ourselves, because we are not being authentic. When we learn to honour ourselves first, and in turn love, honour and trust others, there will be far less greed, killing, lying, deceit or poverty. Our values for the sacredness of life, with a passion for health and vitality, mentally, physically, emotionally and spiritually will instil in our men-folk a greater desire to protect us because they value the feminine and the mother in us, as well as the true masculine within themselves; so much so that they will no longer have the need to fight wars and kill just for the sake of it. Maybe a different reality could show up here on planet Earth. We either have to evolve to this new level of relationship or we will destroy the world.

We need to assert our feminine energy and intrinsic **potency**, not our masculine **force** to make the difference; to continue to develop as the talented, extraordinarily powerful women we have the capability of becoming. We need to do it in a feminine way, using our feminine essence, working from feminine values, not trying to be men in frocks.

Male energy is concerned with completion, with dicing with death, with finishing projects in order to create space for the new – it is the way their body, mind and energy works. In contrast, feminine energy is more concerned with the process of giving life, of fulfilling potential, of creating something more worthwhile, more beautiful, of making things better, of filling the space. We want to show men the beauty of the Universe.

In this male-dominated society, men need us to teach them about beauty, splendour, magnificence, tenderness and love of life, and how to value this in themselves before the planet and humanity suffer any further. Powerful nuturing protective male energy focused together with gentle, intuitive and creative female energy is radiant, extraordinary and brilliant. But we must do it first.

We cannot fully express who we are if we are not in balance. When we put ourselves in harmony with the eternal laws of life, we thus put the world back in harmony. And as the creators of life, it is up to us to bring about this growth, knowing that in our wake is a myriad of others who will be influenced by us. And because we are the mothers of men!

We can inspire everyone we come into contact with to connect again to that life force, that energy, that love which makes us so uniquely human.

Do you dare to listen to the whispers and return to the Source before it is too late? Do you dare to wake up and be a real woman?

Your notes....

Pre - conception

No matter how much searching or personal growth we do, how many crystals or oils we work with, how much incense we burn, how many affirmations we repeat, how much chanting we do or gizmos we have, most of us would admit to feeling we are still not good enough, clever enough, beautiful enough, knowledgeable enough, rich enough, slim enough, young enough, experienced enough or qualified enough. Or worst of all, that one day someone *else* might find out that we are not as good as we think they think we are!!!

We are frightened that we will be found out – found to be a fraud! We constantly think we need to *have* more, *do* more, *be* more, *become* more, *improve* more and *justify our existence* more. We constantly compare ourselves with perfection, and are found wanting. As a result, women are taught to step into their masculine energy and strive harder. We have taken on a masculine lifestyle, with a power of focus that goes against our feminine core, and it is costing us dearly.

But do you know, you've been conned into believing all this non-sense?

This first chapter encourages you to look at your pre-conceived ideas about women and femininity, and to free yourself from whatever may be holding you back from experiencing the flow and dance of life. It invites you to let go of the deep-seated myths which have influenced generations, and change beliefs and thoughts which do not serve you well; those beliefs which prevent you from living at your core energy, so that you can create the life you know deep inside you are here for.

Throughout this book too, I will be inviting you to breathe. Instead of the harsh, angular, short, shallow breaths we have become used to in our hurry-worry world, breathe in as if through your heart, opening up to possibilities, consciously, fully, smoothly. Breathe in love from deep in your belly, involving all of your body. Instantly your body will soften to magnify your feminine radiance, to gentle you back to your feminine core, to connect you with that sense of peace inside.

I wonder if you realise that the woman you are now is the sum total of all your conscious and unconscious thoughts, experiences, beliefs and behaviours together with the actions you have taken as a result of those beliefs? There are choices you have made all along the way which have brought you to where you are now, whether you like it or not.

"Now hold on," I can hear you say. "It's not my fault that this happened or that happened. I didn't choose it."

Maybe not consciously, but at an unconscious level you will be amazed how much unconsciously you contributed to the situations you have found yourself in – but you're right, **it's not your fault**.

Read on and all will be come clearer. The clouds will disappear and you will see that above them, the sun **IS** shining, and the sky **IS** constantly blue.

Who Do You Think You Are?

When we live our lives **as if we know who we are**, all our actions, all our behaviours are performed through that supposition. Can you imagine how it would be if at the end of your life you looked back and said, "But that's not who I really was!" So, if you are living your life as if you are not good enough / clever enough / beautiful enough / wise enough / qualified enough, what do you think your life will look like?

If there are aspects of your life that don't totally bowl you over with excitement and awe and passion and gratitude, then you are not living to your full potential. Let's face it, deep down we all know there is much more to us and to our lives. We just haven't been shown how to access it. Until now! Fear not, it's never too late to change!

We tend to feel safe with our bad thoughts as we get stuck in our own preconceived ideas about the way things are. Yet when you can let go of these sticky thoughts you reveal something else totally. You can start to open to Life the way it is really meant to be.

You can begin to peel away the layers that are holding you back from expressing who you really are - and allow yourself, give yourself permission to connect with your true female self, that energy, that beauty, that magnificence within, and let it shine like a pure-cut diamond. It's time to take off the mask of all the things you feel you have to be in order to be acceptable. It's time to live from your purity. This is not about learning tricks or using feminine wiles to get what you want – that's a false camouflage. The 21st century is about being authentic, coming back to the authenticity in our nature as loving human beings, not about creating yet more masks to hide our true beauty behind.

What Do You Want?

Just stop for a moment, and look around you. Everything you see in the man-made world started as a thought, a vision in somebody's mind. It already existed in thought form before coming into the material. Before bringing anything into your life, whether it's a new business, a car, a frock, a pair of shoes, a kitchen stove, a holiday, a house, a new way of living, a better relationship, a healthy body, you need to decide what it is you really, really, really desire.

Deciding what we want is not always an easy task for a woman, as true female energy is wild, expansive, expressive, pure undirected flow. Can you remember what that feels like? Some of us have never even dared to go there because we get scared of our inner voice, in case it doesn't conform to the way society seems to work.

Often when I ask women what they want, they reel out a list of what they **don't** want. "I don't want another relationship like the last one." "I don't want to be stuck in a job I hate." "I'm sick of worrying about the bills each month." "I can't stand the way my nose/thighs/ breasts look." "I don't want to be on my own any more."

We rarely take time to work out precisely what we don't want and precisely what we do want, so we tend to have to put up with whatever shows up, not realising that we are being dictated to by our unconscious mind.

Let me explain more.

Cave-Woman

Much of our unconscious behaviour goes back to primitive times when we were in our caves. We tended the fire, kept the children safe, made clothes from animal hides with bone needles, created meals from roots and berries we had gathered and stored, and stretched our scant resources for survival. We did all this while keeping hairy mammoths and marauding tribes away, and keeping our man happy, for without him we would have died.

It was a way of life for us to multi-task while our men-folk single-mindedly went off to hunt. Men envy us our ability to do so many things at once, even though they get frustrated at our apparent inconsistencies, so don't chide yourself for doing a hundred things all at the same time - that's just part of the glory of being a woman. Similarly we get frustrated at the way men can only seemingly do one thing at a time, yet secretly envying them their ability to single-mindedly focus.

But our brains are structurally different from men's, and despite all the aeons that have passed, we have scarcely evolved one iota.

In the same way we multi-task, we also multi-think and we multi-process. When we're with our girl-friends, we all talk at the same time and can still follow all the conversations, darting happily from one topic to another totally non-sequitur as we gather as much information as we can about any and every topic. We had to as cave-women, for our continued existence. We needed to know where the food was, where to find the sweetest berries, which nuts and leaves were safe to eat, where the snake in the grass was, where the danger lay, which other woman was a threat to us, our children, our livelihood and our relationship. All in intricate detail. Little has changed!

At some level too, most women are hoarders. Encoded in our genetic make-up, it is a primal need, part of our innate nesting instinct which harks back to those far-flung days. What is it we hoard now we are no longer living in caves? Lots and lots of *stuff* which just clutters up our lives; all sorts of things which may no longer serve us, and are not supportive of who we are right here, right now with what we want to do with our lives and who we want to be. This can be emotions, feelings, objects, people, past hurts, thoughts, songs, memories, injustices, pain, conversations, mementoes, love-letters, old clothes which suited us three sizes ago, even books. Female energy holds onto everything – we feel the energy of everything and find it oh so hard to let go.

When you top up a glass of water that's already three-quarters full, it spills out all over the place. That's the trouble with most of us – we're full up, overwhelmed, so there's no room for change or growth. We need to empty ourselves out before we can fill up again.

On the positive side, our hoarding instinct also inspires us to collect beauty, love, unadulterated energy and freedom with every step, but until we let go of what we *don't* want or need, we can't really shine and show our true colours.

Let Go of What Prevents You from Feeling Peace

When we are born, we know our own magnificence. There is no discord, bitterness or resentment. We are just little, whole and pure. You know how much we love it when we hear a baby laughing and chortling, and how it makes us all smile as we see the total purity and freedom in that new precious being. We ourselves were like that too, before it all got covered up.

The tiniest baby understands love, and expresses it through snuggling close to whoever is giving the love. Even our pets know love in the way we touch them and how we look into their souls through our eyes. That is how we are still meant to be. That is how our spirit is, pure and simple.

As infants, we have twice as many brain connections as an adult, a vivid imagination, a creative mind and a sensitive personality. It takes years of training to change us from that open state to where we are now, years of training the happiness and spontaneity out of us. Strong forces in society, school and home stifle our genius qualities. We're like diamonds that over the years get encrusted with layers of dirt that cover up the sparkliness of our true nature. As newborns, we had only two fears - fear of falling and fear of loud noises. Now it seems we are afraid of almost everything. We make our lives so complicated and lose our intrinsic childlike sense of joy and wonder.

How would it be if you can now let go of what you are not, and just be who you really are? Imagine how that would feel. Then you can have a wonderful open space in which to create your amazing new life. Like a magical spring-clean, it will give you much greater clarity, so you can focus on the wondrous things you really do desire.

Open your mind and empty out the rubbish, all the 'stuff' that has accumulated over the years. Scrub it clean; yes, even the dusty murky corners. Clear away all the junk, all the lies you have been told about not being good enough, so you can reclaim who you really are and what you already know deep, deep within the recesses of your soul. We need to remove the barriers that block love from coming in, and from us expressing it.

So is this brainwashing? Oh yes, absolutely, in the truest sense of the word - washing out the brain. You can free it from all the negativity, conditioning and repetitive patterns of behaviour, worry and garbage that you have taken in throughout your life that keep you from being all that you can be as a real woman.

In order to save you years of your life (did I remember to promise you that you will feel lighter, more energetic and rejuvenated at the end of this book?) we're going to get rid of the junk once and for all. All the barriers that block who you are, all that that has kept you trapped, particularly the things you didn't know that you didn't want! So there will be no **thing**, no **body**, no **situation**, no **excuses**, no **blame** to hold you back - nothing, niente, zip, nada, rien.

At the end of this chapter are exercises for doing just that - but in the meantime, stay with me, because your conscious mind has to understand much more about who you are and how you got here before it will relax sufficiently to allow your unconscious mind to help.

Who Are You Really?

You've got an ego; we've all got an ego. We tend to think of our ego as the part of us that shows off, but our ego also has another side to it. Our ego hangs around with pain, guilt, fear, remorse and lots of 'If only's' and 'Yes but's.' It survives by the juice it gets from all these darker emotions – lots of complaining, comparing, blaming and wallowing in misery. And girls, we're so good at it!

Television thrives on victim-style chat shows, humiliating reality shows and adverts urging us to sue for compensation. People air their grievances with gusto, revel in being the centre of attention for their 15 minutes of fame, and often avoid taking responsibility for their own actions. Ego thrives off it as it gets the attention it so desperately seeks. Even the pain seems worth it; that's its payoff. There is tremendous payoff in suffering and being miserable – it seems to be socially acceptable behaviour these days. Even our love songs convey loneliness and despair, and we listen to them repeatedly so this unhappiness gets recorded and imprinted on our unconscious mind. How we tie ourselves up in our own particular hell!

Your best friend may not know what I am about to tell you, so listen carefully. Although we may not choose the situations that happen to us, consciously or unconsciously we do choose our **response** to whatever situation we find ourselves in.

Everything we do in life, whether positive or negative, has some sort of payoff. The good payoffs make us feel wanted, loved, appreciated, desired and cared for. The not so good ones mean we avoid taking responsibility for our own lives. We then get together with people who share the same pessimistic view as us which just reinforces our negativity; we get sympathy, we apportion blame, we justify our misery, we have ready-made excuses as to why things don't go according to plan and why we have got side-tracked from our life-purpose. If it wasn't giving us some sort of pay-off, we wouldn't do it!

But it's not who you really are!

The Feminine Experience

The feminine experiences all of life. We flow like the ocean, calm and serene one moment, seductive and feisty the next, stormy and overwhelming another. We take little incidents and make them big, we find a gap and we fill it. We magnify to improve things, and yearn to change and beautify where we see potential.

We hold tightly onto the past by reliving it again and again in the present, telling our 'story' to anyone who will listen, rationalising (especially to ourselves) and thereby re-create it in glorious Technicolor in the present moment. So we reinforce what we are trying to get rid of! In other words we are continually creating new memories from all the bad stuff of the past.

Women store every negative event emotionally and can often recall every moment, but the negative stuff gets stuck in our body, in our organs and particularly in our sexual area. What if we learned to manage our memories in a more effective and useful way?

How can I soften the next few questions? But perhaps I just need to come out directly and ask:

Do you like where you are now? Is it fulfilling you?

What pleasure, perverse or otherwise, do you get from being where you are now?

What payoff do you get out of being unhappy?

What payoff do you get out of not having enough money?

What payoff do you get out of being unwell or unfit?

What payoff do you get out of being lonely? Out of not fitting in, out of being uncomfortable, out of looking through lack and limitation? What payoff do you get from overworking and getting exhausted?

Breathe

This might well sound very harsh, but unconsciously our payoff can be quite simply because we just relinquish responsibility – we feel we no longer have to try as we've convinced ourselves that we're no good anyway or that we can't change anything, and that someone somewhere will let us off or feel sorry for us.

When I'm with people who are in survival mode, I'm in my element - I grew up post-war when we had to be very careful with everything. Times were hard, commodities were scarce - that was what I was used to - it became my comfort zone.

Granny used to save bits of soap and press them together to make a new bar, save bits of string, and iron old wrapping paper. My mother would turn collars and cuffs, darn socks and turn worn sheets side to middle, and at Girl Guides I learned how to do the same. My Church used to preach that poverty was a virtue and that God would bless us even more, while the old black and white war movies of scarcity and potential loss made everything seem so romantic and passionately exciting.

When I'm really struggling, I feel virtuous and feel as if I deserve a medal for my thriftiness. It's living on the edge. It feels romantic, like Byron living in the garret as an impoverished but brilliant poet. I can transform a hovel into a palace, and feel really proud of myself. It excites me. It's my pay-off. But it keeps me poor. It's as if I've been seduced by poverty. And when money comes my way I seem to just give it away or lose it. Janie B.

The problem is that our story is actually taking us away from really living; we get so caught up and entranced by the drama and the anguish of our lives, and then watch it like a soap opera as it plays out in front of us. We get morosely seduced by being a victim.

Good things, wonderful things are happening all the time. We should be dancing and singing and congratulating ourselves and each other all the time, yet what people so often talk and grumble about and focus their attention on, are all the bad things and what might go wrong in the future; what I call 'The What-if syndrome.' They create their happiness from being miserable. So if you want to be miserable (and actually, it's quite a good thing for us girls to have a really good wallow from time to time as it releases lots of tension) get a big box of man-size tissues, watch a really weepy movie, be a drama queen, have a good cry and get it out of your system!

Few people believe this, but happiness is the natural order of things. You are valuable and you matter simply because you exist. People who are always grumbling bring about their own misery - they lead a life which justifies their complaints and so their life becomes a self-fulfilling prophecy. People who believe life is wonderful and that they deserve to have a fabulous life often create the situations where they can bring that about. Which do you prefer?

After recovering from a very debilitating illness, I was talking to a young woman confined to a wheelchair with the same problems I had had, and offered to share with her what I had done to get well. She didn't want to know. So then I asked her what she was afraid of if she got well. Her answer was an eye-opener. She told me that her husband doted on her, and was always around to help and look after her. Her fear was that this would all change if she was no longer so dependent on him, and that he might leave. In effect she was manipulating her relationship and her husband's future happiness by refusing to get well.

Life goes by so quickly, like the flash of a firefly, because we're seldom actually conscious and aware enough to notice, experience and appreciate it fully. We're not actually living life, we're existing in our thoughts about life, almost as if we have never allowed ourselves to really be born and experience living fully. We're just sitting on the side-lines and thinking about it instead of participating wholeheartedly.

Woman Talk

Women's talk often sinks to the lowest common denominator; if there's something to moan and complain about, we do. We carry on stirring the misery-pot with our wooden spoons. We've been taught to do so. We conform without realising the true implications of our words, often as a way of self-preservation so that we fit in and so don't stick out and appear different. We tend to talk to everyone about our problems automatically; inside is this lack, and we're looking for someone else to fill the gap and hope they will solve it, or at least let us in to their world.

How quickly can you go from feeling full of the joys of spring, and then meet up with others who are moaning about the state of the world, their health, their children, their partner, their ex, their parents, the weather or their job before your spirits sink? Try the school bus-stop on a Monday morning, or the coffee-machine at work! And on the other hand, those Christmas round-robins, which gloat about their children's success, glowing reports about their house, their work, their husband's promotion, their latest cruise and their achievements which make the rest of we poor mortals feel like hell and totally inferior.

Women teach each other to feel guilt, anxiety and worry. Men may hurt other men – they murder them – but women, we just hurt ourselves! And we do it so well. We think we're going to influence things for the better if we worry about them, but we don't. Worrying is like using your imagination to create something you don't want; we just take ourselves into a deeper downward spiral because negativity takes us into survival mode rather than success mode.

Negative News

When we see bad things going on in the world and it makes us feel awful, we usually try to do something to change it or control it so that we can feel better ourselves. We throw money at it, or we talk about it endlessly. We've been working on that for donkey's years. So is it improving things? I think not. We continually hope that things are going to get better, but hope just keeps suffering in its place because we constantly look to something outside ourselves to solve it. Unless we are willing to change whatever it is inside ourselves that needs to change, we become victims of hope; then when things don't work out, we become hope*less*. It's time to take constructive action.

We live in a world of comparative thinking as we watch TV and read glossy society magazines which sap our energy and life-force, as we compare and contrast what we have or what we do with what's out there. Sometimes this can inspire us to action but more often than not, it causes us pain as there's only a tiny part of our awareness experiencing what is actually happening in our own life. The other part is in our head frantically comparing, contrasting and finding lack, so our mind gets fragmented into little pieces.

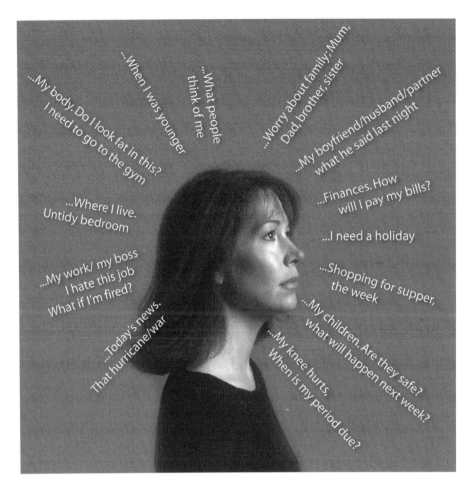

We learn many of our rules of life from our mothers and other women around us: our teachers, our film stars, our icons, even though we recognise at some level that their rules do not work. And when they don't work, what do we tend to do? Try harder, rather than examining the rules we have been living by and changing them.

When is now a good time to stop?

Every time you open your mouth to re-tell your victim 'story,' you re-condition your unconscious mind and instruct it, actually command it, to re-record that same story in your body/mind system. In computer-speak it becomes an embedded command. This may sound really cruel, but it's even crueller to deny what you are actually doing to yourself. Who gives your illness its power? Who gives your poverty its power? Who gives your sadness its power?

So when are you going to give up:

* Whinging about the weather?

* Griping about the government?

* Worrying about war and terrorism?

* Lamenting about lack?

* Interminably talking about illness?

* Sharing your sad childhood saga?

* Blaming your boss, parents, ex-partner, business, life?

* Sabotaging your success?

* Criticising your children?

* Judging other people?

Because it is <u>you</u> that you are damaging! You are starving your essence!

When are you going to start living?

When are you going to allow yourself the life you were born to live?

What will you <u>really</u> allow yourself to have?

All of that stuff you don't want, whether violence, sickness, poverty or pain, guilt, jealousy, frustration, resentment or fear is a by-product of being out of harmony and flow with your real essence, your Source Energy, that Source of well-being, your spirit. It's a refusal to accept the good things in life, albeit not a conscious one. These yukky sticky emotions are like a barometer – they show us oh so clearly when we are not in our flow, because we feel horrid, out of sorts, weepy, grisly … and stuck!

We sort of block off our connection, the same way that otters create a dam to block off the flow of water in a stream. When we complain, judge, justify anything or blame anyone else, we effectively block off the things we really want in our lives, and prevent the good things from flowing in. It's like ordering something really yummy and delicious, and then when the delivery man arrives on our doorstep, we refuse to open the door!

When we focus on what we **don't** want, particularly when we do so with intense disempowering emotions such as fear, anger, annoyance, passion, upset and worry, we get even more of what we don't want. It's like adding fertiliser to the weeds in our garden. We spend more time focusing on what we don't want than we spend time actually living. It's time to **drop** all the false ideas of who you are, **drop** the false preconceptions, **drop** the mask behind which you are hiding, because I promise you revelations beyond your wildest dreams!

How would you like to feel instead? Would you like to feel ecstatically alive, joyful, beautiful, bewitching, dynamic, empowered and delicious? You see, your mind is where the creative power resides, and your body is the exuberant joyful place you can use to take action. When you allow your own mind to shape your destiny, objects of desire, fantastic opportunities and helpful people will start to be attracted to you that will amaze you. They will have no option but to turn up!

Nudges From Life

You know those times when things have gone wrong in your life, when your boss started to criticise you or your relationship wasn't so good? More often than not, this is your life saying to you, "Are you on the right track? Are you being all you can be? Are you doing what makes your heart sing? Are you thinking the thoughts that you love? Are you with the people you love and who truly love you? Are you fulfilling your heart's desire? Are you doing what you're here to do? Are you connecting with your true essence?" The question is, "Do you hear the message?"

If we don't actively seek out those things for ourselves, Life will step in and give us a shove, and it's normally one we don't like. We tend to be very defensive and say, "It wasn't my fault - he did this, she did that!" But by doing so we are giving away our own power. Nobody can do anything to you without your permission on some level. It truly is your choice as to how you respond to whatever is going on around you, and not the event itself.

So what are your thoughts saying to you? Do you say, "Oh, I'm really fed up with this job; it's so boring," and then find you've been given the sack? Do you say, "My husband drives me mad!" and then find he's flirting with someone at the office? Do you say, "I'm exhausted; I need a break," and then trip over your exercise ball and find yourself with a broken wrist? (Yes, this is the voice of experience speaking here!) Do you say, "I haven't got time to stop," and then find yourself laid up in bed for a week with flu?

This is Life nudging you to set you on the road you are supposed to be travelling, which may be to improve your relationship, find work that excites and enthrals you, to exercise before you get sick or rest before you collapse.

Often we fail to notice when we can change things at an early stage while they are still easily manageable. We wait until things become desperate before we're willing to do something about them, existing on a roller-coaster of drama which feels exciting and exhilarating at the time because the intense contrast reminds us we are alive, like hitting your head against a brick wall and finding the intense relief when you stop.

Life whispers at first to us, and when we fail to listen, it gets louder and louder until it's shouting at us. But if we still fail to notice, then sometimes it gives us a very painful and nasty shock indeed before we wake up. This may be the death of someone we love, the diagnosis of a disease or an accident, the end of a relationship or the loss of a job – anything to make us wake up enough to realise that what we are doing is not working, that we have to change the way we are thinking, the way we're behaving, the way we are living.

Breathe

We have been so busy as 'human doings,' that we have forgotten how to connect with our beingness – that place deep within us which organises our every move, our behaviour and our choices. So in order to achieve our outcome here, to reveal the true feminine essence within us and to live our lives with that as our foundation, we need to take a good long hard look at our preconceived ideas about life, and at what is holding us back from achieving what it is we truly want.

If we were living true to ourselves in our feminine energy, we would already have what we desire and a peaceful world to go with it.

The Question of Beliefs

Do you ever wonder why your life is the way it is? Do you wonder what you've done to deserve some of the things that have happened?

A well-known tenet of Buddhism is, "If you want to know your past, look at what you are manifesting now. If you want to know your future, look at what you are creating now." In other words, whatever is happening now is merely a reflection of your old beliefs and habits showing up now. It's like a hangover from the past. It is not reality.

Let me explain. Whatever you think becomes a feeling; feelings become beliefs; beliefs lead to actions; actions lead to behaviour; behaviour becomes habit; habits become thoughts repeated over and over again 55,000 - 65,000 times a day. When we explore what we have been thinking and our belief patterns, we can change what is not supportive of how we want to be. So let's take a look at how we got here.

Although we perceive the same world, we interpret it so differently. Do you know that the only things that can ever hold you back are your own limiting beliefs? Now, what is a limiting belief? A limiting belief is a belief that contradicts what you truly desire in life. That's it! As simple as that!

We tend to think that our beliefs are set in stone and unchanging, whereas in fact your belief is only a thought that you keep thinking, which leads to an unconscious reactive way of behaving. When we re-act (act the same way over and over again) it becomes a thought habit, yet some of these habits are buried so deeply that we are not aware of their existence. It is almost impossible to act contrary to your beliefs, because your unconscious (or subconscious) will not allow you to.

Some of our thought habits serve us really well. For example, if your habit is to think, "Life is just wonderful. I am so lucky, I feel so blessed, I am truly loved. Everything is working out perfectly," these beliefs are in harmony with your true essence, with your Life Source. When you choose (and it really is a choice!) to follow a belief that serves you well and allows your life-force and your energy to flow, you feel invigorated, joyful and enthusiastic; you feel passion, you feel love, you feel appreciation; you feel … well, just great. Sometimes you can even feel a buzzing feeling like electricity flowing through your body as if you could light up a whole city, or you may get a feeling in your solar plexus that feels like hundreds of butterflies are waking up. This is your life-force flowing through you, responding to your good thoughts.

When you notice this, you can learn to choose it more often. When you pursue that connection with your life-force the way you would pursue a love affair, then life will take a totally different course, one of magic and miracles beyond belief, because it is your inner essence guiding you all the way.

Some beliefs really hinder us. How empowering is it if you think that as we get older, our bodies have to decline and become wrinkly and decrepit with bits falling off, accompanied by lots of pain before we die? This belief doesn't serve you, and much research points to the fact that ageing does not have to be like that, but when we believe it, our unconscious mind veers towards it like a heat-seeking missile, locks on, and it becomes a self-fulfilling prophecy.

Beliefs like that hinder us so much, because they resonate at such a different rate from our true essence, our spiritual energy. Every time we hold that negative thought and keep repeating it, we stem the flow of energy that the cells of our body tap into that keep us fit, healthy, flexible and youthful. We literally shut down the body's capacity for rejuvenation, and for producing the hormones and substances that keep us young. And when that happens, we feel horrible negative emotions, the anticipated pains and wrinkles appear and we age very quickly. When we activate any belief that does not serve us well, we feel anger, frustration, fear, defensiveness, jealousy, guilt, insecurity, desperation … and urgency. And then this leads us to take desperate measures, like drugs, cigarettes, alcohol and plastic surgery!

The degree to which you allow your life-force and energy to flow depends on how much you associate with your feelings, and whether they are uplifting or depressing. It is also the degree to which you are connected to your true essence … or not!

The essence of femininity is one of love,

deep abiding generous unconditional love.

Your very essence is love!

So the question you need to ask yourself is, "How do I feel when I focus on this particular thought that I'm thinking now?" And if the answer is, "Not very good," then **whether it is true or not**, it does not serve you well. So you need then to switch your thoughts to something that does make you feel good, and then your 'truth' will shift.

Where Do Beliefs Come From?

We just picked our beliefs up as we grew, and now we cart them everywhere we go like an overstuffed handbag. When you were born, your eyes were like video cameras, your ears like recording devices, and your feelings like a sensor detector. Everything that happened to you or in your environment was recorded into your unconscious mind with no editing whatsoever.

However, as we got older we tended to store the good things as small, insignificant and colourless, and the bad things super-size and in glorious Technicolor. In fact as adults, we store events not as they actually are, but according to our mood and how we are feeling at the actual time. And so when we recall those past events, we filter them through all our present beliefs, justifications, limitations, judgment and childhood conditioning, so it's not what actually happened, but what we **think** happened. Then we re-record the memory based on that. Added to which, because the mind cannot absorb and make sense of all the information available, it distorts, deletes and generalizes according to our belief system. So the memory is not real anyway. Phew, no wonder we have problems and misunderstandings! That's why, when two people describe the same event, it can seem totally different.

Most behaviour gets absorbed into our unconscious minds very surreptitiously from when we are a tiny foetus in our mother's womb to the age of 7 or so. We copy or model the behaviour of everyone around us and because our survival instinct kicks in, accept that this is the way to get through life. This 'conditioning' then creates our 'rules for living,' a blueprint learned from other people, which in turn becomes our own belief system, even if it's untrue or doesn't make sense.

Those very same beliefs have become our limitations; they govern our every move, our every decision. Once our head (our way of thinking) and our heart (our feelings) come together, they create a belief which is far stronger than anyone else's disbelief; and we always act from our belief system. Each belief gets filed into our unconscious mind and we live through that, just like a computer program.

Do you remember as a child feeling you had to change who you were in order to fit in? I remember at a very early age feeling I had landed on an alien planet. While I was enthralled at the beauty of everything, I couldn't understand why grown-ups always seemed so anxious, upset, worried and cross. I realised at a tender age that I had to learn what being 'grown-up' meant if I wanted to survive. I remember watching carefully and copying the behaviour, body language and words of grown-ups around me, and although it felt uncomfortable and made me very sad, I thought that's what I had to do to get love. And I carried on conforming for years, never being true to my real self. When I didn't conform, I was told off for being stubborn. Perhaps that was my spirit reminding me who I really was. In fact, it was only a few years after the end of the war, so there were many things for grown-ups to be anxious about, but unable to rationalise, my unconscious mind had already adopted certain behaviours.

Our parents pass down to us their limiting beliefs which were passed down from their parents' limiting beliefs, passed down from their parents' limiting beliefs, but all with the intention of keeping us safe. That's all it is! We are living with the same belief systems that our Great-great-great-grandparents had some 150 years ago in the Industrial Revolution when times were very different.

We haven't deliberately chosen our limiting beliefs to keep us small and unfulfilled; to cart them around with us and then pass them onto our own children in turn. It's always been about safety and survival, because that's how it was 150 ago and even back in the cave. The main focus was always, "What can I do to keep my children safer? Will it keep them alive?" And we continue to live with the same fears.

Our beliefs drive us in an unconscious way, because we don't realise the power of our emotions. No-one ever taught us that feeling great and happy deep down inside means that it might actually be good for us!

31

It's probably at this point that I need to apologise profusely to my three beloved children for unwittingly teaching them my own limitations. As parents we do what we do out of fear and out of love, because that is what we have been taught in turn. We do the best we can with the resources we have at the time, all with the best of intentions and with all the love and energy we can muster. And in our desire to protect our children from what we have been through, we try to teach them all we know so that they don't have to suffer. Oh the beauty of hindsight!

When I was about seven, I was chosen to present a bouquet of flowers to the Mayor. My mother had spent days and nights making the most beautiful powder-blue voile frock for me with lace trimming, and a full skirt with a large net petticoat underneath which made it stick out like the princess's dress in my favourite story book. I felt wonderful in that dress.

I was standing in front of the mirror in my new frock, just feeling so good inside, when someone came up behind me and told me off, saying something like, "Nice girls don't admire themselves like that. You should learn to be more humble." I felt mortified that I had been caught out doing something wrong when I felt so good and so happy, and really embarrassed and ashamed for having such wicked selfish thoughts. And I thought I was going to be struck down with hellfire and brimstone by the all-seeing punishing God, so I felt scared too.

Being told off always hurt my sensitive little heart. So I learned at a very early age not to admire anything good about myself, to criticise everything I did from the way I looked to the way I thought. My unconscious mind learned to associate feeling good with being punished! But all was not lost. I learned how to change it later on.

The Power of Negative Emotions

Your emotions are purely an indicator of what you are focussing on. They are pure feedback from life. Emotions don't have any power in and of themselves; all of your power is in your choice of thought.

Every time you experience a negative emotion, all it is saying is you're holding onto a fearful belief that is holding back the flow of your real essence and energy. Fear gets you in so many ways; if you feel fear, your mind will have gone to the past because it whisks through its memory banks like the search engine on your computer and comes up with every reference it can find to fear. That's all it is. All negative emotions come from the past, from your 'her-story.' Your past is like a security blanket, something you're familiar with, but what you've done is closed the door to the infinite possibilities of your creative life-force.

Fear is useful when it acts as a natural deterrent to keep us away from things that could harm us – it's that cave-woman instinct coming to our rescue. But inappropriate fear creates a physiological imbalance in your body producing hormones and adrenalin, which in turn set up a whole chain of reactions.

You know the phrase, 'I could smell her fear?' It's true - when we are fearful we send out a fearful message in our vibrational energy, so other people on a similar wavelength are drawn towards us and keep us in that fearful space.

We don't have to fight those old demons of fear and anxiety; just stop feeding them energy with your attention, and instead starve them. Switch your thoughts to something to be grateful for, or which makes you feel really good. In those moments that you focus your attention on something good, solutions will often come to you seemingly out of nowhere. As your negative, agitated thoughts subside and you stop stirring with your wooden spoon, the calmness that comes through you enables you to see with more clarity, and so the fear will lose its power over you. It will just crumble and disintegrate.

It's Your Choice

The challenge is that our minds can only focus on one thing at a time, so we can't guard against the bad stuff and focus our attention on the good stuff at the same time. It's one or the other – your choice! Which one do you prefer?

So therefore the funny thing about beliefs is that they are just that – beliefs, not necessarily the truth. So you don't have to keep holding onto them; just be aware of them. If our awareness is faulty, our actions will be faulty. Every decision we make at any one time is based on our awareness at that particular moment, so if things are not working the way you want, you need to change your level of awareness. Whatever level we are at determines the level of our potential. In other words it either empowers us to, or stops us from expressing ourselves fully.

History and the Power of Myth

Myths abound with regard to women, many stemming from Eve tempting Adam in the Garden of Eden, which through history have led to the burning of women as witches in their thousands, to drowning with ducking stools, to the degradation of female lives all over the world; from Ancient Greece where baby girls were left out on the hillside to die, from China where baby girls were aborted or killed, to terrible atrocities on the African continent. Female genital mutilation is still carried out in certain countries as a right of passage into womanhood for tens of millions of women. And we have had to bear the brunt of this for centuries.

Never underestimate what this history has done for the psyche of us as women. It has seeped into our DNA as we carry the memory of these barbaric events deep within our cells, in our ancestral energy. And even today women are stoned for adultery in certain countries and raped and murdered without thought. This vulnerability contributes to so much of our behaviour, fear and lack of self-esteem at an unconscious level. We feel it more often than we realise.

I Believe...

Here are some of the questions that I ask in my workshops and some of the answers that crop up. When you do these exercises, you may be surprised by your beliefs.

a) <u>What do you believe about women?</u>

For example: women are weaker than men; women have a hard time; women can never earn as much as men; women always have to do everything; women suffer much more than men; women are second-class citizens; never trust a pretty woman; women should stay at home and look after the children; women are manipulative; women need to fight twice as hard to get anywhere etc.

Other questions you can ask yourself along these lines:

What do you believe about men, life, love, health, fitness, sex, wealth, God?

b) <u>What do you believe about being feminine?</u>

For example: feminine women are brainless; femininity means pink and fluffy; feminine women can never make it to the top; you can't afford to be feminine if you want to succeed in the 21st century; you can't be feminine at work or you'll get abused; feminine women get trodden on by more hard-hitting women etc.

c) <u>What self-limiting beliefs do you hold?</u>

For example: If I expose the 'real' me I might lose control; if I show my true feelings I might be judged unfavourably; I have to do it all myself; if I delegate I'll lose control; if I don't do it, everything will fall apart; I must have approval from all the significant people in my life; the nicer I am, the better people will behave towards me; everyone else seems more able to tackle difficult situations than I can; no-one asks for my advice; I never get it right; this is just the way I am – I can't change; I have to be better than others; I'm useless; I'm pathetic; I'm not good enough; I'm only a woman; I'm not attractive enough; I'm hopeless at learning; I'm only one person, I can't make a difference; it's not that easy for me; I've got no choice; I'm not intelligent enough; I don't deserve; I daren't say what I think; I don't matter; my feelings don't count; I'm not loveable; I have to make everyone's life right; I can't cope; I need more qualifications to be taken seriously; I'm not a leader; I'm hopeless at lots of things; I'm not intelligent enough; I haven't got a university degree; if you want something done, do it yourself; if I change, people around me will become upset …

We all will come up with different answers, depending on our personal life experiences and our perceptions. Remember, we see life as WE are, through our own conditioning, not as life really is. My guess is that as a result of asking these questions, you will discover how much you rely on the negative thoughts you have about yourself, your body and your life, and how they mask who you really are. These negative thoughts take up such a lot of energy.

Do you see how they prevent you from achieving what you really want? You may now start to realise that these are just programs, like computer programs, which you have been playing over and over again. They don't contribute to your joy, fulfillment, sexualness, sensuality, serenity, well-being, happiness, self-esteem or femininity.

Whose Belief is it Anyway?

Tracking our current belief system is like going on a treasure trail. Sometimes you will get a flash of recognition: "That's what I was told in Sunday school." "That's what my Mother always says." "That's what I'm supposed to believe if I belong to such and such an organisation / church / political party." "That's what my teacher said when I was 6." Remembering that all our guardians/teachers/parents wanted to do was to keep us safe, now as grown ups these beliefs may no longer be relevant. So now is a good time to let go of ownership of them. They don't belong to you; they are no longer yours.

Ask yourself:

1   What evidence is there that it's true?

2   What exceptions are there?

3   Does this belief increase my energy or deplete it?

4   Is it improving the quality of my life?

5   Is it relevant to this stage of my life?

6   What are the consequences and what is it costing me?

7   What if I choose to ignore this belief?

8   What is a new more empowering belief?

Let me share with you a belief held by one of my coaching clients, and track her thought process. Her belief system was, 'Never trust a man.' Her mother was jilted at the altar, pregnant with Caroline who was subsequently brought up with the idea that all men were untrustworthy.

Everywhere she looked she saw the proof, in glossy magazines, on television, on the news and listening to other women who had been let down. The evidence was everywhere she looked. The problem was that Caroline took this belief into her own relationships, and chose unavailable or untrustworthy men who proved her point perfectly. She saw only what she believed.

When we explored the exceptions to her belief, she admitted to knowing several friends who had great relationships, and even her mother was now living with a really special man. The consequences of her belief meant that she never let a man get close enough to her to find out if she could really trust him, and when things started to get too close, she would run away. Yet all she really wanted was to find the right man and have a family of her own. She suddenly said, "Oh gosh. Is this me doing this? Is it just about my belief? I though it was about them!"

She realised that she had been focussing on the wrong sort of men, and ignoring the good ones who she thought were a bit boring. All of a sudden a whole new world opened up to her, and she started to feel excited and really positive, and couldn't wait to get out there. Once she learned to trust herself, she would bring trustworthy men into her life.

Can you see how a belief can tie you up in knots, while seeing it for what it is can release so much potential?

It becomes almost second nature to take on board other peoples' beliefs about us and live by them as if they were the truth, such as, "You've got to be extra careful because you were very sickly as a child." "You've got your grandmother's thighs." "We've never been rich, and we're happier that way." The permutations are endless.

A teacher told me at 17 I wouldn't get far in life. If I had taken it on as a program, I would not have done so many amazing things. While she stayed in the same school married to her job until she retired, I ventured out and explored the world. But another teacher in my primary school had said that I would be a great teacher in the world. Which belief do you think I chose to hold onto? We need to ask, "Are other people's beliefs allowing me to live my life fully, or are they holding me back? Do these beliefs serve me well?"

I remember my mother telling me when I was a young teen-ager not to let my heart rule my head, so I consciously had to shut my heart down and obey the rules of adults around me in order to survive. I remember how painful that was because I was so sensitive. It wasn't my mother's fault - it was the way she had learned to live in a challenging world and she was just trying to protect me from getting hurt.

Both our values and beliefs can be based in fear and lack, or in faith and trust. So what does it mean by, 'Do they serve you well?' It means are they supporting you and your blossoming life with health and well-being and with what you want to achieve? Are your beliefs helping the world to become more enlightened or less?

Over the years as we mature, our values and beliefs may alter as we move through different phases in our growth and understanding, as we go through our own Eve-olution.

Make contact with that amazing life-force within you – you do matter you know; you really do. Women need to be a vital force for change, so you can't say you're not good enough. If you're saying you're embarrassed, you are denying your essence. If you are obsessed by shyness, inferiority, self-consciousness, you are saying that you don't count. It's cutting into the glorious flow of your life's inimitable essence, like snipping a piece of delicate silk with a gigantic pair of gardening shears. You are robbing your life essence from yourself, which at some level actually affects all the other women in the world at the same time.

Several years ago when I was holidaying on the Greek island of Skyros, a whole group of women came together to sing from Shaina Noll's 'Songs for the Inner Child.' I had never before wept so much in my life. Tears poured seemingly endlessly from parts of my inner self where I had never before dared to venture. The words moved me profoundly and became a catalyst for my change and growth as a woman:

'How could anyone ever tell you, you are anything less than beautiful?

How could anyone ever tell you, you are less than whole?

How could anyone fail to notice that your loving is a miracle?

How deeply you're connected to my soul.'

You'll See it When You Believe It

In the 21st century we are living so much in our heads. In this information age where we are bombarded at every moment with sights, sounds, feelings, tastes and smells, we acquire as much knowledge and information in just one day as our Great-great-grandparents would have acquired in a lifetime. As a result we are in information overload; our minds and bodies are so stressed and overwhelmed with it all and we don't know how to get off the treadmill. This stress affects our female bodies so acutely and throws our hormones out of whack. Thank goodness we are not conscious of it all at once.

The Reticular Activating System

We have within us a special system which allows us to only see the proof of what we believe – it is called the Reticular Activating System (RAS) and works in this way. For example, if you are feeling broody, all you ever see are pregnant women, babies and maternity shops, right down to new-born lambs, ducklings, milk-laden cows, puppies, kittens and trees with bulging buds. The whole world seems pregnant or to have recently given birth! There are thousands of non-pregnant women and people without children, and lots of shops without baby equipment, but all your brain notices is the one thing you are focussed on.

If you go around with the notion that in comparison with you, all other women are skinny, sexy and look like models, then that is all you see. Your brain fails to take notice of all the rest of the women who have normal shapely bodies. Were the skinny women there before? Most certainly. Did you notice them? No, because your mind was too busy absorbing other information. And right now the whole world looks skinny.

If for example you constantly tell yourself, "I'm so unattractive," that's all you will notice. Every glimpse in a shop window or glance in a passing mirror will reinforce your awful belief. You will fail to notice the times people tell you how lovely you look, or the fact that you have beautiful eyes or hair, or gorgeous cleavage, a pretty smile or a sexy dimple. Yet when we get older, we look back at old photos in awe of our youthful beauty, unable to understand why we hadn't taken advantage of that fact at the time.

Similarly if we believe that we are useless, stupid or inferior, our unconscious mind will find millions of ways to show us how useless and stupid we are. Your Reticular Activating system shows you what is uppermost in your mind. It wants to keep you satisfied by proving to you that you are right.

Now you know of its existence, you may like to start noticing more of the things that make you feel really good, really sexy, really feminine, really loved, really loving, really appreciative. Write them down in a journal and invite your RAS to play. You can enjoy looking in this book any time you need uplifting and send your RAS out into the world to find wonderful life-enhancing things for you.

You see, we see what we believe, rather than believe what we see!

Some years ago I was lunching with my dear friend Sandy and bemoaning a decision I had taken which I later regretted. She said, "You can change your mind you know!" I remember saying in shock and horror, "What? Can you say that again?" She repeated, "You can change your mind you know!" Call me daft, but I had been brought up with the adage, "You've made your bed - you lie on it!" It hadn't occurred to me that I had a choice. I wore like a badge of honour the fact that once I had made a decision, I would stick by it. Such is the power of our unconscious belief structure - it rules our every waking moment often regardless of how ridiculous, uncomfortable, illogical and intolerable the results.

I know someone who goes around with a belief system that the world is a terrible place, and that no-one is trust-worthy, so that is all she sees. She fails to notice the beauty, joy and laughter, the goodness and the thousands of wonderful people who are just going about their daily life with good and honest intentions. Everything looks big, dark, dangerous and threatening in her eyes as she unconsciously creates dramas and upsetting experiences, and sees only events that reinforce her belief. She misses out on so many pleasures of life.

Whatever you are willing to put up with is exactly what you will have. Whatever you are open to in life and whatever you are closed to shows up precisely. Instead, if you go around with a belief system that says basically the world is full of good people, and that there is a small proportion that chooses to mess it up, you have a far greater chance of happiness and of creating a phenomenal life.

Your life becomes what you think about all day long. In fact, **you** become what you think about all day long. It's all about where you choose to place your focus. This doesn't mean that you'll be unaware of danger and corruption, only that you choose not to focus your attention on it. When we are tuned into our instincts we will naturally have that awareness.

Louise moved into a pretty market town a couple of years ago. Not long after, she went to have coffee with a new acquaintance, whose house is the most beautiful in the whole town, on the river's edge in an unsurpassed location with stunning views, surrounded by beautiful gardens. Her husband was unexpectedly there and proceeded to talk about how unfriendly everyone was, how boring they were, what a horrible place it was to live and how he hated living there.

In comparison, Louise found the town full of fun, friendly, warm and welcoming people and she loves it there - but then that is how she is! It's all down to perception. It said more about him than about the town. We see what we believe! It all depends on where we choose to put our focus!

Understand that in every moment you are sending out a vibrational energy through your thoughts which magnetises and attracts everything towards you, good or bad. Remember, if you send out a vibration which says you don't have what you want, you will end up getting more of what you don't have!!!

You can change your beliefs in a heartbeat – this is the royal road to a more inspiring, loving life. Once you can relax and let go of all your bad programs and all your limiting beliefs, then your whole life can change. So often women say to me, "But how can I do things differently?" and I say, "Give yourself permission!"

If you find that challenging – and most of us do – on the next page , you will find a certificate of permission to give yourself permission, or you can print it off my web site www.essenceofwomanhood.com. Copy it, sign it, hang it on your wall and carry a copy around in your handbag too, or sign it right here, right now in your book. Look at it every day!

Here in this book we are re-birthing our feminine, re-parenting ourselves in order to bring to the world a beautiful, sensual, strong, healthy, powerful, creative, courageous, feminine woman – **you**. Reclaim your birthright with love and desire, joy, consciousness and deliberation and let go of those old enemies which so sap our strength: fear, lack of self esteem, procrastination and despair. So lighten up, have fun with this process, and see where it may take you.

The Essence of Womanhood

CERTIFICATE OF PERMISSION

This is to certify that I

----

hereby grant myself permission to change my mind to ensure that what I am doing, thinking or believing is serving and supporting my life.

I allow my essence and intuition to guide me in expressing the fullness of who I truly am as a loving, joyful, beautiful, courageous woman.

Dated this day of ---

Expires: ----*Never*---

Signed: --

How Do You Look?

Many things we perceive in life are not actually what they seem. It is always the way we look at them. When we look at life with fear, loneliness, depression or lack, it's just as though we are looking through coloured sunglasses where everything gets distorted. When we drop those limitations and take off those glasses, life becomes full of vibrant and dynamic colour.

> *One glorious sunny day in late Spring, I took my partner to the woods to see the carpet of bluebells which was strewn across the dappled woodland floor. I had seen it a couple of days before and it completely took my breath away. I was so excited to share this beautiful experience with him.*
>
> *I made him shut his eyes as I guided him carefully along the track. When I could hardly contain myself for the sheer beauty of it, I asked him to open his eyes, and waited with baited breath for his response ... Nothing!*
>
> *"Well?" I asked tentatively. "I can't see what you're so excited about," he said. Then I realised he was wearing sunglasses. They had brown lenses, so everything he looked at was tainted with a brown hue, which completely cancelled out the colour of the bluebells. They were just brown stems. So he missed the whole magical experience.*

Your Life is Listening

Your life listens to every word you say. Every word whether spoken or just a thought in your head, is taken into your body just as effectively as if you are writing a computer program; as the adage goes, garbage in, garbage out. The unconscious mind, just like a computer, doesn't analyse or make judgment on the information we put in. It just accepts it as fact.

If you say, "I'm so fat", the computer prints out, "I'm so fat." Likewise your unconscious mind makes sure that every time you see yourself in a shop window or a mirror, all you see is the reflection of a fat person. I used to joke that I could put on weight just by going into the supermarket. My body obeyed – wondrous machine!

"I am…" she said

Every single thought, if reinforced strongly enough with passion, feeling and emotion, goes out into the Universe like a command, and into your central nervous system and unconscious mind at the same time. Every time you say "I am …" it is like a decree, so you have to be very, very careful what you say or think! Pronounce your limitations vigorously enough and they become yours; you take ownership of them. Whether they are true or not doesn't matter – as long as you accept them, that's how you will live your life. Each word strengthens your energy, or weakens it. This is such important information for our lives.

Every single thought is sacred;

every single move you make in life is sacred.

Every move you make

is a commitment to your life.

Even your casual words are very powerful. Because you speak them in a relaxed state of mind, there is no mental block to their manifestation, so they often produce results really quickly.

When we experience failure or lack it's often because of what is uppermost in our own mind. We have accepted unworkable beliefs that are forming our personal world moment by moment. It's time to stop blaming others, face the truth and start having conscious awareness.

The beauty of this lies in the fact that once we have rid ourselves of our limiting beliefs, we will hardly have to make any decisions. The world will unfurl perfectly at our feet.

Recipes and Exercises

In a moment you will find the promised recipes and exercises for getting rid of all your unwanted limitations. You can choose whichever one appeals to you. You may even like to do them all to make absolutely sure you have a real clear out. Think of this like a computer hard-drive defrag, as a mind detox, or even better as a life detox.

How Long Have You Got?

If the thought of doing these exercises horrifies you then find a tape-measure – one of those metal ones is easier to use if you have one. Go on. I'm watching you!

Pull it out to the 82" mark. As women, our average life span is about 82 years, so imagine each year is represented here by one inch. On this scale of 1 – 82, look and see where you are. If you're under 30 maybe it doesn't feel too bad, but if you are over 40 (half way there) or edging nearer the 65 mark, maybe this will be the wake-up call you need.

How much longer do you want to go on living a half-life?

The main thing that stops people having the life they truly desire, is their internal story, so we need to clear out our internal story and give our lives a spring clean. You know when you wash your clothes and you look through the glass door at the front of the washing machine? You may be horrified to see all your clothes swishing around in filthy, dirty water while you were hoping for spotlessly clean clothes. Or when you turn on the garden hose in the spring, you want clean clear water, but what comes out first is a pile of mucky, smelly gunk of old rotting leaves, dirt and wiggly things. That's what we are getting rid of, metaphorically speaking!

The other problem is that - let's face it - we enjoy complaining, we enjoy worrying. It seems to give us a perverted sense of importance. It makes us feel we belong, because everyone else around us is joining in too. It makes us feel right, it makes us feel justified, and it makes us feel as miserable as everyone else! It brings colour of some description to our daily life, albeit grey.

However, it becomes such an ingrained habit that the idea of not doing it any more can be quite scary. What are we going to fill our heads with if all that monkey chatter has gone? Isn't all our grizzly past what has made us who we are? Who will we be without it all? What if there is nothing else there? We make an excuse out of what has 'happened' to us to prevent us from being the amazing women we can be. But can you imagine how amazingly beautiful your life can be when

you can just give it up?

We often keep things so bottled up inside us that they begin to eat us away from inside, and this can be a cause of terrible illnesses. Or we tend to get swallowed up in victimhood, or become passive-aggressive and resentful in our behaviour. As women we need to respond to our feelings and emotions and get them right out of our system, not store them up. Yet one of the main reasons we repeat the same old grumbles and complaints so much is that we don't feel we've been listened to. I mean **really** listened to and heard. There is always someone else vying to have **more** attention, **more** misery and **more** problems than we have, as if we score points for the amount of suffering we are able to endure. That's why hairdressers and nail technicians are so good for us – **they** listen while **we** talk; no-one else seems to have the time.

Thank heaven there is a positive side to discontent; it can act like a springboard to help you jump out to a new way of being. Just know that there is no-one on earth who has escaped pain and loss, suffering and injustices, anger, hurt and disqualification. And there is also no-one on earth who has experienced your life the way you have. To acknowledge it and to be heard is such a blessing and such a relief.

This exercise will give you a chance to really get stuck in, to complain, moan, wail, rant and rave about anything and everything which has ever bothered or upset you. Like a pressure-cooker releasing all the steam, this is a marvellous opportunity for you to let go of all your pain, hurt, anger, anguish, bitterness, worry, annoyance, guilt, judgment, envy and negativity that is bottled up inside you, and which totally wrecks the chemistry of your precious body. Trust me; I know it's lurking there in some deep, dark recesses of your mind!

Let me remind you that we women store most of this emotional stuff in our sexual area, and our best way of relieving this tension is through a full body orgasm. But as most of us have not been taught how to surrender fully to such a glorious experience (it will be in my book on relationship!) we express the stress instead with the rest of our body, with our voice, our actions, and our logic. Then the Wicked Witch of the North appears, and she is us! We've been brought up not to express our feelings properly, either to ourselves or to other people, particularly as we're supposed to be 'Sugar and spice and all things nice.' So it's time to stop being nice, just for now.

I'm going to give you a gift to help you get rid of all the beliefs, opinions, people, attitudes, circumstances, situations and all the limitations that have been holding you back from living the life you truly want, because that is **not who you are at core level**. They are just thoughts - they occur spontaneously, they are just an illusion; and thoughts don't mean anything per se. The only meaning they have is the meaning you give them. Thoughts by themselves have no power, but thought accompanied by intense emotion is like a direct order or a prayer to the Universe. However once you have got rid of these limitations, you will never want to focus your energy and attention on them again.

Remember, we did not come into the world in this way; we came in as pure sacred beings, whole and perfect. There is a Divine reason for your existence which goes beyond our human understanding.

You either love Life and living or you love wallowing in anger, self-pity, sadness and negativity. You can choose to stop suffering any time you want – it's merely a pattern that you have kept repeating over and over again. It is your choice, moment by moment, how you feel. You can choose to play small, or really live. Make the commitment here and now to return to the core essence of who you really are.

This will be the first and last time you will ever need to do this because as you read through this book, your understanding will take you to a much deeper level and connect you to that intuitive loving part of you that may have been hiding for a while.

Government Health Warning

These exercises could seriously improve your health, your well-being and your happiness, so don't use them unless you have really had enough of the bad stuff. After this you will have no excuses!

Recipe for Ranting

Ingredients

2 hours, a willing friend, a quiet space, an overwhelming desire to change, willingness to play full out, box of man-size tissues (girly tissues just aren't big enough for this job!) fresh drinking water, phones turned off, 'Do Not Disturb' notice on the door and fresh air from an open window

Method

Find a willing friend (ideally another woman) who is prepared to totally listen to you without judgment, without comforting you, without correcting you. You may be tempted to do this with your partner, but be aware you may have to bear the consequences if you do! You have a pretty good idea what's in your head and your memories, so choose wisely!

Have an agreement beforehand that whatever passes between you will remain totally confidential. When you do this, it gives your friend permission to do the same herself another time. So it will become a great gift for her too.

Ask her to keep her arms unfolded so you don't feel as if you are being criticised, and to stay **with** you, focussed **on** you, there **for** you. Whatever you come out with, prime her to just say gently, "Tell me more. What else are you mad about? What else makes you angry? What else makes you want to quit? What else really hurts? What else are you sad about? What else do you hate? What else isn't fair? What else are you no longer prepared to tolerate? What else?" She is there to encourage you to keep on, to tell you that you are doing fine and that it's all OK. You don't have to justify anything you've said, nor need it be even discussed again.

Then go for it – just let rip. Get rid of all the 'stuff' you carry around with you.

Like this:

"I hate my job, my thighs are so big, they're disgusting, and Chris at the office is such a bitch and I'm fed up with the way Roger leaves all his clothes all over the floor every morning as if he expects me to clear up after him, and I work so hard and I'm frightened I'm going to be made redundant and I never thought being a mum could be so hard. I'm so sick of smelly nappies and baby talk I want to talk to a real human being, I'm so fat I hate it, I never have any money, my boyfriend just doesn't understand me, and … and … and …

The more you go on about what really bugs you the deeper you'll get.

I'm frightened about terrorists… I'm scared we're all going to die … I can't afford to pay the bills … and my kitchen drives me mad … we haven't had sex for about three months and I want a baby and I think Steven may be having an affair … I'm so sick of worrying… I'm angry that my mum died – how could she leave me? Then I feel awful for being so selfish while people are dying all over the world … and I'm scared my credit card will be rejected … and I feel guilty because I'm enjoying myself again even though my husband only died 3 years ago… and my father beat me when I was a teenager … and I think my son is on drugs … sometimes I just want to run away and I feel I'm a terrible mother… I was sexually abused when I was 9... I've got this pain in my breast and I'm too frightened to go to the doctor about it in case it's cancer… my best friend's got cancer and she's been given 6 months … and the dog's got ringworm and the cat's got fleas … and I was caught speeding last week … and the washing machine's broken down…. and I've got a report I have to get finished by Wednesday…. and my computer keeps crashing … .and…. and … and when I was 13 this man …. and I stole from a shop when I was 8… and I had sex with my friend's boyfriend … .and when I was at school … .and when I was little … .and when my kitten got run over … .and you wouldn't understand what I've been going through … no-one will understand … and it hurts so much and I can't stop thinking about my husband~~~my children~~my work~~~my friend~~my mum~~~my dad~~~my brother~~~my mortgage ~~~my bills ~~~my illness

Don't be ladylike about any of this – it is not about being

NICE~REASONABLE~LOGICAL~INTELLECTUAL

~KIND~LOVING~CHARMING~

It's about letting go! Whatever comes into your mind, whatever grievances, don't judge yourself. No thinking, "I can't say that." Just get it out. Be in your element like a tropical storm. Be fully in the flow, no matter how ghastly or ridiculous or petty the stuff that comes out. Dump the whole lot out.

Even if you are in floods of tears, don't stop, not even to wipe your nose or you will get distracted. Just keep on letting go, knowing you are being listened to, not being judged by anyone. Really dig down and get rid of all the things you've been bottling up for all your lifetime.

You need to do this exercise as if it's the last time you will ever be allowed to complain or moan or be a victim again.

Because…………....… guess what?

It is.

You need to do this exercise as if your life depended on it.

Because……….....…… guess what?

It does!

Find the conflicts in your life and decide, "No more; this is not how I'm going to live my life." Don't just sit there – get in there, move your body, behave like a 2 year-old having a temper tantrum. We've not been taught the value of this, or been given the opportunity to behave like this since we were little, so chances are you may find it challenging to get the hang of it at first. But once it starts it's like a torrent. Play full out, no holds barred. Release all the intensity, the passion, the hurt, grief, frustration, fear, anger, disappointment, sadness, resentment, pain. It's OK; it's all OK. Your friend is there to make sure you come to no harm, and that you feel listened to and really heard.

Woman comes into her own during a rant. Ranting is where you let it all hang out. If you need to thump cushions, stamp on the floor or yell, go for it.

When you are completely emptied out, congratulate yourself for the courage you have shown in doing this, drink lots of water

So how does it work? It's like going on the Internet – type in a word and the search engines go on the rampage and come up with thousands of results based on your input. The female brain is similar in that once you start ranting, it goes spiralling off in all directions connecting with any previous occurrences or situations that are similar. It rummages through all the files in your computer-like brain until it comes up in a rush with the whole lot. Probably not in any rational or logical order, because hooray, you're a woman! We think differently from men. We are much more detailed and link up in our heads in a different way, which is what makes us so fascinating!

If what you come out with is very mild and if you only keep going for 5 minutes, then **start again** - you're not doing it properly! You must have more than 5 minutes of complaints unless you're an angel with exceptionally clean wings. You have to just let rip with everything and anything – what your teacher said when you were 6, what your big brother did at 14, how you cheated at school, where you lied, where you were jealous and so on.

Everything that has ever bothered you needs to be heard. It is so freeing when you realise what you have been carrying around all these years. What do you dare not admit to? What needs to be said that you are afraid of saying? What is so silly and petty that you dare not even voice? Say it. The truth really does set you free.

These areas of control need to be released; events and people have been occupying rent-free space in your head for long enough. Elimination of something from your life is always an indication that something better is on its way. So you need to end the repetition of these limiting thoughts. Chances are you may alternate between floods of tears and laughing your head off because this rant is so liberating to do, and it's so freeing to be heard without someone else trying to calm you down, commiserate with you, stop you, fix you or try to get one up on you by telling you their own sorry saga.

Remember none of this is available for discussion – it's just about releasing it. So often we try to force new things into our lives when we've not made any room for them. Here you are clearing space. Holding all this stuff in makes us sick, ill, drained and unable to function properly. Like wind, better out than in - ooh, very unladylike!

You may feel exhausted afterwards or exhilarated with relief that you haven't been struck down by a bolt of lightning, or the sky fallen in on your head like Chicken Likken. What sheer light-headed bliss - being listened to without being judged, fixed or told off!

Now go and do something really nurturing for yourself. Have a warm hug with your friend, have a delicious bath or a shower, buy yourself some beautiful flowers, go have a massage, lie in the sunshine and snooze. You deserve it.

Queen of the Castle

Nearby where I live stand the ruins of an old castle where I sometimes take my female clients to rant. The walls have been there for nearly a thousand years and have withstood anything that has been thrown at them. They have seen centuries of war and fighting, grief and pain, peace, joy and love. My clients let rip here and rant and rave, yelling and shouting and running around like children releasing their 'stuff.' Where once these walls put up a defence, now they just stand there almost with arms outstretched and absorb all this pain, all this heartache into their amazing stones with no judgment, while I am there to witness. (Thank goodness we always seem to have the place to ourselves.) We all need witnesses to our lives. Once we feel we have been heard, once we feel we have said it all, the sense of peace that comes in is extraordinary.

The point of all this is that you never, ever, ever want to take this 'stuff' into your life again, into your relationships, into parenthood, into your work, into the cells of your beautiful body.

Rather like peeling an onion skin, more layers can come up which cause tears. So if there is anything still lurking in the depths, I suggest you do the next exercise.

Recipe for Spring Cleaning Your Mind

<u>Ingredients</u>

At least 3 hours of time to yourself, a pad of paper, coloured pens or pencils, fresh air, fresh drinking water and maybe an apple or other fruit (do not do this under the influence of alcohol or drugs of any kind)

<u>Method</u>

This is like a rant on paper. Write out all that's been bothering you without stopping - old hurts, memories, grudges, anger, intolerable behaviours, grumps, bad decisions, grief, annoyances, and grievances.

What won't you tolerate in your life any more? What have you had enough of?

I'm angry that ... I'm frustrated about ... I'm hurt about ... I feel guilty about ... I'm disappointed ... I'm sad ... I'm ashamed ... I'm disgusted ... I'm shocked ... I'm frightened ... I hate ... I can't stand ...

Keep writing ... keep writing ... all the horrible gunky stuff that has been festering inside you for so long that you have not dared to express, things you don't think it's right to say, things you feel if someone knew about you they would never speak to you again. All the pain, damage, abuse, slights, memories which you have stuffed down deep inside – let them out, get them out, like vomiting them onto the paper with no judgment, no opinion as to whether you are supposed to feel this way or that way, no "I can't possibly write that," or "I shouldn't be thinking this," or "I thought I'd got over that," or "That's pathetic." If swear words come up, let them. Use language you didn't know you possessed without putting in the bleeps or the asterisks. No holding back. No censoring. Tell it like it is. This is not the time to be ladylike or polite – it doesn't mean you're bad, just that you're having a cleaning session exactly the way you'd clear out a blocked and smelly drain. This is about getting rid of everything that is not the real you.

Dredge it all up from the depths and get it out of you. Keep breathing as you may find some of what comes up surprises you, shocks you, even horrifies you, but that is what you have been carrying around for all your life so far. Don't stop, let it pour out on paper with no editing, no dotting 'i's or crossing 't's. Just let it flow.

Keep breathing

We women are wild, passionate, stormy creatures who have sat on our feelings and emotions for so long, often with no one around to hear or acknowledge them. You only have to look at some of the heroines we admire on film to know that when they spark with fire and passion and feistiness, we sit up acknowledging that we too have that inside us. How too we long to be able to let rip! Remember Scarlett O'Hara from 'Gone With the Wind?'

The more you write, the more liberated you will feel as you can now express what is truly in the depths of your pain – AND IT'S ALL OK. Don't judge yourself for having any of these feelings no matter how unpleasant they may sound. Just write all over the page, in the margins, everywhere. Now turn the page upside down and write all over what you've just written so you can't read any of it. This is not a record to be kept for posterity. Pour out whatever you are feeling - just keep the pen writing, don't look up from the page and don't stop the flow.

If you feel stuck, put on some music which makes you weep so you can really get in touch with those emotions. Enter that vale of tears and let them out – sob, wail, cry and shriek. We often keep them so bottled up but our tears are full of amazing healing chemicals. You need to **really** empty out so all those negative emotions have been expressed.

If you find you're not empty, delve deeper and find out what it is. You need to take some time over this process to get deep enough.

While men have been brought up not to show their more tender and vulnerable feelings, many women have been brought up not to express any anger because 'Nice girls don't do that.' (Please don't write in and tell me of the exceptions - I know they exist!) What we do typically is exchange hurt thoughts for angry ones, but hurt is not the core emotion. It's not healing for us expressing hurt when we really feel anger, and it leaves us either feeling misunderstood, or still pent up, feeling that we can't move on. If you don't express your emotions fully you will not be fully alive, and we've been taught to hold it in. Unhappiness comes from being incongruent with yourself and your deep needs.

When you think you have finished, go deeper still and allow your unconscious mind to bring up anything else. Keep asking yourself, "What else? What else hurts me? What else haunts me? What else am I angry about? What else am I jealous about? What else am I frustrated about? What else am I still grieving about? Who else did I really love that I haven't confessed to? What else still rancours? What else pains me? What else daren't I admit?" Ask the questions over and over again until you are really emptied out. Then put your pen into your other hand and carry on writing. You may find that this hand says very different things as it accesses a different part of the brain.

Put crudely, this was like verbal diarrhoea. All the stuff you have just written **is not who you are**. It is what has **prevented** you from being who you really are all this time. Now it's out, it doesn't have to be inside you any more, devouring your feminine energy.

Do not read what you have written – it is no longer relevant. It belongs to the past, to the former you, and need no longer concern you. Close that door, turn the key and never bother to go back there again. It has helped you on your way to being who you truly are and it is time to let go of it.

For many women, the relief of getting all this out is enormous. They never realised they were carrying around so much guilt and pain, not only over major events in their lives, but seemingly insignificant events also. We get to see, express and acknowledge all that is holding us back from getting on with our lives. Can you see how we hold these grudges against people, partners, parents, family members, teachers, church, society and people in authority? We carry them around with us all day and all night, twenty-four hours a day, seven days a week, and we wonder why we cannot get on, or why our mind is never tranquil.

The interesting thing is, most of what causes you anguish is to do with your response to other people, where the real you is hiding behind the mask of your personality. All that energy tied up with other people's stuff. How it distracts you from dealing with what is actually happening in your own life, and how well you have been taught to do this! And you will start to see the pattern that you have played over and over again, just in different guises.

Once acknowledged, these thoughts need never trouble us again unless we choose to give them renewed energy. How would we do that? By thinking about them and focussing on them. It would be like paying a fortune to go back and see a film you hated over and over again. Who in their right mind wants to focus on pain and hurt and deprivation? In their wrong mind yes, and many of us do, but it's not an intelligent choice. It doesn't make our lives happier, healthier, more prosperous or more loving. This is the chance to get rid of it all for ever, to say, "I've finished with all that suffering." A clean mind inside is the only way to be happy, and isn't happiness what we all really want?

Farewell to the Past

Now take your pieces of paper and scribble all over them as if you are scratching a CD till no word is left visible. You are wiping out the pain and the hurt of the past.

It is over. It is done. It is just a story. It is not who you are.

What follows may sound completely daft, but it's incredibly transformative, so just humour me and go along with these ideas. They are very powerful. The more you play full out here, the more satisfying and life-changing it is.

Find a shoe box to represent a coffin, or make a box out of paper. Put your writing inside, and any old unwanted letters, photos and any old memories you no longer want. Now seal the lid, and write 'Rest in Peace' on top. Find some flowers to decorate the lid, even if it's just daisies from the garden, and give your 'old stuff' a send-off funeral fit for a Queen.

Do it in glorious style and splendour! You can even create a proper service with a song, a hymn, readings and poetry if it inspires you, and play some suitably funereal music. Light a fire in the garden or safely in the fireplace, and ceremoniously put the 'coffin' on the fire and release it with gratitude, giving thanks to all those thoughts and memories which no longer serve you.

"Thank you for being in my life and for teaching me

what I had to learn.

I lovingly release you forever."

What, gratitude for all the pain and hurt? Yes. After all, these thoughts have been with you for so long they are almost a part of you. They don't need to be denied, they need to be honoured for the part they played in your life. Yes, because they have brought you to where you are now, this strong, powerful, tender, loving, sensual mystery of womanhood on the brink of being ready to acknowledge and reveal the truth of who you are. Without that contrast, we would not know what it is we truly want in our lives.

Penny, my client, cried her way through a box of tissues but she was amazed and astounded by what came out. "It wasn't the first stuff that staggered me, the stuff I knew I was upset about, but all the other things that were hiding behind my present pain. I remembered things I hadn't thought of since I was a child. It was like blowing up a dam - all this muck came crashing out, all sorts of tiny little grievances that I just didn't realise were still affecting me from years ago, like I'd crammed them away in a cupboard and shut the door without looking at them. No wonder I always felt on overload with all that stuff running around my head. Burning the papers was amazing - I felt lighter than I had in years. Brilliant. And the pain has gone."

You can also do this with any old emotions you no longer want to have, any old habits, behaviours, repetitive thoughts or a love affair which needs completion. My ex-husband and I created a ceremony like this together beside the river when we were working on resolving our differences before we parted. It was a very transformative, healing, moving and loving evening.

Fire is very cleansing – it transmutes. Like the phoenix rising from the ashes, it creates space for a new way of being. Feel the calm and cleanness as the flames burn away all that is preventing you from being who you really are. Allow the tears to come – these old habits of self-pity and blame have been a part of you for so long, it can be a wrench to let them go. Know that each time you do this exercise, you are letting go of all the things you **don't want** in order to make room for the things you **do** want.

If making a safe fire is not an option, tear up the paper into tiny little bits and flush them down the toilet with absolute gusto. This is a powerful tool for handling these old useless trains of thought, particularly for difficult issues which need resolving. **You** are not hate, anger, grief, annoyance and hurt. Those are just thoughts which you have focussed your attention and energy onto.

The ego has learned how to live off negatives. From birth until about the age of 2, there is a hormone in our little body and in our mother's body called oxytocin, which ensures her unconditional love for us. Sadly this wears off about two years after birth, when we hear the first dreaded "No," and from then on, we hear far more "No" than "Yes." Our ego then learned how to live and survive through worry, fear, scare tactics and negativity. But lucky you! You now know how to give it all up.

Afterwards, stretch, jump, dance, hop, move anywhere to shift the energy in your body. You may want to go for a walk and be in nature, and then have a luxurious bubble bath with candles and soothing music. Drink lots of water and have as early a night as you can. Be gentle on yourself – you've just had major surgery!

17 Seconds Away

Holding on to bitterness and hurt is only a thought program, like a computer program, and thoughts in and of themselves have no power, only the power we attach to them – provided you only think that thought once. If you keep thinking the same thought over and over again and imbue it with emotion, then it sprouts wings and flies off to do your bidding.

Do you know it only takes 17 seconds for a thought to become active, to grow a neural pathway in the brain? Then each time you re-think that thought, it goes zooming down that same neural pathway until it has formed a well-worn channel, like the Channel Tunnel. These thoughts than become very powerful like angels with beautiful wings, or horned demons with a three-pronged fork, according to whether they are **con**structive or **de**structive.

If you hold a negative picture in your mind as to what you **don't** want, your dominant thought reinforces that negative situation into your memory so you keep experiencing it over and over again. Like a computer, your mind is literal in translation. It doesn't try to work out what you really want; it just goes with whatever you put in. So if you don't like a particular situation, 'Cancel it and let it go, yeah sister!' (For those of you too young to remember, this is a line from the song 'I'm gonna wash that man right out of my hair!' from the film 'South Pacific') Say "Cancel, cancel, cancel!" or "Delete, delete, delete!" and replace the bad thought with the thought of something you really like. Trust me here – this works!

Anytime we see something as a threat, it's only because we are feeling insecure; and when we are insecure everything threatens us. Because for so long you've been holding onto the idea that other people are responsible for you feeling bad, it can be a bit daunting to let go of that idea. But nobody else can change their behaviour enough for us to not feel threatened. It is not about them; it is about **you**. Everything is about you. It always is. Everything is about the way **you** are focusing your attention and energy. You can't change past events no matter how hurtful or painful they were, but you **can** change how you now choose to feel about them.

Our natural feminine state is one of pure love but when we take on a personality of fear and anxiety, it drains our energy not only from our own lives but also from the whole world. Can you imagine what effect each of us has on the rest of humanity? We are all one, part of the One Song, the Uni-Verse. What affects one of us affects all of us; so the beauty of this is when we contribute to ourselves, we contribute to the whole. When we let go of this stuff that troubles us, our serenity affects everything and everyone around us, like the beautiful ripples on a pond. You do matter. You do make a difference.

Must Not Haves - exercise

Now you've cleared out what you no longer want from your past, sit down quietly for an hour or so and write out a list of your 'Must Not Haves.' For example: "I must not have a partner who yells at me, I must not have low standards for my life, I must not have a dirty home, I must not have people around who do not support me, I must not have a job I hate…"

This is not about moral judgement or what other people say you shouldn't have. It is about what you are no longer willing to tolerate in your life. You need to have clarity as to what you **don't** want in order to discover what you **do** want.

The Dance of Transformation - exercise

Oh how I love doing this. We've cleared out our bad memories, but all that emotion can get stuck in our muscles, our skin, our cells, our molecules. Colonic cleansing is fantastic and believe me, really clears out all the old unwanted waste. Massage is wonderful but these are both where things are done to us, rather than us participating fully in our own cleansing. Exfoliating in the bath with delicious oils and salts is invigorating but doesn't go deep enough. But this dance moves me in a way that gets me out of my head and intimately connected with my core.

Read through this exercise before you start.

Do this exercise accompanied by some special music. I use 'On Earth as It is In Heaven' by Ennio Morricone, taken from the film 'The Mission.' You will be able to download the music from the internet.

Ideally stand with feet slightly apart and with your knees soft, so you are steady and balanced and your energy is grounded. If necessary you can do it sitting or lying down. Gently closing your eyes and keeping your mouth half open (this relaxes all your internal muscles down the central core of your body) beginning with your head and hair, start to peel off all the outer mask of who you no longer are. Sometimes I do this really gently stroking my skin; other times firmly pressing and pulling quite hard as if I am peeling off a mask like an actor in a play, or pulling off tight rubber gloves or a wet-suit. I need to feel it going into my muscles and cells, so it is not a massage or a caress.

Release each layer into an imaginary pile in front of you, pulling the mask off your face … your neck … your arms … your hands … your breasts … your back … your buttocks … your sex … your legs … your feet … every part of you as if it has been stuck on you for years.

Keep breathing

After the music has finished, gently rest your hands on your chest and feel your heart beating. Now slowly open your eyes, gather that imaginary pile in your arms and release it out of the window for the Universe to deal with, or if you have an open fire, put it on the flames.

The relief afterwards is glorious, and it leaves me with a delicious sense of wonder at my own life; I feel completely renewed as the stuck energy is removed. Sometimes I will do this if I have been on the underground in London as other people's energy can easily get stuck on us; it's like a shedding of a skin that doesn't belong to you. Try it – it's amazing.

What Do You Say to Yourself When No-one's There? - exercise

For the next two days, without judging yourself, write down all the bad or negative thoughts you are thinking about or saying to yourself. Please, really I urge you to do this and see what you are saying out loud or inside your head. This is really important because the way you talk to yourself shapes your life.

Ok, I confess, I have heard myself say, "Stupid woman. What's the matter with you? What are you doing? For goodness sake why are you so useless? How can you have messed up again? What's wrong with you? Why can't you get it right?" and other such endearing things. I wouldn't talk to my best friend like this, so how come I'm talking to my precious self in such a way? (If you say you never talk to yourself, you're telling little white lies!!!!! I can see right inside your head!)

Once you see your pattern of self-talk, throw it away and resolve to be kinder, gentler, more loving, more encouraging to that special person in your life, because if you aren't, how do you expect anyone else to be?

Spiritually we are unbelievable creatures and so full of love, yet we talk to ourselves in such a derogatory way. Who is doing the thinking? Whose program are you running?

Look things squarely in the face and realise this is not who you **are**; this is how you **behave**. This type of thought suppresses your spirit and squeezes life out. We make the thoughts look real and we look after them, feed them and nurture them like favourite plants in the garden, but in fact the thoughts are killing you. They are like voracious weeds.

It's not doing you any favour to listen to your negative thoughts. We treat them as if they are important and really they are not, they are just passing through. So dig them out by the roots like nasty old weeds, particularly the clinging bind-weed (repetitive negative thought) which wraps itself around you and literally chokes the life-force out of you.

Learning to Say "No" - exercise

Women are great people-pleasers, and the idea of saying "No" to someone may be quite challenging for us. We like to appear to be nice, to be indispensable, and to help others before ourselves. It's a behaviour wired deep within our psyche, purely as a survival mechanism.

Every time you focus your attention on upsetting or distressing reports in newspapers, on television, or listening to other people's troubled sagas, you are giving them energy and adding to their pain as well as actually including them in your own energy frequency. You are not contributing to the solution. Remember, whatever you give your attention to grows, good or bad. You create an energetic attachment to whatever you focus on. So when you pay attention to something that makes you upset, fearful, embarrassed or not feeling worthy enough, it keeps it in your potential as well as theirs, and blocks off the energy you need for your personal growth, health and creativity.

Nothing is going to change in your life until you say "No" loudly enough to what you **don't** want in order to evoke an exultant "Yes" to what you **do** want, so that you then can turn your loving attention toward the "Yes." When you tell the Universe exactly what you are not prepared to put up with any more, it will listen. Otherwise you are sending mixed messages. It is all about you making up your mind and being single-minded instead of double-minded. It's about wrapping all of your mind around what you really, really desire and not allowing any part of your mind to be left over to disagree or say the opposite.

How many of us have said, "I'm not putting up with this any longer," then we give in? If our head and our heart are divided we can't get results. We need to be congruent; your head (your thoughts) need to be aligned with your heart (your feelings) and aligned with your sexual energy (your potential for action and creativity). It is our Holy mission to do what makes our heart sing. That is where the word holistic comes from – whole, Holy, holistic.

Practice saying "No" very quietly, then increase the volume bit by bit until you are shouting the word "No" at the top of your voice. (You might like to play some loud music so the neighbours don't come rushing in, or warn them in advance!) Use your arms and hands to express your rejection of what you do not want, to push away what is no longer acceptable to you and to your life. Now decrease the volume of your voice bit by bit down to a whisper until you can say "No" authoritatively, confidently and quietly.

As I travel through this wondrous journey of life, I understand that we need to have experienced what we **don't** want in order to be able to choose and be discerning about what we **do** want. We need to have experienced the bad in order to choose the good; to have experienced the dark in order to appreciate the light. We need the contrast in our lives otherwise everything would be a monotonous grey colour. Be grateful for the "No's" for without them we would not be able to decide on our "Yeses". Like a sword being tempered in the flame and then plunged into freezing water, we have to go through challenging times in our lives to create the strength of who we are. Then it's time to release them, and focus on the best.

Once you have mastered this, you will never again have to say "No." Instead, only say "Yes" to what you **really** want in your life and focus only on that.

Saying "Yes" to Life - exercise

Now try saying "Yes" to Life – first whispering, then progressively louder and louder until with the greatest of glee you are prepared to be all you can be, opening your arms wider and wider to embrace all the good that life has to offer. I appreciate the fact that this may sound like that orgasmic moment in 'When Harry Met Sally,' but that makes it even more enjoyable and fun. Now bring the volume down until you can say "Yes" with joy, determination, gratitude and excitement. And now practice whispering "Yes" seductively! Mmmmmm! Well done!

The Hot-Air Balloon - exercise

Imagine there is a giant hot-air balloon in the middle of the room. Accompany this exercise with some fast-paced music, (I use 'End Titles' from Blade Runner by Vangelis) and closing your eyes imagine that you are going from room to room in your home, collecting all the things that you no longer have use for – things that you have not looked at for at least a year, things which you do not absolutely adore or that no longer give you pleasure, things you have grown out of or that you have no sentimental attachment to.

Allow the music to empower and inspire you as the tempo swells and grows. As you stand there, gently open your eyes and actually physically mime collecting all those unwanted things and throwing them into the basket of your balloon. You need to really use your body here. In your imagination take things off shelves, out of drawers, from the loft, the garage, your wardrobe, your car, your handbags, your school reports, your filing cabinet.

Now clear out the people who are not supporting your life. We all have people in our lives who rocket us to the stars or who sink us like stones, so put the baddies in the basket – head first or feet first: your boss, the tax man, the noisy neighbour, yes, even your mother-in-law can go in too. Be assured that you are not harming any part of anyone you pop in the basket; it is just your negative attachment to them you are removing, and you will be amazed that they don't bother you so much in the future.

Now put in any left-over beliefs, thoughts, habits, memories, fears, bad relationships and limitations which you just discovered are holding you back from being who you really are. Throw away unkind remarks, fat thighs, spots, grey underwear, lack of energy …

Do this with style, dramatically, with great glee. I have had clients and students laughing and crying as they have done this, rubbing their hands with delight, and manically chucking things and people in. It's so good. Actually feel the weight of what you are putting in – let your body feel every action, every move.

At a certain point, the music increases in intensity and you know it is now time to cut the cords that keep the basket tied to the earth. You can either untie them or use an imaginary golden axe to chop through the ropes. Now once again WITH GRATITUDE for their presence in your life, what you have learned and the choices that you have made as a result of these things being in your life, watch the basket rise up and fly out through your ceiling. See it in your mind's eye going up... up... up... higher and higher. Look out of the window now and see it going further and further away... soaring among the clouds... until it becomes a tiny, tiny speck in the distance... and then...finally ... gone!

Now you may be ready for a glass of champagne. Celebrate!! Cheers!

Clearing the Clutter - exercise

When you've done the emotional side of clearing your clutter, the material side is often much easier. Maybe now is a good time to go through your drawers, wardrobes, bookshelves, attic, garage, your handbags, your purse, and throw away or recycle any things which are not enhancing your life. De-junk your life! If you need an extra hand, call one of the excellent clutter-clearing coaches to support you in your mission. You will feel simply amazing afterwards!

Empowering Beliefs - exercise

Now take the old beliefs you had and create something more empowering out of them. Give up your old ideas and be willing to open to new ones. The faster your energy is moving, the more important it is for you to release those limiting beliefs. What can you say instead?

1. Take three of your old beliefs that hold you back

2. Write out a more empowering belief

3. Now create a way of expanding your comfort zone in this area

4. What will you now say to yourself?

5. What will NOW be like when you comfortably hold this new belief?

6. How will your behaviour change/ your results change?

Old Belief 1	Old Belief 2	Old Belief 3
New empowering belief	New empowering belief	New empowering belief
New comfort zone	New comfort zone	New comfort zone
New self-talk	New self-talk	New self-talk
What will <u>now</u> be like?	What will <u>now</u> be like?	What will <u>now</u> be like?
New behaviour/new results	New behaviour/new results	New behaviour/new results

Professional Help

If you are struggling with some very deep issues in your life, I recommend that you find some appropriate professional help. These are some of the sites I recommend. Rather than telling your 'story' over and over again which in fact just reinforces all the issues into your cells like a tape recording, **Co-counselling** (www.co-counselling.org.uk) gives you the opportunity to just get rid of all the emotional stuff in a few sessions. You can rant and rave and yell and get it out of your system rapidly – far better than lying on a psychoanalyst's couch for 20 years.

Life-Coaching (www.noble-manhattan.com) takes you from where you are now to where you want to be rather than wallowing in the past and reinforcing the problem. It rapidly helps you to find the habitual behaviour pattern with which you have been running your life so you can literally transform it.

Regression Hypnosis and NLP (Neuro-Linguistic Programming) (www.tophermorrison.com) (www.changeintelligence.com) will take you rapidly back to the point in your life where a behaviour pattern originated, which may be a traumatic incident, an event or even as simple as an overheard comment which can affect the whole of your life. Releasing that quickly and easily can transform your life in just a heartbeat.

Emotional Freedom Technique (EFT) (www.emofree.com) and some other similar therapies are enormously useful to free up your energy.

Little Gems

✳ Look for the solution rather than the problem

✳ Face challenges with a clear mind free of anticipated negative interpretations. They have no power and life energy unless you give it to them.

* Worry is a choice. Life supports us only if we let it. You are never powerless unless you think you are powerless

* Life is like a mirror – it reflects back to us whatever image we present

Whatever you are putting your attention on,

past, present or future,

actively seek out that which feels good.

So we have removed many of the blocks which prevent us from living in our female essence. You have done the hard part now. All the rest is plain sailing. There may be times when you need to return to this chapter, but for now let's move on to the moment of conception.

Your notes....

Conception

Now we know what we **don't** want in our lives, it's time to conceive what it is we **do** want. Simple really, because it is often the opposite of what we do **not** want!

You have a choice here; in fact, you always have a choice. If you want to go back to pick up those horrible habits and old belief systems that you've just thrown out, you can do so – but it will be like rifling through a smelly old dustbin collecting all the little scraggy ends that no-one else, let alone you truly wants, and you might as well stop reading now.

If I get very excited when I read something, then I know my personality, my ego, is responding. On the other hand, when I feel myself letting go, almost sinking with relief into the understanding, surrendering to it while a deep sense of calm settles upon me, then I know my soul or spirit is welcoming it with open arms. There is a knowingness of truth at the deepest level. So as you read, start to notice the energy change in your body. Feel it beginning to slowly light up like a glorious sunrise. You will have greater clarity and understanding, a calm knowingness as you find yourself nodding and agreeing as the realisations sink in. Then you will know you are on track to realising who you really are.

This chapter is about conceiving what it is you really want in your life, not what others want or expect from you, but going on your own treasure trail of discovery to uncover your deepest desires. It talks about male and female energy and helps you see where you are spending most of your time. It shows you the power of your thought and how you can use it to create what you really want in your life. It gives you the opportunity to dream, to really dream.

Still with me? If so, I pay homage to the essence within you, and trust you will stay the journey.

The Act of Creation

Today we are going to employ all the forces of the Universe to create what we truly desire so that we can bring it into being. Conception is an act of creation, an act of absolute love, the most powerful and beautiful force in the Universe. The Universe started, so it is said with a big bang, and if you'll pardon the pun, so did you! Life is the merging of two Universes, the union of sperm with an ovum, the fusion of male and female, of Yang with Yin. There is an awesome sense of unity behind the manifestation of life.

Imagine a microscopic egg containing all its potential for growth being sought out and literally bombarded with millions of sperm, each determined in its vitality to penetrate the outer shell and become the catalyst for growth. Yet only one is successful. Within seconds of fertilisation, the cells divide again and again, and thus is the beginning, the genesis of your existence.

Out of all the millions of possibilities, it is **you** that has been created and generated. There is a whole lot of sperm and ova that didn't make it, that aren't reading this book, that aren't here right now. The chances of you being born were zillions to one against, yet how often do we appreciate that our arrival on this planet is nothing short of a miracle? In fact **you** are a miracle.

Creation whispered a prayer –

you were the answer.

Life took its first breath –

and the promise was born.

That promise was you!

And there is no one in the whole of the world, no one in the whole of the Universe among those zillions of stars and planets and life forms, quite like you. No-one looks like you (unless you are an identical twin or triplet) no-one has your voice, no-one walks, talks, or thinks exactly the way you do. You are unique! How extraordinary!

So there is no point whatsoever in comparing yourself to anyone else because there is no comparison! Yet in that uniqueness, we also share a common bond, a connection as human beings, as living creatures which binds us together on this small round spaceship called planet earth, as it hurtles through space.

The Perfection of You

A few years ago I went to visit Gunther von Hagens' BodyWorlds Exhibition in London which displays the anatomy and physiology of the human body. While very controversial at the time, for me the exhibition was enthralling, shocking, beautiful, distressing, amazing, horrifying and awe-inspiring all at the same time, reducing me to tears at some points and opening my eyes with absolute fascination at others. What struck me most was how individual each person is.

The display that took my breath away was of the central nervous system. This above all was the most exquisite masterpiece I have ever seen, an intricate interconnecting weave like a loose lacy garment of nerves feeding and nourishing every part of the body. It was so beautiful and almost ethereal in its utter perfection, and completely transformed the way I looked at life. The most powerful computer fed by the most powerful minds on the planet could not engineer anything as remarkable as that. Absolute exquisite perfection!

Now here's a thought. Whatever your religious convictions, put them aside for a moment and consider this. What if, as the wise sages of old tell us, Life / Energy / the Divine / Universal Intelligence / God Force / Goddess / Universal Life Force / the Great Incandescent Soul, whatever you like to call that energy, that power that is greater than us that most of us feel or at least have some awareness of, has designed and created us with perfection? What if we have inside us the same attributes, abilities, powers and potential as that very Life-Force itself?

Alternatively you can choose to believe that your existence is just an accident of evolution, and that our bodies are just biological adaptations due to our instinct for survival. But at the end of the day, which belief gives your life more meaning? Which belief makes you happier? Which satisfies you at core level? Which one gives you the life you truly desire? Because we only get one chance (this time round) and this is it!!!

And because, after all, it is only a belief!

What if we are not inferior, unworthy creatures who have to strive to be perfect? What if we are already perfect, and what if we believed it? What if we are gods and goddesses in embryo, an expression of Life wanting to express itself in all its glory? What if we have all that in us and we are not using it, but instead preferring to believe all the clap-trap about being inferior, about needing to be more, about needing to earn grace, needing to become worthy?

Can you honestly imagine a Creative Force designing something imperfect or inferior? So try this on for size. What if we really have everything inside us that we will ever need, only the majority of us are just not living up to our potential? What if all we have to do, instead of striving to become more, is just uncover our enormous latent possibilities and who we really are at our core essence? Can you imagine how that would change the way we behave and change the way we see life?

The problems come when we start to interfere with our perfection, when we start to distort it by failing to recognize who we really are through modesty, guilt, feeling unworthy, self-criticism, inferiority, our conditioning, lack of trust in ourselves, listening to others' ideas of how we should be and so on, all of which leads us to be less than we are capable of being. And we women are particularly susceptible to this.

Beautiful Womanhood

What are the beautiful attributes of a woman? In my workshops, women have come up with:

Sensual, loving, warm, dark, passionate, like juicy fruit, wild, seductive, tender, powerful, curvaceous, moist, compassionate, flexible, delicious, surrendering, intuitive, emotional, deep, encompassing, like a flower bud, caressing, secret, smouldering, honouring life, reliable, dependable, truthful, earthy, voluptuous, sexy, warm, soft, open, embracing, fluid, bowing and bending, seeking equilibrium, strong, beautiful, thoughtful, funny, with a quiet hidden nurturing side that is at the centre of our feminine nature. And yet at the same time, she can be mischievous, childlike, frivolous, petulant, saucy, wilful, playful, one moment a harlot, the next moment the lover, the teacher, the healer, the mother.

All of these and so much more are within us, but how often do we let the world and those we love see all these parts of us? This is both our strength and our vulnerability, but it is not until we share this magnificence of who we are with the world that the world has the opportunity to change.

As Marianne Williamson says,

"As we let our light shine,

We unconsciously give other people permission

To do the same."

We are so different from men - thank heaven! What a beautiful contrast. Aren't we fortunate to have the diversity of maleness and femaleness? When we remember our feminine nature, truly remember it, we become well-rooted, strong and enriched, as it gives our creative spirit the chance to soar and be free.

Tired of Fighting Dragons!

How many of us are truly living at this magnificent core of our feminine essence? Woman's natural state is to feel vulnerable all the time, but because we are scared to let go of control and allow a man to take care of us, our fear makes us behave in strange ways instead of using that vulnerability to generate something even more beautiful, even more powerful, and to be our real selves.

Many of my female coaching clients come to me with problems involving relationship, sex and intimacy, lack of confidence and self-esteem, health issues, weight problems, career challenges and stress. Almost always, it comes down to the same thing – they are striving in their masculine energy and it is just too much. Penis envy? I think not! Perhaps it is time to return that part of the anatomy to where it belongs!

Sadly most women under 40 have been taught 'Never rely on a man,' yet many women secretly admit that they too are tired of fighting dragons. How we long to have real men to take responsibility for some of our decisions from time to time, so that we can be in the power and flow of who we really are as women. And if at this point you are screaming, "No, that's not what I want," I don't believe you!

Let's explore this a little further. When we look at masculine (Yang) and feminine (Yin) core energies, we can see how special our differences are, and how superbly they are designed to work harmoniously together.

Yin /Yang Energy

This ancient Chinese Tai-chi symbol from the Taoist tradition represents the balance of male and female energy. Yin is the female energy - the dark, hidden, internal, just as our sexual organs are hidden away. Yang is the male energy - the light, warm, visible, the external, just as his sexual organs are outside and visible. Yin is empty, secret and cold wanting to be filled and is represented by the earth; Yang is hot, full of passion and is represented by the sun.

With no harsh dividing line between the male and female energies, they are complementary rather than conflicting. There is a synchronous flow, a beautiful undulating curve as they mould and meld one into the other, supporting and caressing the other, creating a wholesome oneness. It's not a static equilibrium – it's fluid, graceful and dynamic. The perfection lies in the fact that each has within it the germ or seed of the other energy to give balance and harmony. It has a symbiosis, thus transforming this relationship into one of inter-dependence, rather than dependence, independence or co-dependence.

Each needs the other; without the masculine, the feminine is not only incapable of expressing herself outwardly, she also remains unexpressed internally. Likewise without the feminine, the masculine is incapable of expressing himself inwardly, and also remains unexpressed outwardly. So Yang has to contain some Yin, Yin has to contain some Yang in order to be whole. Without that there is no spark, no energy, no creativity, no power, no vigour and no growth.

In other words, a man in order to be whole needs to have a connection with his poetic, creative, gentle, nurturing, feminine side, but this is not his primary energy. A woman in order to be whole needs to have a connection with her strong, achieving, productive, focussed masculine side. But this is not our primary energy – this is not where we should live. Both masculine and feminine need to come together in order to be whole. Like a bird needs two wings in order to soar off into the heavens, Life needs the two wings of masculine and feminine, both within us and in our external environment.

In Diana Cooper's book, 'Discover Atlantis,' she talks about how priests used to read the auras of prospective couples before marriage to ensure that each had sufficient of their core masculine or feminine energy, so that any offspring would be brought up in balance and harmony. That is how important it is!

Polar Opposites

The Universe is an indivisible matrix of cosmic force always seeking expression through the union of its opposite energies, hence light and dark, hot and cold, love and fear, praise and criticism, maleness and femaleness. Perhaps spiritually we are androgynous, neither male nor female; who knows. But both maleness and femaleness are necessary for us to have our human experience of the Universe here and now, and this time round you were born in a female body to experience fully what it is to be female. Neither is better nor stronger than the other; they are just different, which allows us to complement each other and celebrate those differences.

Problems arise when we overdevelop one set of energies that is not our true essence, and under-develop the other; the dynamic gets distorted and it harms us at a very deep level. So when we take on the same energy as a man, we lose that intimacy, passion, desire, tenderness and creativity in our personal relationships. Like two batteries in a torch, our light can only go on fully when our polar energies are aligned in an opposite fashion. Where there is polarity there will be a juice between each other all the time.

Unfortunately, our culture is really messing us up – it is conditioning men to get too much in touch with their feminine side, while women are striving even more to keep up with and overtake men. And (I know I'm sticking my neck out here, but at the risk of repercussions, I am going to) we are more often than not being influenced by gay icons who are designing our clothes, makeup, hair and décor, and who themselves may not be living in their own true core energy! Buyer, beware!

As little girls if our feminine essence wasn't encouraged and nurtured, we learned to cover it up by being sensible, analytical and logical. For a girl who sees any weakness of her mother as being feminine weakness, she will often put on a masculine mask. Later when she wants to connect with men, if she is in her masculine energy and they are masculine, they will not be attracted to her at all. So she has no choice but to get her satisfaction from business, art, sport and other occupations. She's calling the shots but she can never be totally free and open; she then finds feminine men to be her assistants. Some women stay in control because they haven't found a man masculine enough for them, but we have trained our men to be that way!

Gender Energy Chart

Take a look at the chart below, and place a tick in the box which best describes your behaviour and abilities. We develop a pattern growing up, whether through modelling someone else, or because our talents lead us in a particular direction, or because something has happened which leads us to consciously choose to behave in a certain way for our survival. Whatever the reason, it shows up in our behaviour and communication. This is not about our sexuality, but about our energy.

With 0 being neutral, and with 5 being very strong, see where your tendency lies.

Behaviour and abilities	5	4	3	2	1	0	1	2	3	4	5	Behaviour and interests
adventurous												cautious
aggressive												passive
ambitious												security oriented
analytical												integrative
assertive												tactful
competitive												co-operative
decisive												ambivalent
disciplinarian												going with the flow

Behaviour and abilities	5	4	3	2	1	0	1	2	3	4	5	Behaviour and interests
dominant												submissive
exclusive												inclusive
goal oriented												process oriented
good at maths												good at art
good at science												good at literature
independent												interdependent
individualistic												interpersonal
leader												follower
logical												intuitive
objective												subjective
philosophical												practical
rational												emotional
self reliant												consults others
sexual												sensual
strong												tender
thinking												feeling
worldly												domestic
MASCULINE												**FEMININE**

So do you find yourself veering more towards the masculine characteristics on this chart than you had previously been aware of? The biggest challenge we have in our personal relationships is lack of polarity. If we are not living at our core essence, the polarity in our romantic and intimate relationships is artificial; and if it's neutral, there is no creativity.

You and I know that a woman can do virtually anything a man can do, but it's not sustainable for very long, or at the same level. Designed in different ways, we have smaller hands, smaller frames and differently wired brains. The corpus callosum, which separates the left side from the right side of the brain, is thinner in women so we can access both sides of the brain more readily, which explains our emotional sensitivity. Our neural pathways intermingle more than in men, yet when we get older, around menopausal age, this tends to swap over in both sexes; women get more focused and men become more in touch with their emotions.

Generally we are suited to different labour than men. We can't work equally because our hormones dictate that we need to rest more. We can produce just as much as men, but how much better if we do it in our own special way, sharing labour with each of us doing what we are most suited to according to our capabilities and talents?

We came to this planet with a sexual energy for a reason - to activate each other! How easily we slip into male-oriented tasks ourselves, but it leaves nothing for the men to do, when in their hearts, often their greatest desire is just to make us happy and to provide for us.

Whilst our highest prerogative is to belong, his highest duty is to protect; it's in his internal wiring. But our dedication and determination to our independence not only makes masculine care and protection unnecessary and redundant, but also we both lose out. Our masculinised lifestyle with its power of focus, resolve and tenacity works against the natural attributes of a woman. We're behaving as though women are inferior and as if we still have a need to prove ourselves, and so have been socialised to use more of the energy which is not at our core.

Masculine strength and endurance are attributes which often we shamefacedly admire, actually drool over. You only have to look at the advertisements on television or the latest James Bond movie to see what makes our pulse rate speed up. Most of us at heart know we would love to have protection from a strong, capable, masculine man so we don't have to be fearful, (this is the truth – come on, confess! I dare you!) And we don't know how to ask for it, as we're taking over so much of the male role both at home and at work.

And lack-a-day, men are no longer our chivalrous knights of old because we have now become so capable, so efficient and so independent that we no longer appear to need them. We have left them without a role and feeling inadequate. Justifiably wary of being chivalrous lest they have their courteous and gallant deeds contemptuously hurled back in their faces, they are now losing respect and admiration for the sex that birthed them. Yet most of us have been brought up on heroic tales where men slay dragons for their women, and always rescue them at the last minute. Deep down many of us wish they still would. What a conundrum!

Our impenetrable, tough exterior only leads to misery where achievement becomes everything, but in turn, how we suffer. Many of my more successful female clients are overworked, overwrought and overwhelmed in their pin-striped suits, distraught that the nanny gets to witness their children's milestones. They despair that they are losing connection and intimacy with their partners, continually suffering from stress-related illnesses, knowing deep down that there must be more to life than this but terrified to let go of their status and high earning capacity.

What Men Want

Can you imagine how it must feel to a man when we are in our masculine energy? It really turns him off and literally repels him, and we wonder why we fail to impress him! Real men in their core masculine energy are interested in real women. They live for truly feminine women, so much so that in fact they would kill for them. Young women are still innocent and free, and men drool over freedom - which could give you a clue as to why men run off with the younger version!

Men's ideas of feminine perfection are different from our ideas. What we admire in women is rarely attractive to men, and yet what we ignore or condemn in other women are sometimes just the characteristics that make her fascinating to men. How blind we are to our own charms!

While we're inclined to appreciate poise, talent, intelligence, cleverness and artistic beauty such as the shape of the face and nose, and of course clothes, men have a different set of values. They appreciate girlishness, tenderness, sweetness and vivacity, and place more importance on a feminine manner, on that sparkle in the eyes, smiles, freshness and radiance. And that angelic quality that some women possess can awaken in a man such deep tender feelings, almost like worship, bringing him peace and inner happiness in contrast with his own strength. The more feminine a woman becomes, the more he will offer his care, attention and protection, and so his love and tenderness grows along with his self-esteem. He won't offer his care and protection unless a woman needs it!

So am I saying we need to become simpering, weak and feeble? Not at all! Men don't want a pathetic specimen that they can push around; they seek women with an inner passion, someone with an inner fire and dignity. A dynamic woman is really attractive because she creates energy which he can feast on, whereas someone with no energy will have no attraction at all.

So don't be cajoled into thinking that femininity translates to weakness. Our feminine side is a force that can conquer all. There are times when we have to be strong and forceful, creative and energetic, powerful and courageous – the word 'courage' comes from the French, 'rage du coeur,' the rage of the heart which we have in abundance. There are times when we need to employ our female Yang energy, when we are taking our work out into the world for instance, making important business decisions or pushing our babies out of the womb. But too much Yang creates havoc with our hormones and menstrual cycle, creates problems with fertility, and also with holding on to pregnancies.

While love is more important to a woman, admiration is more important to a man. When we stop admiring them, they stop being masculine; when we deride them, they cannot perform as men; when we nag them or over-protect them, we sound like their mothers. Can you see where we're going wrong? And when we help too much, when we take over where they should be, men get weaker and more aimless; we leave nothing for them to strive for. They begin to see themselves as less which leads to resentment; then they bite the hand that feeds them, and we wonder why!

When we are not in our Yin flow, a man cannot express his masculine Yang energy and so we both lose out. If we are in the same polarity, there is no dynamic spark, no magnetic draw, and no real eroticism in love-making. It becomes either a battle ground like two stags in combat, or a luke-warm, watered-down version where passion just flies out the window.

When we're not living at our healthful energy core, we have nothing to offer.

We simply lose ourselves in an imitation of men,

which kills our spirit.

Perhaps now we have proven ourselves, we can stop striving so hard, give in gracefully at last to our natural instincts and come back once more into our soft, yet powerful, loving feminine. When women start to really understand and appreciate this, they so often cry with years of pent-up emotion and relief, longing so much to be released from the constant struggle we have set ourselves. When too we can bring our men back to a place of self-reliance, our relationships will flourish.

A Buddhist sutra from the 13th century states, "A cherry is a cherry. A plum is a plum." While this may sound blindingly obvious, it is in fact very profound. A cherry is not a plum, nor ever masquerades as such. Similarly a woman is not a man. We are individual and unique with our own special characteristics, and designed to be so. When we continually struggle effortfully to adapt to an energy which is not who we are in essence, we create so much pain for ourselves; we're not being honest and authentic, and as a result we just cannot function properly. No wonder we have so many problems in our relationships.

When would now be a good time for us to wake up and make our relationships more meaningful?

If we don't have a great relationship with ourselves, we can't have a great relationship with anyone else, because we can only share with others what we have inside ourselves. Your relationship with yourself is your relationship with another human being. Imagine how amazing that will be when you make that relationship with yourself something really special!

Designed To Be Different

Men and women are designed to be different yet complementary. In human beings it is like a Divine marriage of the masculine and feminine. We are all connected at a spiritual level, but as men and women we are different expressions of life, and as such create a fuller, more rounded expression of what life truly can be.

When we take nature as our teacher, it all becomes so blindingly evident. In the kingdoms and queendoms of bird, fish, animal and insect, the female of the species doesn't copy the male – she stays true in her female power. The female has power over the male sexually; they know it and we know it, but as sentient beings this is for us to honour, not abuse (unless of course you happen to be a black widow spider!) In the realms of the human, it is women who have the power to bring a man to orgasm – he can only bring us to orgasm should we desire it and when we can relax sufficiently and trust.

Within any encounter or relationship, as one partner becomes more Yang, the other needs to become more Yin in order to create a balance, but we're doing it back to front, inside out and for far too long. At heart we are searching for our complementary energy, which is where many relationships fail. We recognize there is a void - tragically one of our own making.

This lack of polarity totally wrecks relationship. As women are becoming more masculinised and forceful, many men are fighting to regain their masculinity, sometimes by being antagonistic which leads to passive-aggressive behaviour, or in desperation becoming aggressively macho and even violent. Some men are just not bothering at all, failing to connect with their own potentially powerful masculinity, becoming weak, ineffective and somewhat pathetic. In turn they seek out strong, capable women to look after them, a complete role-reversal to nature's intention, while pornography, paedophilia and fetishism are on the increase, possibly because of the lack of connection between the male and female. And because we feel we cannot relinquish the role of protector to our men, we have to get stronger. Then we complain, and test them all the time!

Yang Dance - exercise

How does it feel to be in our Yang energy? Kick your shoes off and dance it.

This dance can be accompanied by music taken from the last part of Prince Igor from the Polovtsian Dances by Borodin (National Philharmonic Orchestra Tjeknavorian.)

This is rather like a dance of the Indian god Shiva, at one and the same time the destroyer of evil and the regenerator, with his strong, masculine energy, able to go out into the world and put into practice all that he is inspired to do.

As you hear and feel the music swell, feel that strong energy rise from deep inside you. Yang energy is directed outwards into the world. With eyes open, let the music rouse you to move with strength, courage, power, force, determination and intentionality. This is an outward, dynamic movement; feel that potency and vigour build up inside you, a force to be reckoned with. Feel the tone in your muscles, the throbbing of life-force in your veins. Feel that erotic instinct full of vitality that permits us to convert our dreams and ideas into reality and to bring them into the world, an instinct that demands expression.

After the music has finished, walk around slowly and get your breath back to restore your heart beat to normal.

Keep breathing

While exciting, stimulating and exhilarating, and even though women are very good at this dance (sadly often much better than the men!) this energy is not sustainable for women for long periods of time. We rapidly become exhausted because we give so much of ourselves to it, so much of our emotion and expression. Yet we live at this level much of the time.

Somehow when men do this dance, they conserve their energy in a different way. This is a Yang dance using masculine energy, too much of which diminishes our personal charm and our capacity to express our eroticism with delicacy. It's a reflection of our stressful Yang environment derived from fighting and competition.

When we too can learn how to conserve our Yang energy and draw on it through the sensitivity of our Yin only when it is necessary, we will become so much happier and more fun to be around.

You may like to try a Yang dance later using different music, but this time using your Yin energy – it will feel very different.

Relight Your Fire

So what lights your fire? Do you thrill at the sight of a man mopping his brow as he sweats over a computer, or stripped to the waist and dripping with sweat as he chops logs? Morris dancing, or sweeping you away in his arms, cheek to cheek, and taking you to the floor in a tango? Playing badminton or champion tennis? When a real man in his masculine energy enters a room, we feel it. Our energy shifts and our bodies respond as we recognise that strength and power. Our female cells sit up and listen - his pheromones are at work!

When we become more Yin within ourselves, honouring who we really are as women with tenderness and sensitivity, this then gives our men permission to grow and hold fast in their true powerful masculinity.

I have witnessed this happen over and over again as I work with men to help them reclaim their authentic male energy through movement, voice, and through thought and intention. The word 'real' comes from the word *regalis* meaning royal - rather apt here don't you think? Real women swoon over real men, just as in those romantic novels of the 18th century. Mr. Darcy, eat your heart out!

The transformation is astounding to watch as the repercussions permeate every aspect of the men's lives, from their sexuality and intimate relationship to their career and self-expression. It is the polarity, the differences that create the dynamic, where they once again are living from their intrinsic strength. We as real women can then surrender to the joy, freedom and eloquence of our feminine. Respect, honour and integrity return where once they were lacking.

Take a look in the lonely hearts columns in the Sunday papers; men are crying out for sensual, genuine women, tender yet spirited, loving and caring, interested in the arts, the countryside, walking, log fires and conversation to share life's riches. Women on the other hand tend to describe themselves as independent, successful, smart and intelligent. And then at the end of our day, we go home and talk endlessly about work! We are using men's language to try and attract what we want, but all we will attract is a feminine man who needs a strong partner.

Deep down, men are looking for what they had as babies at the breast: the warmth, comfort, and enfolding unconditional love of a woman, plus a sexual intimacy where they can totally let go and forget about day to day troubles. They want to be loved for who they really are, as do we all. Most men are not instinctively attracted to successful career women, although the financial advantages are undeniable. In most men's hearts there is a desire to serve, to worship, and to honour the connection with the 'mother' in us. When that is belittled, it destroys their pride; it demeans their very own existence. The instinct for them, though buried deep, is still to be providers of that masculine strength so that we can grow and blossom within their protection.

Yin Dance - exercise

In Indian mythology, Shakti represents the inner essence of woman, the intuitive, abundant, enduring, receptive, creative nurturing element which balances out the strong masculine Shiva. She is the Divine Force, destroying negative forces and restoring balance to the cosmic order and the order in one's personal life.

What does it feel like to be in our Yin energy? Bare-foot on the carpet, on the grass, on the beach or in a chair, relax into this dance and feel it permeating every part of you, every organ, every tissue, and every cell.

This beautiful dance gives us the possibility of returning to that interiority, that beauty and connection within, that place of exquisite tenderness, to our inner essence. Our inner sanctum, like our sexuality, is hidden away in the depths of our being, and this dance brings us back to the inner self. Remember, spiritually you are an extraordinary creature. You came here with a beautiful soul; your amazing body is the home of your forgotten spirit, and when you reconnect with it, life transforms.

For music, I use Schubert's 'String Quintet in C Major,' or 'Prelude' from Yanni's album 'Tribute.' With feet slightly apart to create a steady base, and with soft knees, eyes gently closed and mouth half open, beginning with your hands over your heart, allow yourself to surrender to the beautiful music and receive it in every pore of your skin, vibrating and resonating in every cell.

Moving very, very gently and in slow motion, let small, gentle, flowing movements of your arms, hands and body express with great sensitivity, gracefulness, delicacy and tenderness the precious and timeless beauty of the inner you. Tears may well up as you reconnect intimately and compassionately with your true self, as you acknowledge that part of you which has remained unexpressed for so long, and merge with that inspirational, primordial impulse to dream.

Breathe

When the music finishes, place your hands gently back on your heart and feel the steady beat of life pulsing through you, and slowly, slowly in your own time, open your eyes and return to the room.

Our Inner Female

We are the inspiration - or can be again when we remember how. We have the power. If we want to create a successful, harmonious, intimate relationship with another person, then we have to create a close relationship with our own inner female first. It is that fundamental nature which allows our body to nurture and grow a baby; it nurtures the seed, nourishes the foetus and protects our unborn child within the womb.

When we fail to honour and value the feminine in ourselves, in response men fail to honour it in us too. We have shown contempt for our own values as we moan and complain about men, then not only copy them, we go beyond. Where a man would just stop and rest, we go on beyond endurance until we are exhausted! Losing ourselves in an imitation of man, we grow sterile and demonic, killing our truly creative, intuitive spirit. The fiend of inferior masculinity can so easily devour our womanhood as we grow afraid of our femininity and shut off from it. But unless we get rid of our fear, we cannot acquire this all important polarity.

When we can learn to appreciate our own honesty, dependability, kindness and love, our sweetness, our gentleness, our prowess, our passion, our sensuality and our joyful eroticism, we will attract into our lives just those sorts of people who will directly complement those energies. And yes, we can still do and be this as powerful successful business women! When we step into our true female power, our sovereignty, we will stop wounding the masculinity of our men. We will encourage men to step into their true masculine power which is not one of brutality, war, aggression and anger, but one of protection and provision, of love and honour.

Letting Your Yin Speak - exercise

When you connect with your inner Yin as if it is a lover, the poetry that falls from your pen may astound you as you reach into that innermost part of you which has seldom if ever been voiced before. Try it and see; write a letter and see what emerges. These have come from my workshops:

"Welcome home my lover. At last! Where have you been hiding? I almost forgot your existence. I remember you as if in a far-flung dream, yet no matter how hard I tried I couldn't find you. You were lost in a labyrinth somewhere far beyond my reach."

"Now I feel you surrender, graciously, joyfully and with such a sweetness, sensitivity and tenderness. My voice is powerful even when gentle and quiet. It knows as I know."

"I go beyond my physical body vibrating into Source around me. It is time to nurture yourself my sweet, to feel the dewy moistness of your tears as they fall unfettered."

Now write to your Yang energy from your Yin, as if it were a lover.

"Love me, protect me, keep me safe so I can expand into the fullness of my being. Honour me, trust me, hold me, respect me. Let me be the fullness of who I am, then I can give you your heart's desire."

"Let me be the woman to your man. Let me dance, let me shine. Allow the strength of your passion to be released so that I can release the beauty of mine."

"I struggle so and the wild woman needs to come out to play. Don't hide me any more – let me be the free, wild, tempestuous, adoring, passionate, sensuous, dynamic being that my soul yearns for. Don't keep me small – un-prison me, set me free to fly then I can fly back to you. Don't keep me like a caged bird for I cannot sing with these bars around me."

Integration of Yin and Yang - exercise

When Yin and Yang are disconnected, they cannot complement and harmonise each other. We each come into our own in the presence of the other, unveiling who we really are. Woman in the presence of man reveals her true self; she sparkles. That is when we shine our glorious light, our true essence. Man in the presence of woman, is potent.

Balancing the Yin and Yang within ourselves allows our creativity to express itself. Our sensitive, poetic, creative Yin can then go out into the world expressed through the powerful Yang. Without Shakti, Shiva would be inert, aloof and inactive. Combined with her energy, he manifests his full potential. They complete each other, two opposites coming together as one.

This is about finding peace within, resolving conflict and creating harmony within chaos. This is a marriage of polar opposites. This is harmonious interdependence, the ultimate reality and balance of truth, the perfect balance of spirit and matter.

When you dance this music, you will know what I mean. For this dance I use Seal's 'Kiss from a Rose.' Don't be tempted to sing the words, for that takes you back into your cortex, the thinking part of the brain, while this is an intense living experience. When I am teaching dance, this living experience in present time awareness is called 'vivencia.'

Take off your shoes and dance bare foot. Leaving your mouth half open, let the sound and vibration of the music enter into your body and move you, allowing your soft gentle Yin movements to be expressed with the eyes closed and the more powerful Yang with eyes open. Let the music direct and guide you. In fact, let go. Just be, and become one with the music, with its strength, passion, flow, power and ultimate tenderness. Allow it to gentle your Yin and impassion your Yang.

Breathe

The Female Yang – The Female Yin

Like a beautiful tree growing strong, we become well-rooted when we tap into the deep feminine aspect of ourselves and our creative spirit is freed to create untold beauty. At the essential core of the feminine being is such a compassionate loving heart. No simpering mushy emotion this - it has severity, ferocity and a boundless depth to it, as well as a quiet, tender nurturing. After all, there is nothing stronger in nature than a mother bear!

When we acknowledge this powerful female Yang element inside us, and once again connect with and learn from the female Yin of nature's intrinsic rhythms and splendour, we allow our spirit to soar and our creativity to re-awaken. Our contribution to what this world is now lacking will be extraordinary.

Be gentle with the earth and with yourself. Unless we allow our feminine to be truly seen, we are in danger of a whole generation of girls missing out on the joys of real womanhood and our true nature. Laddish culture means the innocence, elegance and joy of femininity is lost to them, and the whole world becomes poorer for that.

Men and women have learned to challenge each other, to be combatants rather than collaborators. It is now argued that evolution has flourished because of co-operation, not because of competition.

103

Imagine how far-reaching the implications of this might be, and how wonderful it will be when we learn to live in a loving space!

Where is Your Energy? - exercise

Slightly different from the earlier exercise, look at the words below in relation to the way you currently tend to live your life in your present or your previous **intimate** relationships. Circle the nine words that characterise you and how you tend to operate.

Focussed	Pleasing	Purposeful	Leading
Letting go of control	Powerful	Trusting	Fearless
Owning	Surrender	Allowing	Decisive
Dominance	Accommodating	Non-demanding	Powerful
Protective	Acknowledging	Nurturing	Leading

Now take a moment to look at the words you have circled and map them onto the chart on the following page on the right-hand side labelled **Female**. What is your current predominant energy? The higher up the scale you are, the more masculine energy you are expressing. The lower you are on the scale, the more you are living in your feminine energy. But, if you are down at the very bottom, living mostly in non-demanding, accommodating and surrender, the more likely it is that you will behave as a victim which can lead to passive-aggressive behaviour towards your partner as your innermost needs are not being met.

Having completed this, it may be helpful to choose the nine words which represent where your present or your last partner or partners expressed themselves within your relationship, and chart it under the side labelled **Male**. Similarly, if their energy is near the bottom of the scale, they are living predominantly in their feminine, and may themselves become passive-aggressive as they try to reassert their force. Too near the top and chances are they will be macho or aggressive, which could in turn lead to violence as their innermost needs are not being met. So you will see how the polarity works in your relationships. If both are in the middle, this will be more like a friendship with little or no passion, and probably a very weak sexual attraction.

MALE		FEMALE
Macho/Aggressive	off the scale (unhealthy)	
Dominance		Dominance
Fearless		Fearless
Total Strength		Total Strength
Purposeful		Purposeful
Owning		Owning
Focussed		Focussed
Powerful		Powerful
Leading		Leading
Driven		Driven
Decisive		Decisive
Protective		Protective
Nurturing		Nurturing
Trusting		Trusting
Pleasing		Pleasing
Acknowledging		Acknowledging
Letting Go of Control		Letting Go of Control
Allowing		Allowing
Non-demanding		Non-demanding
Accommodating		Accommodating
Surrender		Surrender
	off the scale (unhealthy)	Victim/Passive-Aggressive

Reprinted here with kind permission from www.tonyandnickivee.com

Imagine here that the top segments are blue and the bottom segments pink, with the middle section - Decisive and Protective - neutral. If both are in the blue, it will be like two stags fighting it out. Both in the pink will be wishy-washy. Ideally the male will be mainly blue with a little pink, and the woman mainly in the pink with a little blue. The middle is a shared area where both need to have access, both able to make decisions and to be protective of their own energy, each other and the relationship.

It may be quite an eye opener to see in fact how far you have veered towards your masculine energy and how you may have suppressed your feminine. Do you see why so many of us struggle? And as we get older, women tend to become more masculine and men more feminine as our hormones lose their power, but fear not, this can be changed. Growth hormone stored in our pituitary gland can be stimulated by the right sort of exercise (www.educogym.com) to rejuvenate and balance our hormones as well as paying consideration to diet. Biodanza™ (www.biodanza.co.uk) too can help regulate and rebalance the hormones while helping to reinforce your true identity.

When we constantly live out of balance with our sexual essence, we feel unfulfilled deep down, which is why we over-exert ourselves to try and fill the gap (masculine energy) instead of relaxing more into our deep feminine (being receptive to being filled).

Am I suggesting that you cannot be a scientist, a mathematician, a train driver, an engineer, an inventor, a lawyer, a scientist, a bricky or a plumber if you're a woman? Not one iota. (I know a young woman who is a fantastic plumber who dresses in a pink boiler suit as her trade mark!) What I am suggesting is we be all that and more, but in *our* way, in the way of woman. Do what you do in a feminine way, not by taking on the attributes of a man, not by competing with him. By giving all that you do the feminine touch, you can enrich society in a beautiful way.

Most personal development courses are run by men where the content is very masculine, goal-oriented, focused, analytical, ambitious, rational and success-driven. After seminars with these hard-hitting single-minded guys, I used to come away fired up and raring to go, and it was not until a few weeks later, exhausted and feeling a complete failure, I realised I was out of synch with being a woman. My feminine essence is not cut-throat, driven and forceful. Yes I want to be successful, but in my own way, honouring my own energy, being true to my femininity and my inner self.

What screws us up, is not being who we really are at our core. I believe that the purpose of life is to give full expression to who you are as a person – for you to be you – the ultimate you where every moment you can feel the exuberance of being fully alive. Once fully expressed in your feminine essence, you can contribute so much more to others, and be a way-shower. We have so much to teach the world. This is the ultimate eve-olution.

As the oracle at Delphi stated:

Know thyself!

To which later have been added the phrases Be thyself, Love thyself.

Conception of Thought

The word conception means not only genesis of being, but also of thought. Our ability to think and reason is what separates us from all the other animals on this planet, and it is our ability to think that can lead us to destruction or majestic evolution. As you have learned, how we think empowers or disempowers us as women.

The mind is an instrument of the soul; the body is an instrument of the mind. Ultimately all three - body, mind and soul - can function in unison. When you really understand and learn how to use the power of thought and mind, this is called Mastery. (I wish there was a feminine version – perhaps I shall call it Miss-tery!) Then your life will transform.

Conception takes place in one micro-second – it's the creative spark that sets off a phenomenal process. So let us re-ignite that creative spark and re-awaken your feminine essence to re-mind you who you really are.

It is at our moment of conception that our life begins –

☯ conception = thought

☯ our beliefs determine our thoughts

☯ thoughts and feelings determine our behaviour

☯ our behaviour determines our actions

☯ our actions determine what happens to us and our destiny

So we need to be very, very careful what we think, what we believe, and what actions we choose to take in this precious life.

It is a choice. Every moment is a choice. You can continue to do the same things the same old way ad infinitum but don't expect any different results. Alternatively you can do things anew with greater wisdom and marvel at the difference; as Einstein said, "There are only two ways to live your life. One is as though nothing is a miracle. The other is as though everything is a miracle." Which do you choose?

Creating Your Own Reality

We have heard for so long that, 'You create your reality.' When I first heard that years ago, I was incensed, beside myself with indignation.

"You mean I created the abuse I've just received, the illness I've just had, the death of my friend, the loss of my job, the difficult birth of my baby that nearly killed us both, the war, the famine, the atrocities..." You can hear me now ... and I bet you've all said it too. It is so convenient to blame other people!

Things happen – there will always be natural disasters, man-made disasters, circumstances beyond our personal control, but what we *do* have is the ability to *respond* as opposed to *react* to whatever is happening in our lives. This is what the word responsibility means – the ability to respond to whatever we are experiencing. We create our experiences by our choices; we create our choices by our thoughts; we create our thoughts by our beliefs; we create our beliefs by our conditioning. We continue to reinforce our conditioning by the words we use out loud and to ourselves with our inner talk, and by the feelings and emotion behind those thoughts.

Despite what you've been brought up to believe, the Universe is neither punishing you nor blessing you. It is an intelligent loving energy that is responding to your attitude and the vibration of the thoughts, feelings and emotion that you are emitting, constantly reflecting back to you what you are transmitting. It is a perfect feedback mechanism; the more joyful you are and the more positive your attitude, the more well-being and good things flow to you - and you get to choose the precise details of how they flow, moment by moment. Airy-fairy nonsense? You know it's true; we've all been there, done it, got the T-shirt. When we are in a bad mood, or scared, everything seems to go wrong. When we're in a good mood, even if things don't go according to plan, we shrug it off like water off a duck's back.

The problem is, we tend to *react* (go over again) to what we are witnessing in front of us, so when we see horrible things happening, we focus our attention on them. We attempt to control circumstances and people around us, which only feeds our feeling of frustration and vulnerability. The truth is we can't control all circumstances; all we can do is control how we feel about it.

Thinking of Good Vibrations

Aware that I am simplifying somewhat to make a point, according to quantum physics, we live in a vibrational Universe where everything pulsates, literally a dynamic dance of matter. We too are vibrational beings. Looked at under a microscope, our trillions of cells are vibrating at a particular resonance or frequency according to whether we are well or ill, relaxed or tense, vibrant or apathetic, loving or warring. Everything about us in our environment too vibrates, even the chair I am sitting on as I write is not inanimate – it has molecules and atoms and sub-particles that are zooming around at a phenomenal rate to create what appears to me a solid object - and in between there is just space, all held together by energy.

And just as the cells in our body vibrate, so too our words take on a vibration. When we speak out loud, the vibration of our words does not just stop at the four walls which surround us. It permeates through the walls and the roof and out into space vibrating in both waves and particles of energy.

At an unconscious level, we are able to sense the vibrations coming from other people. For example when we say, "I didn't like his vibes," or "He's on a different wavelength," or "It doesn't resonate with me," or "He feels creepy," it is our instinct at work. We sense fear in a wild animal's eyes, we sense danger in a dark alleyway, we sense atmosphere in old houses.

Not only do we have our five senses of sight, hearing, touch, taste and smell, but another hundred or so senses that we are not even aware of. We have this incredible ability to sense and translate at an unconscious level much of what is going on around us. The clues are all there, and in an encounter with someone else, their body language, which is an energetic expression of what is going on inside the person, accounts for about fifty-eight per-cent, and we pick it up!

Even our unspoken words, our thoughts go out into the wide blue yonder. We are like radio transmitters. The vibration of our thoughts and feelings go out to be picked up by the equivalent of a satellite-dish receiver, which may be another person or object vibrating and pulsating at a similar frequency, tuned in at the same wavelength. When they receive our signals, we pull them into our life experience.

You know how sometimes you may be thinking of someone in particular and the phone rings and it is them, or you wonder how to solve a particular problem and the book with the answer you are seeking falls off the shelf at the library? Or you switch on the television and the answer comes to you in a snippet of the film that is being shown, or you see an advertising hoarding with the exact words you need to hear right now? When the vibration we are emitting is in tune with what we really, really want, coincidences and synchronicities seem to occur over and over again. We feel in the flow, on our path, content and at ease, as if there is an unknown support mechanism protecting and guiding us.

Your Life is always listening.

You always get a response

even though it may not be

the one you think you want.

Imagine a stringed instrument – a beautiful Stradivarius violin – and you strike the open G string. What tends to happen is that all the other instruments in the orchestra with a G string will also start to vibrate in harmony. This is called entrainment.

So too with us. We don't only attract the good stuff towards us. When we play our chords of misery, poverty, lack, heartache, despair, loneliness, fear and illness, we resonate with other people or situations on the same wavelength, and all of a sudden these people or situations appear in our lives. They seek out the same 'musical note' so we can play our misery chords together.

As women, we tend to easily pick up the vibrational resonance of people we are with as we empathise readily with their sadness and pain. And we think we are helping them by being sympathetic. But you can't get sick enough to help sick people get better; you can't get poor enough to help people in poverty to thrive. It is only through creating your own health, well-being and abundant loving energy that you have anything to offer anyone else.

Your life can be as wonderful or as horrible as you allow it to be. It all depends upon the thoughts that you practice, because we do practice thought, much like practising the piano, over and over again. And therein lies the basis of anyone's success:

How much are you practising thoughts

that bring you love, joy, friendship, abundance,

health, harmony and happiness,

and

how much are you practising thoughts

that bring you pain, lack, loneliness and misery?

Can you see now why we have to clean up those old fearful thoughts, which is why we did that exercise in the previous chapter? Like the weather, we need to clear away the fog and clouds to create a perfect mental climate, because above the clouds the sky is always a beautiful cerulean blue.

In turn, your thoughts dictate your energy level. What you allow into your life on an energetic level can be life-changing or just another passing experience. It's completely up to you how much beauty and joy and well-being and abundance you let into your life. If it's just an experience, once it's over it's over.

Once you can understand, this information can be life-changing for you.

Taking Command of Your Thoughts

The average person is a product of their thoughts. We are literally hypnotised by what society dictates, by what we see on TV and in magazines, and it doesn't help when we continue to hypnotise ourselves with our own self-talk.

All you have to do is take command of your thoughts to change your personal life and your global life. The more you understand how your mind works, the greater control you have over your destiny. Become the mistress of your mind – when you take command of your thoughts everything changes. If you don't control your thoughts, you can bet your bottom dollar that someone else's thoughts will control you. If your life is not the way you want it, it's being controlled by someone else; even if you are infatuated by someone or you resent someone, they are running your life.

Undo everything negative you have ever learned about yourself. It's like unpicking the threads from a tapestry – cut the negativity out, because your success or failure depends on how you structure your thoughts.

We get trapped in thought that has become solidified like jelly which takes on the shape of the vessel it is moulded into. It leads to problems in our personal world, which in turn we pass onto our children and thus get perpetuated ad infinitum. When we become 'at cause' of our lives rather than being at the effect of it, we empower our lives dramatically, opening the portal to an unlimited number of choices as we change our perception and interpret things in a more constructive way.

Mind What You Are Thinking About

Most people don't understand that you get to control the way you feel, because you get to choose the thoughts you think moment by moment. It's so easy to forget this, and then we get swallowed up in a downward spiral of depression and misery. So remember:

You have the ability to control the power of your thoughts!

You have the ability to control the power of your mind!

Remember that in every moment you are sending out a vibrational energy through your thoughts which is attracting everything towards you like a magnet, whether it is good or bad.

Now you understand this, it means you now have the ability to choose and create your dominant thought, your over-riding feeling, your dominant vibration to resonate with the frequency of whatever you prefer and desire. You really do; that's all it takes. And that's all any successful person ever has done; they just wanted something, wrapped their whole mind around it, believed it was already on its way, behaved in a way which was in keeping with what they wanted, and hey presto, it arrived in their lives. It's a simple system, which I'll explain a bit more about later. It is so vitally important, because your innermost dominant thought becomes your reality.

How to De-activate Negative Thoughts

The problem with what we **don't** want is, if we focus on it, we give it energy. Having done the exercise in the previous chapter, hopefully you will have given your all to it, so there is no whining or whinging left in you – you've done it all, got rid of all your rubbish. So from now on, you can choose to take your energy away from all of those negative things, and just ignore them.

Beware, because if you send out a vibration which says you **don't have what you want**, you will end up getting **more of what you don't have!!** Purely because you focused your attention and energy on it.

Whatever you focus on expands!

When you say, "I'm not going to think that thought," or "I don't want to feel like this any more," for that split second of time, you're focusing on that very thought. When you pay attention to what you don't want, you feed it and wake it up, like waking a pet vampire that sits on your shoulder, because as long as it's got your attention, you've activated and given energy to what you don't want.

The only way you can de-activate a grizzly negative thought is by withdrawing your attention from it, and by putting all your focus on something else instead. When you show appreciation, love, praise or pleasure towards something else entirely, you open the gateway to allow good things to come pouring in. Focus on things that make you feel good. And smile!

The interesting thing is whatever you're thinking about is literally like planning a future event. So:

When you're angry, you are planning.

When you're miserable or depressed, you are planning.

When you're worrying or frightened, you are planning.

When you are upset or hurt, you are planning.

When you're going over your past, you're planning.

When you're appreciating and enjoying, you are planning.

What are you planning?

What is your predominant thought and feeling?

We are such worriers. But the more you don't worry, the more Life has a chance to come in. There is no sense whatsoever in worrying.

If you can do something about it, do it and then there's nothing to worry about. If you can't do anything about it, there's no point in worrying, because you can't do anything about it. Simple huh!

The more you ignore the things you don't want, the more that power and hold they have over you will decrease, because you stop feeding them energy. Most problems sort themselves out and defuse their energy of their own accord with little interference from us. I'm not talking about ignoring urgent bills or ignoring a pain (a pain is a signal from the body that something is not quite right) nor am I talking about ignoring abuse or violence or cruelty. I am talking here about ignoring those inner feelings which used to wind us up so much, those negative emotions that keep trying to trap us and sap our loving feminine energy.

Our present culture is characterised by so much hate and fear, greed and jealousy all fed by the media. Because we have been focusing on negative forces and energy, it makes us prone to accident, disease and crime, which only attracts similar forces. The evidence is all around us.

As women we have a tendency to want to clear up the 'issues.' Don't go there girls! You know, and I know, that paying attention to a *problem* will not solve it. We've tried that for most of our lives and it doesn't work. We can't use the same thoughts to *solve* the problem as we used to *create* the problem – we have to do the opposite.

Trust me on this one – I struggled with it for ages, and then gave up, completely surrendered. We are trying to solve problems by what has already happened in the past, by our own old experiences. Instead when we give up or surrender, what we don't know seems to take over because we've let go of control. It's as if some unknown force sorts it out, and usually in ways we could not even have imagined. So in moments where I just don't know what to do, instead of struggling and getting anxious and upset, and making sure I hedge my bets, I now say out loud:

"I give up. I completely let go. Unconscious mind, Life, God, the Universe, Angels, whatever goodness and wisdom is inside me and out there, please help me as I've done all that I know to do and I now surrender to the best possible outcome. Thank you."

And do you know what? It works. It really works! Something happens which is way beyond my ability or my thought processes to fathom out. By letting go, by stopping trying to control things my way, Life seems to step in and defuses or sorts out the problem. It never fails to amaze me. People and situations arrive which you could never have engineered with the limited capacity of your own mind, and you will feel joyously free again. You will be amazed how often problems disappear – or at least diminish in importance and urgency – if you just take your mind off trying to solve it.

Make the best of this moment

and this … and this …

Tracking Your Thoughts - exercise

My brother used to have a toy train that went round and round a track when he pressed a switch. That's just like our thoughts, they go round and round until the train derails. The question is, do you want to go round and round until you get derailed, or do you simply not bother to get on the train at all? When we're in negative mode we dredge up all the evidence we can find to support us in our misery. We play the same old pictures, films and sound tracks over and over again inside the cinema-screen of our mind to help us wallow, and we do it on the biggest screen possible in glorious Technicolor. We sit hunched up in a way that increases our misery, we use grizzly language and a miserable voice tone to help us feel even more of a victim, and focus superbly on what will make us feel terrible. In fact, we could win Oscars for our daily performance.

The solution? When you notice the first negative thought, make the choice not to repeat it. Don't get on the train in the first place, and don't press the on-switch. It's so simple – not necessarily easy, but certainly simple! Our tendency is to give importance to a thought, and then grab hold of it for dear life. Then we feed it and grow it. But it's only a thought! It doesn't matter unless you make it matter.

How do you **not** get on the train? Go and do something you enjoy doing or that's fun instead. Play some music and dance, jump up and down on one leg, go outside and pull up some weeds from the garden, clap your hands, stamp your feet, drink a glass of water, paint your toe-nails, sing in the shower, phone a positive friend (not to moan!) and demand that she cheers you up, read a page of a juicy novel, jump on your man, kiss the milkman, clean your teeth, massage your ears, anything to distract your mind from that train of thought. You may have to 'train' your mind to get off the train, but it won't take long once you've got the hang of it, and it's so much nicer than seeing that same dreary old scenery going past yet again.

Even better, make the best of what you're actually doing right here right now, because how you deal with NOW is actually creating your future. If each and every moment you're making the most of what is actually going on, no matter what it is, your present and your future just gets better and better and better. When you do, your mind relaxes and opens up to other possibilities, which often resolves the original problem as your intuition steps in to guide you.

Be here, now, where you are.

Focus completely on whatever is in front of you, whether it is eating an orange, cleaning the bathroom, sorting your accounts, putting on your makeup, washing the dishes, playing with your child, making love. Look at what's there; see the colours and the textures, hear the sounds, feel the air around you, smell the aromas. Use the power of all your senses to pull you into present time awareness, and the murky thoughts will diminish in their power. This is being in the now, the gift of the present. This is where life actually happens – not in the past, not in the future, but now this very moment. And life becomes so exquisitely beautiful.

Children teach us so much. Look at a two year-old fighting over a toy. When you substitute the toy with something more interesting, the tantrum will stop and the child will smile again and forget what she has let go of. Your mind is just the same; it behaves like a two year-old having a temper tantrum, so substitute with something more interesting, more beautiful, more exciting, more fun. You see, your choices of action at any given moment may be limited, but your choices of thought are not! There are infinite possibilities!

"But," I can hear you say yet again, "that's not reality! That's pretending the bad stuff doesn't exist." Not at all. We've trained ourselves to focus on the ghastliness of what we call day to day reality.

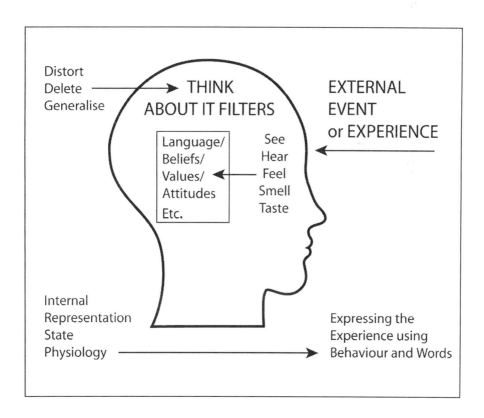

We've trained ourselves to tell the truth as **we** see it, filtered through our experiences, through our conditioned eyes. But remember, in order to cope with the 2 million bits of information it receives every second, the brain distorts, deletes and generalises and so it may not be **the** truth at all, but just what you are choosing to focus your attention on.

When we understand this, it makes even our accepted history seem questionable – through whose eyes was our history written? How different would it have been written if it was her-story?

You honestly don't score points for seeking out horror and misery in your own life and scaring yourself with awful thoughts. So focus instead on lovely things that make you feel good - a beautiful sunset, a rose, photographs of loved ones, a painting, a tree, the sky, whatever fills your heart and soul with gratitude. Why? Because it alters your vibration and makes you more resourceful and able to deal with anything that occurs.

Our Extraordinary Mind

The mind is so vast, so amazing, so awesome, so omnipotent that we cannot conceptualise it until we break it down. I use this beautiful picture of an iceberg with my clients to explain the difference between the functions of the conscious mind and the unconscious mind. The conscious part of the mind is like the tip of the iceberg – it is the logical part where we make decisions, where we analyse things, but it is only a small part, some say as little as 1%. And it can only hold a very limited amount of information at any one time – apparently seven things at once, plus or minus two.

Our unconscious mind on the other hand is about 99% of our mind. That's the part that while you are playing the piano, is breathing for you, growing your hair and finger nails, beating your heart, maybe growing a baby, keeping the rhythm of your fingers on the keys, smiling, digesting your croissants, healing your cells, listening out for the children, balancing your hormones and performing millions of other miraculous tasks all at the same time, without you even having to think about it.

When you can understand what I am about to tell you now, it will make an enormous difference to your life. You see, the unconscious mind can't tell the difference between what is real and what is imaginary. So you could be just pretending to play the piano, or really playing it, because when you fully participate, even in your imagination, you produce the same vibration and your unconscious mind is responding as if it is true.

I suggest you read this paragraph a few times and let it sink in. The vibration of the thoughts you are thinking or imagining, accompanied by the intensity of your emotions while you're doing it, go out into the Universe seeking something vibrating at the same resonance. So, what you are thinking and what comes back to you is always a vibrational match. Your emotions are like your Satellite Navigation System; they tell you what's on its way, good or bad. So if you're feeling grim, know that you're in the process of attracting grim stuff, people or events. If you're feeling fabulous, all the goodies are coming your way.

So how you are vibrating, attracts more of the same!

Are you getting it yet? Amazing huh? But also extraordinary as it means we can be in charge of our lives. This makes such a difference to who we are as women. So how can we use this untapped resource more fully?

Easy as ABC

Three little words that have been used so often have been given to us from the great Andrew Carnegie who said "Whatever (wo)man can conceive, whatever (s)he believes, (wo)man can achieve."

Conceive ~ Believe ~ Achieve

I would turn them round to read the other way, because it is your imagination, your words and feeling that hold the power. Imagine you have already achieved what it is you truly desire, believe it has already come to pass, then conceive whatever it is you need to do in order to ensure it comes about.

Achieve ~ Believe ~ Conceive

Then be open to receive when the Universe comes to deliver. And keep doing it over and over again.

This powerful word 'conceive' also means visualise, imagine, picture, envisage, conjure up (just like a magician!) When our unconscious mind gets involved, and we really believe that what we want is not only possible but that it has already happened somewhere in boundless time and space, even though we may not see it YET, the Universe seems to conspire to ensure that our wishes are granted.

What Do You Really, Really, Really Want?

If you have seen that hilarious movie 'What Women Want' with Mel Gibson, you will recall that he is able to listen in to the thought processes going on in women's heads. It drives him crazy with the non-stop chatter, unrelated thoughts and high emotion in contrast to his ordered masculine mind.

So if we are sending mixed messages as to what we want out into the Universe, guess what? We will get a mixed response back. If we're not specific enough, the Universe is unable to decipher what we really want, so we need to conceive carefully. This literally determines the course our life will take.

You see, we tend to take out a mental insurance policy on what we say we want, just in case. Let me tell you a story. A woman goes to heaven, and as she is moving through the beautiful halls, she notices side rooms full of objects covered in dust sheets. Intrigued, she asks her guardian angel what they are. He tells her there are millions of rooms like that in heaven. "Every time you want something, the angels hear your request and get so excited as you go off into your dream world picturing and imagining what it is you want, and they prepare everything ready to deliver to you. Then you go and say things like, "I don't suppose I'll ever get it. I'm not good enough," so the angels put everything away. Then a bit later you say, "But it would be so nice!" And so the angels take off the dust sheets ready to deliver to you. Then you say, "But if I get the job maybe I'll have to spend too much time away from my boyfriend; then we'll split up, and I probably won't get the job because I'm not experienced enough … and anyway I don't really need a Porsche … and how can I be thinking like this when there's so much poverty in the world?"

And suddenly the Universe, in all its wisdom and desire to give you what is uttermost in your mind, withdraws its support from your original dream to give you what your new request is, **not** to get the job because that's what you've just requested. Then when you don't get it, you say, "I knew I wouldn't get it, I'm just not good enough." And it becomes once more a self-fulfilling prophesy."

Who do you know who does this?

It's like going to a certain burger bar, (you know the one I mean!) and ordering a burger and fries, which are identical whether you order in Prague, Amsterdam or Brighton, and hoping instead to get Steak Diane with a delicious green salad, sauté potatoes and a glass of Cabernet Sauvignon to go with it. No chance. You get what you order, whatever is uppermost in your mind.

Your Must Haves

In the previous chapter we wrote down our must not haves. Now write down your all your dreams and desires, your must haves. Make a list of what you really would like in your life, material objects, relationships, career, health, family, wealth. Put it all down, no judging, no saying, "I don't deserve this." No saying, "I couldn't possibly have that." Let your imagination soar.

What else? … What else? …

This is important as you will find out in a later chapter.

Dream a Little Dream

This is a vital ingredient of deliberate creation. If you really want something, program it into your unconscious mind when you are totally relaxed by day-dreaming in vivid detail. And then get out of the way. In other words, don't do anything to prevent it happening. This is never about using will-power. Really imagine that you already have your desire and are already experiencing it. Take it as read, that it is just a fact of life. At the same time let go of any attachment to the outcome, so you're not yearning for it. Then inspired by your vision, begin to take steps towards your outcome. It will happen at the perfect time. It must **be**; it can be no other way. It's the way this incredible Universe works. The CD that accompanies this book will help you do this effortlessly.

When you put your request out into the Universe as an intention, as a decree, it will happen. When you allow it to, when you put yourself vibrationally in harmony with what you desire, and when you follow through by taking action towards your outcome as if you already have it, your emotions will tell you whether

you are allowing or resisting it right now.

The seed of your desire contains everything necessary for it to blossom to fulfillment, just as a seed or a daffodil bulb contains everything necessary to create a beautiful flower. Your job is just to give it a fertile growing place in order to put roots down, expand and bloom.

As women what we need to do is enjoy ourselves (find that inner joy), please ourselves (find that which pleases us at a deep level) connect with ourselves, be ourselves and love ourselves in the essence of our femininity. A far cry from the way we have been brought up – 'You have to suffer to be beautiful,' and 'Put everyone else's needs before your own.'

What I am suggesting here may sound selfish, but it is vitally important because until you can connect with your authentic self, love yourself, enjoy your life and share that essence with others, you have nothing to give to anyone else. As the air stewardess says, "Put your own oxygen mask on first before going to the assistance of anyone else."

My middle name is Joy, and while I hated the name when I was growing up, I now realise what a blessing it is. My joy is at my core and is the greatest gift that I can give to anyone. When I am joyful, it spreads to everyone in my presence and goes out like ripples on a pond. I know that when I fail to look after myself, to honour who I am and forget to treat myself with the love and respect that I deserve, when I look outside myself for approval from others, then I become not only a burden to other people but I give my power away. I make other people responsible for my life, my happiness, my joy, when that power and joy is inside me all the time, just waiting to be unlocked.

Your feminine essence is like a beautiful diamond buried in a lump of carbon. It is there wanting to shine brilliantly. All you have to do is chip off the outer covering to reveal it, polish its multitude of facets and marvel at its brilliance. When you discover it, it will lead you through life in the most wonderful way.

Like mining for diamonds or mining for gold, mine each moment for something that feels good, something to appreciate, something to relish, something to savour. That's what the moments that make up your precious life are about. It's not about justifying your existence; your existence is already justified because you exist! It's not about proving your worthiness; you're already worthy. It's not about achieving ultimate success, because, guess what? You're never going to get every single thing done that you want to in this one lifetime. So RELAX and enjoy the journey!

Choose the truths that really serve you well. We create our own truths; they're not static and set in stone, but fluid and dynamic. I have seen women pulled down by their truth of illness, failed relationships, loneliness, bitterness and misery, and others uplifted by their truth of friendship and warmth and wellness and love and happiness and abundance, even if what is showing up in front of them belies their beliefs. They know they are creating their own future.

What you are living and how you are living it is your truth.

Return to Sender - exercise

If all you do is look for things to appreciate you will live a joyous, spectacular life, the life of being who you really are at your essence. It's the only thing you ever need to do. Can you imagine how the world would be if most of us did that? Not la la land, but somewhere so extraordinarily beautiful, peaceful and loving.

Ignore anything that does not please you, just don't pay attention to it, and allow your eyes, ears, feelings, touch and taste to feast on what feels good, and keep practicing until it becomes a habit. Practice feeling good, and the more you do it the more you will manifest what you truly desire.

savour ~ appreciate ~ enjoy

S.a.e. This is like a self-addressed envelope - when you can savour, appreciate and enjoy, it comes back to you multiplied. Our lives and our attitudes towards other women are a reflection of the way we think about ourselves, so if it is not working, stop doing it. It can't be right.

We have had to fight to get to where we are – but enough is enough! It is time to stop fighting and being defensive, take off our armour and just BE. Allowingness is what it is all about. When we respect, honour and support the feminine in ourselves, we in turn will be respected and honoured. It's time too to champion and support other women rather than be competitive with them as well. This awakening process is a chance to blossom and to grow.

Who is Wrecking Your Life?

Why won't people change the way they behave? Why can't they behave the way we want them to? We get so frustrated and annoyed with other people: our mothers, our partners, our ex-partners, our children, our colleagues, our bosses, our politicians. They seem to be out to get us at every turn. Don't we matter enough for them to change their conduct and their attitudes? Ouch! It really hurts!

But when you realise no-one else has to change in order for you to feel fantastic and to blossom, life becomes a totally different game, because you are in charge of your thoughts and feelings. No-one else. Just you. What absolute freedom!

It's not about them. It's never about them. It's always about you and your response. It doesn't mean you have to hang around trying to persuade someone else that you're good enough; it's not about you lowering your standards to someone else's scarcity fears; it's not about you making yourself small to accommodate someone else's ego.

When I feel people are not being as kind to me as I would like, I say,

I don't deserve that.

And I'm not doing it to myself any more.

Show Me Your Friends and I'll Tell You Who You Are!

We become who we hang around with. If people around you are a constant drain on your energy or keep telling you that you can't do something that's important to you, then spend less time with them or change your set of friends to those who support and encourage your growth. Other people have different agendas for your life which is not necessarily what you want for yourself, and when you open your lives to change, so often it feels like a threat to those around you.

As women we don't like to upset the status quo and we get anxious not to offend other people. But to have your precious energy sapped from you is not going to benefit your health, your life or the world. My closest friends and I have an agreement that we will point out to each other if we're going back into our old patterns, using negative language or behaving in a way that is not true to who we really are. It means the days of tea and sympathy are over, but the days of joy and laughter and extraordinary happenings have become a way of life for us.

Be with people whose energy level is good, and only stay with people whose energy is less than yours if they are willing and wanting to change. Negative energy is like a parasite – it sucks the juice out of you, so don't stay long in that presence or it will make you literally sick. If you are not surrounded by uplifting people who think you are great, you sink to their model of the world. Don't waste your precious energy. When we are with the wrong people, our light literally goes out. Politely and gently, GET OUT OF THERE!

During the last few months of my marriage, I used to get an awful feeling of pressure around my head when my husband came anywhere near me, as if I was being hit over the head with a wooden mallet. He always looked so angry, in a black funk. It felt as if he'd stuck a vacuum-cleaner hose into my guts and sucked the life-force out of me. Being in the same room with him left me exhausted and drained, feeling useless and very vulnerable.
Catherine.

Bad energy makes you feel queasy. You literally can't stay in mental pollution created by yourself or others. It's time to get rid of the negative talk. Put up notices around rooms in the house, particularly the bedroom and dining area to remind you.

Do the things you love

With the people you love
And think only the thoughts you love!

Bring people into your life who will celebrate who you are at any given moment, not just on birthdays and anniversaries but because it's Thursday or Monday, and because you are you, and that is who they are celebrating!

Maybe this sounds like cloud cuckoo land. "It's just like Pollyanna," I hear you say. "It's not reality." But actually it **is** reality. It's fear that causes poverty, war and deprivation, stock-market crashes and depression, famine and fighting and all the other horrors in the world. Fear causes people to act in horrific ways both at an individual and collective level.

Reality is not clouded with resentment, sadness, guilt, bitterness, anger, greed, fear, defeat, argument and lack of respect. Reality is free of all these things, free of conditioning.

When you are truly at your best, you have the wisdom and energy to make a powerful difference in the world.

Energy, like people, hangs around with that which is similar, so positivity hangs around with positivity – negativity hangs around with negativity. This is not about positive thinking – that doesn't work. Like the American success coach Anthony Robbins says, you can't go out into a garden full of weeds and claim, "There's no weeds." You have to pull up the weeds, and focus on, water and nourish the flowers.

Your Satellite Navigation System

The Universe responds to how you are feeling and the vibrations you are sending out right now, this minute … and now … this minute. The Universe can't tell the difference between the vibration of some event that you are actually experiencing, some glorious juicy memory, or your imagination.

Vibration is vibration is vibration

As I touched on earlier, your feelings and emotions are like a Sat. Nav. System. They tell you everything that you need to know about your relationship with your true feminine essence and Source Energy, and whether you are in the flow of allowing and receiving or not. What we've been living by is all learned behaviour. We learned at our mother's knee that the world is a frightening place, and how we need to protect ourselves by hiding who we really are and what we really think and feel. But Life responds to our every vibration. So how would it be if today you can make a new decision about what you really want your life to be about, and make that new vibration dominant? How would it be if we come out of the closet as real feminine women? Don't you think you're worth a little bit of effort? I do.

It's not to do with will-power. When we exert our will-power, it becomes a battle between the conscious versus our unconscious mind where all our habits and conditioning are stored; that's our personal blueprint, and the Unconscious mind always wins. That's why we have so much trouble sticking to New Year's resolutions. Our blueprint decides our life. Once you have let go of the old useless conditioning and you program the right material into your unconscious mind, you can influence and change your blueprint. Now is a good time to replace the old stuff with a new positive input.

So what does it take to do that?

Little Gems

❋ Daily focus on what you desire – use your imagination to daydream

❋ Concentrate on what you want to become – ignore what you don't want

❋ Demand more of your life – Life supports you all the time; you only have to notice

❋ Raise your standards – be all you know you are inside

❋ Expand your beingness by using a conscious deliberate thought process

When you recognize who you really are – a feminine loving woman with so much to offer – you will know that you deserve to have anything you desire. Create your own reality by conscious intention. Affirm its possibility gently and in a relaxed way until belief sets in. Create an ideal of how it is to be and expect its manifestation. It cannot help but show up.

What are Your Rules of Life?

One of the biggest challenges in life in this rapidly changing information age is choosing what to do in our lives, what to focus on and what to spend time and energy on, particularly when we have such a large range of choices on offer every day. Having a clear purpose allows us to do that.

The trouble is we have rules for ourselves and others, but our rules often get in the way. People who are successful have fewer rules. If you have lots of rules as to how other people should behave, how life has to be in order for you to be happy, the less happy you are going to be. So if your rules say in order to be happy you have to have a perfect relationship where your man tells you he loves you 100 times a day AND £1,000,000 in the bank AND be a size 10 AND totally fit AND have an immaculate home AND be Managing Director AND have the latest sports car AND the most well-behaved children AND be invited to a party every weekend AND have 3 exotic holidays a year, you may find some of these things may let you down! Try substituting OR for the AND, or create better rules, and see how much happier you already are.

The happiest people are those who are grateful to be alive, who appreciate a smile, who find delight in adventure, joy in a simple action, who love being with other people and also love their own company. If you can find joy in small things, the big things are a bonus.

How You Look at the World

When we look at the world through eyes of anger even though it may be justifiable, for example anti-war, anti-poverty, we join our energy to other people's state of anger or lack in the world. There is so much anger and resentment in anti-war marches, people willing to do battle in the name of peace. You cannot create peace that way. Even watching the news and getting upset or angry about what is going on in the world adds fuel to the fire. As a young teenager I remember going to a ban-the-bomb rally thinking I was marching for peace – it was terrifying and disturbed me for years.

If it all makes you feel powerless, do something constructive. Take action; befriend someone who needs some encouragement. Your help towards changing one life could be the one life that in turn saves thousands; you just never know. If you want peace, think calm loving thoughts; if you want wealth think abundantly; if you want health, think healthy thoughts rather than those of illness. Go on a joyful walk for peace, a workshop on abundance, a talk on health. Do what makes you feel good. Smile at strangers and spread a little happiness.

Neurologically, when we contribute toward the higher good in the world, the pleasure centre lights up in our brain, and it encourages us to do more, so we get constant feedback when we are on track. When we decide what our contribution is, what our purpose is, our life becomes like a beautiful song.

Vision and Purpose

How would it be if you jump into the unknown where creativity and potential live, and create something really special for yourself? We are creators. We really can do almost anything we set our mind to.

Happiness is not dependent on what has already happened. It's about what we individually really want. It might be the pursuit of money, but money for its own sake is usually an empty purpose; it is often just not enough! It might be a beautiful home or a business venture, having a family or an ambition realised, a special relationship or a talent explored. But more often than not, pursuing your life purpose will in turn bring you those other things anyway. Only you can decide what will really make a difference to you; that when you have it, will completely transform your life.

I believe as children, we come with a knowing of what we are here for, what our purpose is, where our true desires and talents lie, and it is those desires that are like the seed part of us which will grow. Sadly we are then often educated out of what really matters to us, and we often end up doing something to please others, which bears no relation to our true calling. So ask yourself, "**Who** am I going to be and **how** am I going to be?" Because it really is up to you.

We need a vision for our life or we won't know which direction to go in, nor if we've got there. When people tell me all they want to do is retire, I know that is a death sentence. We all need vision and purpose, and as women we can do so much good in our lives. This inner quality, this inherent purpose is deeply touched when we follow our dreams.

The Universe rewards those that are living their lives **on purpose**, particularly those who include the well-being and happiness of others in their vision. If you are aiming for your own happiness, include that of your family. If you are aiming for your family's happiness, include that of your community. If you are aiming for your community's happiness, include that of your country. If you are aiming for your country's happiness, include that of the world. If you are aiming for the world's happiness, include that of the Universe.

When you discover your true purpose and begin to live it, you will just be joyous and present in the moment, because anything that fills you up with joy is effortless. There is no place for "I'm not good enough" when you are on purpose, because you are just fully alive. When you are in the flow of life, you are passionately involved in what you do and full of excitement about the future. Motivated by enthusiasm and inspired by creativity, you are fully self-expressed, fully alive. You feel as if you are indeed in the right place. You are guided; everything just flows as you draw into your life the people, situations and circumstances you need, and it feels as if you just can't go wrong. Even challenges seem to melt before you as you shine your light into the world.

So what is it that calls to you? What is the mission that is powerfully calling you into being? When you can discover it and answer its call, put your life into it, your heart and soul, your whole being into it. Yes it takes courage, integrity and passion, but as you have already discovered, you have this in abundance.

All your worries and anxieties will melt away, as you begin to focus single-mindedly on accomplishing your vision for what you want to see happen in the world. When we live our lives **on purpose**, we find ourselves. It's like coming home. We find balance and inner peace.

Many of those old conditioned 'programs' that we've adopted, cover up our spirit. Our natural state when you take away the programs, is one of peace and of being in the flow. As soon as you are in the flow, you are so much happier; worries melt away, you experience euphoria and you get the benefit of whole brain thinking.

Enjoy your life. Move into what you're supposed to be doing, and connect with your spirit. When you align yourself with your true purpose, your life path, life becomes effortless and success arrives with grace and elegance.

What are your dreams? Discover what you are you here for... and then do it! Take action. Understand who you really are and what you are here to do!

Your Life Purpose – exercise

Ask someone to read this next part out to you and guide you through the process. This exercise gives us so much insight as to what we are supposed to be doing in our lives.

Close your eyes and think what you wanted to be when you were growing up. Go back to a time when you were 5/6/7/8/9/10 yrs old. Ask yourself, "What did I love doing when I was a little girl? What did I want to be when I was a child?" Write it down.

Who were your role models? Whatever you wanted to be, why did you want to be that? What were your feelings, what were the sensations? For example maybe a singer, using your voice and being on stage. Maybe an archaeologist, making miraculous discoveries and finding something unique to share with people. Maybe a dancer, explorer, teacher, doctor, vet, artist, athlete, scientist, inventor, making things with your hands or looking after other people.

Why did you want to do that? What feelings did you hope it would give you? What did you want from it?

Now remember a time at any age when you were really on a roll, where you felt incredibly well, things were effortless, when you felt, "Wow I really love this. This is what life is about. I want to feel like this forever." Step back in your mind and in your body, just as you were then. Look through your own eyes as if you were actually still there. See what you saw, hear what you heard.

What are you doing? What are you feeling? What was the state you were in? What were you experiencing?

Think about it. Was there anything in common with this and with what you wanted to have in life? With how big you wanted to grow, or what you wanted to create, or contribute, or discover, or expand, or challenge or love? What were you feeling? What were you doing?

When you get a sense of what that was, then think of another state when you were on a roll and when life was really flowing and you felt, "This is it, this is what life is about. I love this." Step into it right now. Look around. What were you feeling, seeing, tasting, and smelling? What were you doing? Were you creating or writing or acting or making something or studying or helping or teaching or working or on a beach or climbing a mountain? How were you feeling? Were other people involved? What was the process? How were you being, and what were you doing? Feel it in your body. Is there anything similar between this and the last experience, or this and the feelings that you wanted to experience when you were growing up and the things you wanted to be?

Feel it. Capture it. Now do it again – remember a time when you felt incredible. This is it. Step into it. What were you doing? What were you feeling, creating, sharing? Feel those feelings, really feel them.

Ok now open your eyes.

Maybe you are not doing what you originally envisaged but doing something similar. The most important thing is that you need the ESSENCE of what you really want. This then becomes your purpose.

When you feel you have it, write it down. You may need to spend a while getting it really right, until it makes you feel absolutely amazing and it resonates with your inner being.

The purpose of my life is ...

You need to say it in a few simple phrases, brief and emotionally charged; how you're going to be as a person, what you're going to do and how it relates to others.

Your job is not to be perfect, it's to be excellent. And it's not about the future. This feeling is something to achieve every day, so life takes on a whole new significance. What must I have in my life? What must happen in order for my life to have been worthwhile? What is the one thing that I must have or do, that will knock everything else into touch?

Put a copy on the wall, in your purse. And keep checking in by asking, "How can I live my purpose more? Am I on track? If this was going to make me into somebody more, what can I do to make it more?"

Often this is not about getting your dream – it's giving you your destiny. We have come through many pitfalls to get where we are now, and when we look for the benefits in seemingly impossible or distressing events, we will find them and realise that somehow they will have served us.

Inside each one of us is the desire to live passionately. When we are doing what inspires us, thrills us, makes us feel amazing, when we use our unique talents it will give us the greatest sense of fulfillment.

Enjoy the life you have. Touch the people around you. Live your life's purpose.

This is your life. Make it matter.

An average life lasts for 2,475,576,000 seconds.

Don't let yours be average!

You can turn your life around

in just one heartbeat!

When you fulfil the promise of who you are, Life will support your every move and you will attract the right people towards you. And always remember, although you have a purpose in life, don't take life too seriously. Don't take yourself too seriously.

Gratitude Journal - exercise

Buy yourself a beautiful book to write in. Every morning write in it ten things you are grateful for, and in the evening write in it ten things that have happened during the day that you really appreciated. Find things that really count and appreciate them till you have tears in your eyes and as you realise just how blessed you really are. The more you do this, the more magic and miracles will appear.

Now you have far greater clarity and understanding, it's time to rest and relax and learn how to nurture and enjoy your beautiful feminine energy.

Your notes....

Gestation

Gestation is a time of growth, of nurturing and development, of expansion, of tender care and protection, our growing time in the womb of our creation. While masculine energy is more like a science in its efficient rigidity, feminine energy is more like an art in its dreamy flow when we give it the freedom to be. A woman who is free in her feminine energy is so appealing; if she's already happy, babies gurgle, animals become docile. Then, like it or not, men show up in their droves.

This is a time of celebration of who we are. Being happy is the cornerstone of your existence, and you can achieve this with a clear mind. You have a gift that is uniquely yours, intertwined with the attributes of the feminine with all your intuition and mystery and beauty and love. Give yourself permission to develop these greatest of female gifts because intrinsically we already know how to be this way. Laugh, play, sing, dance, rest, relax and love with the celebration of who you are and of the magnificence you are becoming day by day. This is how we can bring about change; this is how we can make a difference right here, right now.

This chapter is devoted to learning how to cherish our feminine energy, being true to our intrinsic nature, loving and honouring our lives in a gentle yet powerful way. It talks about how to enhance our femininity by the way we look, by the way we eat and by the way we exercise. Some of this information may be blindingly obvious; some exercises so simple it almost goes without saying, but the power lies behind the combination. Put it all together and you create something truly awe-inspiring. It will teach you things you do not yet know; it will remind you of things you already know but are not doing. As the Chinese proverb says, 'To know and not to do, is not yet to know.'

When visiting my friend Simon's family in Australia, his adorable little daughter Christie fascinated me and taught me so much about femininity. At age three and in a household with three older brothers, she would flirt with anyone passing by with her long fluttering eyelashes, her engaging smile, her rapt focussed attention and her sweet girly wiggle. Her soft voice meant that her brothers had to be quiet to hear her, and when sitting on someone's lap, she would cup their face in her hands and turn it towards her to give her their total attention as she tilted her head on one side to talk. She was never aggressive but charming and delightful, and the boys showered her with affection and adoration and really looked after her. This was Christie's intrinsic feminine nature combined with her instinctive cave-girl need for survival, and of course she had men wrapped around her little finger.

Yet she could be fiercely demanding if she turned her mind to it; she could shriek like a banshee until she got attention, would burst into tears, stamp her foot, and talk baby talk in a way that made your heart melt. This is the storm of the feminine that passes just as quickly if acknowledged. I'm not suggesting that we should employ her tactics, but she 'did feminine' in abundance.

Femininity has an extraordinary appeal to a real man in contrast to his own strong and firm masculinity. The more feminine we appear, the more masculine men can be. When he realises and acknowledges his own strength and ability, he feels a great sense of pride in who he is and a deep desire to protect, because we awaken his tender feelings.

When our femininity disappears, his romantic feelings disappear so it's the risk you take - love it or leave it. He may respect and admire a woman who has lost her femininity but it won't be the same. For him, it will be more like having a mate rather than a lover.

So who is this ultimately feminine woman I keep talking about? In my workshops, women have said:

"Not needing to be tough and ruthless, powerful and aggressive, dominating and forceful, she is naturally oriented towards her womanhood. She is soft, gentle, warm, loving, sensual, sexy, passionate, caring, compelling in her womanliness; one who revels in being a woman, who allows the beauty and vulnerability in her to be revealed. She can relax into her softness and her pleasure of living, her voluptuousness and her warmth, to be Yin to her partner's Yang. Female energy is everywhere, in the dance, in the flow, in every colour, hue, taste, flavour, smell and movement. When she follows her heart, her life transforms."

And that is only the beginning!

Falling In Love Again

We are, I believe, coming into the age of awareness, consciousness and enlightenment. It's now time to inhabit our bodies in a new way. Our physical body is the way our essence expresses its presence in the world, so it's time to fall in love with our bodies, the home of our spirit which we have so tragically neglected. Remember that women are deeply connected with love and spirituality. We come with a beautiful soul, so where it is housed really matters.

At the core of many of our problems as women is the notion of perfection, and we chase after it thinking that the perfect body equals the perfect life. Right now, the fashion seems to be for a size 00, where bones protrude and eating disorders proliferate. We are designed to go in at the waist and out at the hips, yet fashion dictates that slim boyish hips are more attractive even though it puts us more at risk for producing babies.

All this competition creates such intense pain, instability and desperation, and yet again we have bought into it. Body hatred is recent; until women got the vote, soft rounded hips and thighs and bellies were perceived as desirable and sensual without question. The more powerful women become, it appears the more pressure there is to get rid of all the padding and curves that make us inherently female.

We certainly have proof that hating our bodies doesn't work, otherwise the health and diet industry would not thrive. When we lash out at our bellies, our hips, our thighs, our cellulite and our breasts, we're lashing out at what makes us uniquely female. Saying the same hateful things to ourselves day after day and year after year has not made us healthier or slimmer or happier. Nature has designed us this way for a purpose, and when we hate our bodies we hate ourselves.

In contrast, when you surrender to enjoying and accepting yourself wholeheartedly, like magic your body will change anyway as you learn to respect it more and feed it with loving thoughts. So if something is not working, don't do it harder; do it differently.

What would happen if women stopped hating their bodies? Can you imagine how powerful and unstoppable we'd be? We seem more comfortable with self-abuse than self-love, but contempt seldom inspires change. Get over it. Stop talking about it and instead move into your body. Re-inhabit your body with genuine love and understanding. When you feel love rather than hate or fear towards your own body, you will feel gloriously powerful and completely independent of the opinions of others. Enjoy the body you're living in – luxuriate in it, worship it.

Let go of finding fault with yourself and also with other people. Don't wait till you complete that class, loose that weight, earn more money. You are the perfect you at the perfect time, right here, right now. How can others see the glory in you if you don't see it in yourself first?

So let's get out of our heads and our judgment and come gently into our heart. Live with more integrity and see yourself as an expression of the Divine; and when you do, you will naturally take greater care of your most precious possession, and it will transform almost by magic.

Your Beautiful Woman's Body

From the time that we are old enough to understand, instead of learning to respect and enjoy the wonders of our body and the magnificent destiny of our womanhood, the messages we girls receive about growing up, menstruation, sex, giving birth and ageing usually teach us that it's inconvenient, messy, embarrassing, shameful, painful and frightening. Our nervous system takes this on board and thus we become programmed with an irrational fear. For each and every one of those threatening thoughts, a chemical and physiological response occurs within our body which causes the strands of our DNA to tighten up like wringing out a T-shirt. In turn this creates internal stress which we carry around with us every minute of our existence.

Books, television and magazine articles abound with advice and advertisements on which pills to take, which surgery to have, which exercise regime is best, which apparatus to buy, which cream to put on our face, which products to choose to make ourselves thinner, sexier, younger, more desirable as if there is something fundamentally wrong with us. Is it any wonder we suffer from low self-esteem? But none of these external agents will truly work by themselves. Even the good book says, 'Love thy neighbour as thyself.' But that depends on loving yourself first.

The Body Beautiful

Female energy is about energy everywhere. We thrive and brighten and come into our own when we receive praise and attention from others. Once you give that same praise and attention to yourself, it will also fly towards you from other sources.

What make us uniquely female, are our bodies. So much about us is internal, not only physically with the way our sexual and reproductive organs are hidden, but also emotionally as we focus on our feelings and emotions more internally than men. Just by the very nature of the design of our female bodies, we need to treat ourselves in a different way from men.

Our body is a wondrous miracle and can be an absolute joy, yet sadly we don't take much notice of it until something goes wrong. Overnight illnesses, like overnight successes, have taken years in preparation. We're given so many warning signs but fail to take notice when we are overworked, overwhelmed or are not looking after ourselves sufficiently, and here I speak from experience. Many times I have failed to listen to its urgings, whisperings and yearnings to relax and play, and have overworked until my body has just given up. Enforced rest is not much fun after the first couple of days!

The Pharmacy Within

Take a moment now and think about your body in all its extraordinary magnificence. Within your body lies the power to heal and transform itself which far outreaches any modern remedies, when you assist and work with it. Enormously resilient when you take care of it properly, your body is literally a powerful chemical factory which has within it the ability to manufacture anything that's created in a pharmacy. It is able to mix far better medicine than your doctor can prescribe, in the right proportions and in the right strength to heal your ills without any nasty side effects. All you need to do is learn to access that ability, and while you will not find all the answers on these pages, I hope it will give you the encouragement to seek further knowledge and understanding.

Girls Must Be Girls!

In order to awaken our feminine in a strong healthy way, we need to be in great shape physically, mentally, emotionally and spiritually. Some of us have had to grow up so fast that we've missed out on the ease and simplicity of childhood, and with the age of innocence stripped away by fashion, films, television, games and technology, we may also have missed out on that time of playfulness. This time of re-parenting ourselves means that we can treat ourselves the way we really want, be a loving parent to ourselves, give ourselves all the love and joy we desire and have enormous fun at the same time.

Walking through the city of London, I see young women who are so stressed that their bodies appear almost tortured. Their release is in alcohol, cigarettes and cocaine, late nights and unfulfilling sexual encounters. They seem unable to access that part of themselves which is beautiful, peaceful, loving, creative, dynamic and life-enhancing.

So it's time to take stock. If you are out drinking pint for pint with the lads, have sexual encounters which leave you feeling empty inside, or if you have just forgotten what it is like to feel deliciously feminine, then now is a good time to return to the well of female wisdom, time to be true to your authentic nature, and be lovingly devoted to your outcome.

I must tell you that my very first coaching client some nine years ago was a 'working girl,' or as she so proudly told me, 'a prostitute,' and I had the greatest admiration for her. She was amazing, looking after men with disabilities who normally had no opportunity for a sexual encounter. She had incredibly high self-esteem. I know a couple of other women too who for one reason or another have chosen the oldest profession in the world, and I respect and honour their choice.

But for the rest of us, you know when things are shallow; you know what satisfies your soul at a deep level. And you know instinctively whether something is good for you. So while alcohol and drugs might feel good in the moment, we know deep down that it is affecting our energy at a cellular level. Having sex may feel good, but a woman who sleeps around without the love of her heart and the respect of her body betrays the very essence of her being as a woman. This is not about morality; it's about what enhances our inner self and what diminishes it.

We hear so many stories of pop stars and actors who have used all the drugs, parties, alcohol and sex to try and reach a place of fulfillment within themselves, and they just cannot access it. A rule of thumb – if it makes you feel bad somewhere inside, you know it's wrong for you.

Girls must be girls. Even if like me you also enjoy auto-cross, motor-racing, lifting weights, winter sports, snooker, sailing, diving, fishing and other typically male pursuits, realise that your inner female needs extra special consideration and nourishing. Many of us spend more time planning our homes, cars, careers and pastimes than we do our lives, our health and our well-being, but as women we need to take extra special care as our reproductive system has far more sensitive areas than men have.

Our beautiful female bodies are not designed for really hard continual manual labour; that's man's work, because of our smaller hands and smaller frame. Yet in many countries of the world, women toil out in the fields while the men sit around drinking coffee discussing the politics of the day. And in the more industrialized cities, women drive themselves beyond endurance. We have too much ambition, too much pushing beyond our natural limits and too much activity that depletes the body's nourishing yin element, all the while still trying to justify our existence.

A number of my female clients run marathons and participate in iron-men challenges, mountain-bike racing and triathlons competing with men, and wonder why there's no energy left for creativity, or why their sexual impulse seems to have vanished. Running is one of those exercises that can deplete our precious yin energy, and if you are thin to begin with, there is insufficient yin to waste. While we want to enjoy a healthy diet and lifestyle, it's all too easy in these competitive arenas to overdo it to the point where it can outweigh the benefits. Too much aerobic exercise in women can lead to depletion in female hormones; menstrual periods stop and chances of fertility lessen. It is our body's feedback. When are we going to listen? Because we do have a choice.

The stresses of pregnancy, birth and raising children can also drain a woman's nourishing yin essence, especially if other factors in life are demanding and the woman is over-working or over-exercising. When we deplete our yin energy, it can lead to reduced flexibility, drying of the tissues and a constricting influence in the body which in turn can lead to cardiovascular heart disease. So we need to nurture, gentle and protect our precious vital force much, much more.

When we're lacking sufficient yin, the best medicine is to build more by sleeping well, exercising moderately, breathing properly, eating freshly cooked or raw whole foods and reducing stress. It's fine to use our masculine yang energy when it's appropriate, but don't get so seduced by it that you can't get back in touch with your feminine.

Just stop what it is you are doing that prevents you from being whole, and do what gives you true joy and a sense of well-being. Go walking, swimming, dancing, horse-riding; rest, read, paint, play the piano, love well, nourish your body, play with friends, laugh, be in nature, pick flowers in meadows, roll in the grass, dabble toes in the water.

So what else can we do to re-awaken our true feminine? In the information and exercises that follow, let your intuition guide you. Your inner tuition is a direct line to the greater part of you and the Universe, and it will show you where you can make simple changes and reap great rewards. If you're here on the planet to be and to experience love and happiness, why would you do anything else?

Look like a Natural Woman

When we look like natural women, it brings out a very favourable response in men; in turn the feedback and respect we receive makes us feel even more feminine, more appreciated and more cherished.

Look in the mirror and notice your facial expression. Sometimes we can look so hard-faced as our busy lives take such a toll. Crazy though it sounds, soften your face and practice gentle tender looks without scowling. The beauty of this is it makes us look ten years younger, so we won't have to spend so much on face-creams. Hooray!

Longer hair often makes us feel more feminine, but even if your hair is cut short, there are ways of making yourself appear softer, more approachable and exceptionally attractive. There are so many ways of enhancing our looks and how we feel about ourselves, from creams, treatments and make-up, to the colours we wear. When we take time to care for our skin and our body, we feel a million times better.

Dress like a Natural Woman

In these days of unisex dressing, we're encouraged to dress like men in jeans and shirts, pin-stripe suits and military-style clothing in masculine brown, grey and khaki, and often in the same fabrics used for men's clothes. Our femininity goes out of the window and while we're not looking, they're wearing pink and yellow! It's time to accentuate and enjoy the differences between the genders, not emphasize the similarities.

Only a very feminine woman can get away with wearing masculine-style suits because it's really hard to feel feminine when dressed like a man. The only time it works is when we look cute and pretty. What man can resist a woman in an oversized men's shirt? It makes her look small and defenceless and very appealing.

When we fail to look feminine, men notice and we feel it inside. In total contrast, when we wear pretty clothes that accentuate our femininity created with fabrics with a soft and silky touch to them, embellished with jewellery and make-up, we inhabit a different realm. It's not just a modern trend; women have been enhancing their looks and their femininity for aeons.

It's interesting to know that when we wear a skirt, the energy from the earth comes up in a spiral vortex into our sexual organs and regenerates us. The sway of a skirt creates gracefulness as we move and keeps us in our feminine flow. When we give up wearing the trousers, we give it up metaphorically as well. My clients report dramatic changes in their feelings and sensuality, and dramatic response from the men around them when they change from trousers and jeans to skirts. Try it and see.

Throw out all your old greying underwear and treat yourself lovingly with gorgeous underwear that makes you feel good. You will know the moment you put it on whether a garment is right for you, without even looking in the mirror.

Expand and enhance your self-esteem by looking good from the inside and out. It doesn't have to take hours, but taking care of ourselves makes us feel good, and it shows. No more saving the best for a special occasion. Each day of your precious life is a special occasion. No more putting off until tomorrow!

Behave like a Natural Woman

Appearance is one aspect but our manner is even more important. Aggression, excessive competence, fearlessness, coarse crude behaviour, hardness, defensiveness, taking command, masculine strength and masculine capability don't belong in our feminine domain.

We behave like this at our own peril. It's a question of what makes you feel good inside. Do you want to keep having to do it all, to carry all the burdens? Don't you, like me, long to stop for a while and let someone else take over so you can relax and let go of all the responsibility?

We create our own vicious circle. The more we do, the more is expected of us and the more we deprive men of their competence. We're missing out here. It's not about being submissive or useless; it's about the quality of our lives and the quality of our love.

Learn to be patient, be gentle and be a bit more forgiving. Let go of jumping in and solving men's problems, of doing things that they are struggling over that you know you can do easily and more efficiently. They can sort it out – it just may not be in your time frame, or in the way you would choose to do it. Trust them to find the solution. So am I saying you'll have to bite your tongue rather a lot here? Yes, quite probably, and your fingers and thumbs as well in order to not interfere. But it will make such a difference to your relationship with the opposite sex.

Our true feminine nature reflects love, kindness, compassion, sympathy, concern, joy and playfulness in contrast to a man's vigour and firmness. Look at the way you express yourself with your hands, your face and your body; in fact your total manner.

You can regain the charm, sweetness, poise, dignity, grace and courage of our feminine nature and learn to relate to yourself and others in a more tender way. You already know how to do this - you may have just forgotten. You may find you absolutely adore being this way the more you let go, as you retrieve the flow of an unshakeable inner happiness.

Move like a Natural Woman

The body never lies. We reveal our biography in our every movement, in the way we hold ourselves, the way we walk, our gestures and the way we dance (or not as the case might be). Unbeknown to us, we are constantly sending unconscious messages out into the ether for others to pick up, simply by who we are and the vibration of our energy.

Whatever you think and feel is expressed not only through your words but also through your body language, whether it be depressing or uplifting, suffused with pain or deliciously happy, shamefully secretive or imbued with integrity, lacking hope or overflowing with intense desire, not knowing which way to go in life or gently yet powerfully on purpose.

When we walk, we show the world exactly what's going on inside us mentally and emotionally. It's in our body movement that our femininity is predominantly lacking. When you have released all that was holding you back and start to re-awaken that dormant, gorgeous, feminine, connected self, you will walk and move in a light graceful manner.

When you start to notice the way other people walk, you will see how many are living in their heads, thinking, thinking, thinking, and so disconnected with their body's natural rhythm. We walk as if we are permanently constipated, as if we never have sexual feelings, as if we have no connection with anything 'down there,' as if we are not truly alive. When you cast your cares aside and experiment with different ways of walking that bring you back into your beautiful body, you will find you walk more joyfully, with your vision for your life leading you, courageously, lovingly, sensually, with awareness, in celebration of life. You can share the moment with someone else and be totally present.

Mother Nature really does know best. We have a natural undulation to our womanly curves created by the shape of our pelvis which beckons our men towards us; a natural wiggle which is an attractor, a sway from side to side designed to rock a baby gently in the womb. But not only that, it stimulates our hormones, lubricates and massages our inner organs as they slide over one another and keeps our hip joints gliding smoothly. We are designed to walk like a woman for our overall health and well-being.

Walking like a model does you no service at all so please don't be tempted – it creates an air of stiffness, arrogance and falsity. So let's go girls! Next time you walk anywhere, give your head a holiday, enter your body and walk like a real woman; feel your hips, feel your thighs, feel your buttocks, feel your belly and feel wonderful.

Feel Like a Natural Woman

We replenish our energy, our voluptuousness, our sensitivity, our feeling of oneness, our sensuality and our juiciness when we reconnect with Nature. Bathe in the warm waters of the Greek islands, the tropical seas of Hawaii, those intensely female places. Jump in the waves, run along the beach, lie in the glorious rays of the warm sun feeling its nourishment permeate every cell.

Do Tai Chi in the olive groves; pick walnuts, pomegranates and figs. Eat juicy fruits straight from the branches in the orchard, blackberries, raspberries and plums. Dance in the meadows; kick piles of leaves in the woods in autumn; plant a flower and vegetable garden; scoot down snowy hills on a toboggan; splash in puddles, wade out into the streams, sit by waterfalls, go out in boats and trail your hand in the water. Share moments of eternity with your lover as you watch the sun go down; lie out under the stars; roll down grassy slopes. Do anything out in Nature that fills you full of the joy of living.

Own Your Own Body

In seminars, we bring women onto the stage to dance so men can reveal to us what they find attractive. No matter what their size or shape, without exception the women they choose naturally radiate their love of life, their pleasure in movement and their enjoyment of the sensuality of their body.

It's never about their external appearance, but what is inside shining through. The sexiest woman is a happy woman - ask any man. Smiles will melt any man's heart. He will tell you that you reveal your true essence when you smile, when you laugh, when you pour your glorious life energy into everything and everyone around you. It's the smile men go for first - if he feels that she is happy, then he will be happy too because it makes him feel successful! There is nothing that will turn a man on more than to see a woman enjoying herself naturally with all her femininity and beauty radiating from within, with no need to artificially draw attention to herself.

Just imagine how it would be if the size and body shape you have right now was the height of fashion. What would you do differently? Go and do it anyway, because it's never about your breasts, bottom, legs, face or age. It's about the way in which you own your body.

Feminine energy is naturally found in very young women, but as we get older (and I mean in our 20's!) we have to learn to surrender to our feminine. It's not about being submissive. It is where we relax into and give way to the pleasure of being who we really are. This is the key to femininity – it is the key to total freedom.

Own your body, own your sexualness and own your life! Emotions are expressed through motion, through our physiology and through our body language which entices relationships towards us. So learn to feel that connection with your body and move in the way only women know how.

Speak like a Natural Woman

Do you know our voices have dropped as we have even copied male tonality over the last few years? The musicality and the lilt we used to have is disappearing as we have adopted monotonous, crude, vulgar, critical and harsh overbearing language styles which have been reinforced by the media. We talk far too much drivel, talk too loudly, too aggressively, and have forgotten the beauty and expressiveness of our language. And laughter has all but disappeared.

I was watching an exceptionally romantic old black and white film the other day where the women spoke in an attractive, alluring, appealing and unbelievably sexy way, even though the accent was very British 1940's. And they were listened to! The men were enthralled by them. Maybe it's time for a voice revival – what fun!

So slow down, modulate your voice tone, soften up, remember how to giggle, remember to breathe and enjoy more silence. If you don't like the sound of your voice, there are some wonderful voice coaches who will help and guide you to sound more naturally feminine. (www.drvoice.tv)

Touch like a Natural Woman

We all have a need to be touched and held. We even use the phrase 'deeply touched' by certain experiences because touch affects us at such a profound level. Much research points to the vital importance of touch for our survival as babies. Without touch we die, physically and emotionally. Touch nourishes us inwardly - the loving gesture of another's touch on our skin is absorbed by every cell and regenerates it, enlivens it and harmonises it.

Be gentle on yourself. Envelop your body in warm fluffy towels as you step out of the bath or shower; hug those you love and be hugged and caressed by those you care about in a warm loving embrace. A woman's touch is naturally healing. Learn to touch others the way you like to be touched; learn how to enfold those you love in your arms in a way that makes them feel treasured. Hold them to your heart and express your love through your gestures, through your caresses as well as through your language, because touch is a reciprocal gesture for the body receiving and the hands giving as energy is passed between the two.

In truth, we all still seek the warm fleshy comfort of our mother's body which greeted us after birth. Being embraced and held close by other women where we can snuggle and relax into their arms nourishes us at our core. It fulfils a primordial need for nourishment which we never quite received enough of as infants. We all still crave that closeness and don't receive enough - no amount of air-kissing can make up for the lack of contact and touch. This is not a sexual encounter but a sensual one, as women's bodies are so soft, tender and comforting. In our politically correct society we have forgotten the importance of touch, that vital, life-giving, tender, unconditional caress which mends our wounds and heals every hurt.

There are some wonderful therapies available these days which help shift our energy and heal our modern day stresses, like Huna massage (www.huna-massage.com) Reiki, Moxite (www.moxite.co.il) and many others that deal with energy. I urge you to explore them or learn them for yourselves.

Weep like a Natural Woman

As women, we spend so much time trying to be strong, holding it all in, turning the other cheek, biting our lip, keeping on top of everything and putting on a brave face. But that can really harm us. Part of our letting go requires that women weep – this is an essential strength we possess. There is such strength in our vulnerability. I'm not talking about wallowing in self-pity here, but so many women have forgotten how to weep that they have lost the meaning of tears.

On the other hand, we have gone into compassion overload with all the devastating stories brought to us by the media that our minds are unable to absorb and respond to it all, hence for our self-preservation, we have learned to shut down. When we shed tears, we release tension and stress, we soften into our feminine, we awaken our compassion for ourselves and others and allow our vulnerability to emerge, while giving others permission to weep as well.

Love like a Natural Woman

When you remember the treasures of your heart and share these with people around you, your natural ability as a woman to love, to truly love, will be revealed. Bring your thoughts and your feelings through your heart as you breathe, and release your words with love. Surround yourself with love. **Be** love!

Smell like a Natural Woman

Our personal scent permeates out into the atmosphere and broadcasts very subtly from our skin in tiny molecules. It's nature's way of transporting our pheromones, all designed to catch a suitable mate.

Each area of our body has a different though subtle aroma: behind our ears, our neck, our hair, our armpits, our sexual area, behind our knees and of course our feet. Each of us also has our own distinctive scent, our unique signature which can alter quite dramatically depending on the state of our health and our emotions, what we eat and drink, where we are in our menstrual cycle and whether we are fertile. Someone who is vegetarian or vegan will smell very different from someone who eats meat or fish, while someone who eats processed foods with all its hidden chemicals, or who smokes or drinks excessive amounts of alcohol will emit the smell of toxins built up in the tissues.

This also affects the way we smell in our vaginal secretions. Woman's natural smell and taste here is like the ocean, but is very much affected by what we eat - try melons, chilli peppers, Thai curry, garlic, fish, figs, strawberries. Which is more appealing?

Man's nose, when his instincts are intact, is geared towards finding the perfect mate to mother his offspring because his cave-man impulse needs him to perpetuate the species through his personal genetic fingerprint. In South America for example, when men greet you, they breathe you in deeply. But if we cover up our natural smell entirely with artificial perfumes and chemicals, his nose gets very confused and we can end up with partners who are wrong for us. These magical pheromones of ours are designed by nature to draw to us the right partner. The ecological couple who would naturally come together to create strong, healthy offspring has all but disappeared.

Seduced by the aftershave of her boyfriend and not entirely convinced about him as the right choice, a client of mine decided to let her head rule her heart, intellect overtook instinct, and she married him. Twenty-two years and four children later, she left the marriage after years of struggle and unhappiness. She actually couldn't stand his real smell; it was nature's way of deciding for her if only she had listened. Later she chose a partner whose body scent was strong and almost overpowering but she revelled in sleeping with her head under his armpit, and slept with her face buried in his T-shirt when she was away from him. Had they met earlier, their off-spring would have been absolutely amazing.

In my early teens, I was taught to be embarrassed by our natural body smells. Perfumed vaginal sprays came onto the market so we were constantly anxious and embarrassed about our personal scent. How wrong can we get? We have deodorants, perfumes, powders and body sprays for every part of us - our hair, our breath, our armpits, our vaginas, our feet. While cleanliness may be next to godliness, when we mask all of our true smell, we destroy nature's innate intelligence.

With our bodies losing up to 2 pints of sweat daily, we will of course want to smell enticing and delicious as opposed to smelling like a farmyard, but the many natural deodorants on the market will keep the most offensive bacterial smells at bay without completely masking your own unique perfume. And your man, if he is the right one for you, will be very turned on by your smell and you by his.

Menstruation – Blessing or Curse?

How do most women look at this time of the month? We call it 'the curse.' Poor Eve – so much blame! In tribal cultures where they are more in touch with nature and its seasons, menstruating women spend time in peace, quiet and solitude to allow their bodies to gently deal with what is going on internally.

This tiny little speck of an ovum is phenomenal. It houses the energy to create life and when we can harness that energy for our own life, the benefits are enormous. Our intuition is at its highest when we menstruate, so this is a perfect time for meditation, to connect with the goddess within; not easy if we are leading frantic lives, but if at least we can change the way we feel about menstruation and experience its mystery, we will feel very differently about ourselves.

When my periods suddenly stopped at forty-two due to the stress of my failing marriage, I was amazed at how much I missed them. Through meditation, dance, and a new loving relationship with a partner and ultimately with my inner self, my body came back into balance, my periods started again and it was then with great joy that I celebrated my menstrual cycle. I nurtured myself, gave myself extra rest and care and connected with my inner feminine at such a deep level; in return he treated me with such honour and reverence at that time. Now post-menopause, all has changed again and the wise woman emerges in absolute freedom.

We seem to feel noble in beating ourselves up for being imperfect, which takes us back to the myth of Eve and original sin. But how can we expect men to be respectful and gentle with us when we are so disparaging about our natural bodily functions? When we can learn to honour our menstrual periods and greet them with a feeling of appreciation and loving acceptance, the attitude of our men folk will change towards us. Ultimately men can find women's power to give life frightening, but when we value and respect it, and look with awe and wonder too at our miraculous bodies and share it with them, imagine how they will change!

Our body gives us feedback all the time. PMT is our body's way of warning us that we need to take extra care of ourselves, exercise gently, spend more time in nature, eat well, rest and be gentle. When we can do this for ourselves, pills and potions become unnecessary.

Our Beautiful Breasts

There is an energy field of unconditional love in the breast area of women, because we give unconditional love when we suckle our babies right next to our heart. So this is part of our body to enjoy, to revel in, to feel proud of.

Our breasts differ depending on our genes, our diet, the distribution of our body fat, our muscle structure, how we exercise and even our attitude and beliefs. Yet look at what we do to our breasts – we compare them to those surgically-enhanced and airbrushed celebrity photos in glossy magazines, and then criticise our own breasts for not having the same attributes.

In today's image-crazed world, our breasts can really affect our self-esteem. We can get so obsessed about our bodies that there is even a name for the phobia some women develop called 'body dysmorphic behaviour' which affects as many as 1 in 100 women in the UK. It stops women going out and getting on with their lives as they spend so much time worrying about the perfection of the shape and size of their breasts together with the rest of their body, and this obviously has a knock-on effect in personal relationships. Particularly prevalent amongst models whose status depends on their appearance, they worry that their breasts are not pert enough, big enough or round enough, because breasts make us feel feminine. They agonise about how they would cope if their breasts started to go south, as can happen with the joys of motherhood and forces of gravity, which can alter the shape and position of our breasts. So now is the time to have a good relationship with your breasts.

One of the greatest killers of women these days is breast cancer. Far-fetched as it sounds, one of the best ways of looking after our breasts is to talk kindly to them. When we stand in front of a mirror and complain about any part of our body, it will respond – it is the way of any organism to respond. If you stood in front of a friend and told her constantly that she wasn't good enough, she was too small, too big, ugly, deformed, pathetic, droopy, fat or called her awful, horrible, crude names, how would you expect her to respond? Would you see her glowing with joy and pride at your rude comments? Of course not – and your body responds in the same way.

If you don't believe this, try giving up the negative talk and start loving and praising your breasts for three months and see what happens. Don't just shove them in a bra - as much as possible allow the natural bra of the body to support them if you are not too heavily breasted, and let them out to play giving them fresh air and sunshine where possible. Apparently 90% of us are wearing the wrong size bra, so find a specialist to measure you so you're fitted correctly, and beware of harsh under-wires as they may constrict the blood supply to the breasts.

When you exercise, wear a sports bra to stop the muscles stretching beyond redemption. A good personal trainer will guide you to the exercises which will restore firmness and good muscle tone to the surrounding supportive muscles.

Massaging Your Breasts - exercise

Breasts respond beautifully when you massage them; it tones the underlying muscle, stimulates blood flow and wakes up your hormones. You can do this massage after a bath or shower, or get your partner to do it lovingly for you before you go to sleep. Using the flat of your hand, your thumbs and fingers and some pure massage oil, massage in circles all the way round in one direction then the other, ideally every day for a few minutes.

Now make a fist and get your knuckles in and under each breast and massage gently – this helps to keep all the ducts and glands free and healthy. At the same time, say kind words to your breasts, love them, thank them, appreciate and adore them. Sing, "Love, lift us up where we belong." Anything to enjoy your beautiful breasts. It is possible to enhance breast size through hypnotherapy, through connecting with your unconscious mind and its blueprint of your body and the cells, so imagine what wonders can be achieved by this exercise.

I make no medical claims but massaging from the outside-in may in time enlarge them; massaging from the inside-out may make them smaller. Experiment and see.

I heard a heart-warming story of a woman who had breast cancer, and rather than focus on the illness, she spent hours talking and stroking her breasts back to health along with her medical treatment. Another woman who had a mastectomy, chose to have beautiful pictures of flowers tattooed on her chest in honour of her womanhood.

Following Your Feminine Heart

Our heart centre really is the seat of our emotions – it's not just a fairy tale. How incredible your heart is. There it sits beating away in your chest nearly 100,000 times a day, pumping all of your blood around your body once every minute. In one day your blood travels a total of 19,000 kilometres – that's the distance between Britain and New Zealand; and in an average lifetime will pump about 1,000,000 barrels of blood through your precious body.

Do you realise that the heart pumps blood to itself first before pumping to the rest of the body? When you follow its example and you look to your heart first, you realise that when you love and take care of yourself, you have more to give to the world. Your body knows the answers – listening to the messages it is telling you guides you to a place of harmony. Treat your heart with tender loving care, because our hearts behave in a different way from men's. Intense grief for a woman can lead to heartbreak where part of our heart literally dies.

As women we tend to put everyone else's needs before our own. Let me ask you a question. If you are cooking, who takes the last or the smallest portion? If the piece of fish or meat falls apart or the egg breaks, who takes the broken piece? In my workshops when I ask this question, the women laugh and the men look totally baffled. While it doesn't matter to them, they haven't cottoned on yet to the fact that it's one of the ways we express our love!

So it's time to put yourself first and listen to your heart. Learn to love you!

Health and Vitality

Your health, physical, mental, emotional, sexual and spiritual is under your control. The way your body responds to different foods, exercise and activities is exclusive to you. Each of us has a unique blueprint from birth which is why we react differently to climate, food and circumstances. Our uniqueness is both our magic and our contribution.

Imagine the difference to the life of a child consciously, deliberately and joyfully conceived by healthy loving parents, from one born from a frantic coupling where the parents are in poor health themselves. So if you are going to re-awaken your feminine, doesn't it make sense for you to be healthy?

Life in the twenty-first century gives us myriad choices, and good health can be one of them. Health is our natural state. Without a healthy body and a healthy mind, we are nothing. All the knowledge in the world, all the skills and abilities, affluence and wealth, material objects and status in society amount to nothing at all if we are not healthy enough to enjoy it.

Barring genetically inherited diseases and accidents of birth, in babyhood we have all the potential if fed well, nurtured, loved and encouraged, to grow into totally healthy human beings. It's not until we start putting chemicals into our body, additives, preservatives, pesticides and pollution alongside unresourceful mind-sets, that we disrupt the delicate balance of the body with its subtle energy systems and start to jeopardise our potential for well-being.

Health isn't just an absence of disease, but a vitality, a state of vibrancy, a living energy system which regenerates, rejuvenates and keeps us looking towards the future. Health is in our body, mind, spirit and soul, and only when they are in balance can we consider ourselves truly healthy. Health is where there is potential at all times to do whatever you desire, to be clear-headed, to move with fluidity and flexibility, to have clear skin and functioning organs, to be able to use your body sufficiently well during the day so that when you go to bed at night, you have nourishing sleep and awaken the next morning feeling well-rested.

Rejuvenation

You can't turn on your television or open a magazine these days without discovering yet another product for anti-ageing, particularly for women. In fact there are medical conferences going on all over the world with scientists and eminent physicians researching anti-ageing, let alone cosmetic companies. If we weren't so enlightened, it could lower our self-esteem!

The information that follows ranks among the most leading-edge knowledge and is based on scientific research, so what you are about to read could change the way you view both ageing and exercise forever. How amazing will it be if you now can move beyond indifference about your body to being your own raving fan?

As cave-men and women, we used our muscles all the time, hunting, moving rocks, chopping wood, climbing trees and lifting heavy weights which strengthened our body structure. Nowadays our sedentary life-style means that we only get a fraction of the exercise our body needs to maintain its health and vitality.

As we age, we lose 30% of our muscle mass. Unfortunately this also means that the muscle in our vital organs such as our liver, pancreas, brain and heart also gets depleted. An additional problem is that our metabolism, (the rate that we burn food for energy) also slows down; therefore for every 1lb or 1kg of muscle we lose, unless we reduce our food intake, the lost muscle-tissue gets replaced by fat. All of this may lead to cardiovascular problems, poorly functioning organs and reduced hormonal secretion, so we start to age from the inside out.

When people find themselves becoming overweight, they generally reduce their amount of calories which does indeed cause weight loss, but what we haven't been told is that much of this loss, rather than being fat, is actually muscle-tissue. Often they then start doing aerobics. Research shows that an hour a day of aerobics depending on how vigorously we exercise burns 400-500 calories a day, which does cause weight loss even if the food intake is not reduced, but unfortunately much of this again seems to be muscle.

When you lose muscle-tissue in this way, you could be seriously damaging your health. It exhausts the internal organs, depletes your immune system, knocks your hormones out of whack and fails to build up sufficient muscle to keep the body in shape. This means it's particularly bad for women. The composition of the body then becomes similar to that of an older person, and so in fact you've speeded up the ageing process.

Because you've been misinformed, you've wasted all that will-power and hard work. However the good news is that research shows that when you build an extra 1lb of muscle, it burns 50 calories a day. So if we replace some of the fat on our body with just 10lbs of muscle, the muscle alone burns approximately 500 calories a day, even if we are just sitting, relaxing or sleeping!

This in turn helps to restore lost muscle to our vital organs and they begin to regenerate, which rejuvenates our system and affects not only the way we look, but our emotions and how we feel about ourselves too.

If up to now you have lost muscle, if you want to rejuvenate your system you simply have to do exercises to gain back the lost muscle. Even if you are young and beginning to acquire too much fat, you should increase the muscle to correct the problem. If you are already in good shape, the most anti-ageing step to take is to maintain your muscle. (www.educogym.com)

When we feel the strength in our bodies, we become lean and sleek and centred. This really does work; when you do this in conjunction with good natural food and supplements and a positive mind-set, it tones your body and keeps you more youthful and vigorous. You naturally rejuvenate as the hormones come under control, you feel fantastic, more at peace inside, clearer headed, you sleep better and you have greater health all round.

Nourishing Your Female Body

Part of loving ourselves, is to watch what we put into our bodies. We wouldn't feed those we love with poison, yet that is so often what we do to ourselves - toxic foods, toxic environment, toxic thoughts, toxic relationships. New books constantly give us the latest fad diet, yet look at the first three letters of this word – it reads DIE and that is what so many diets do. They kill us because we are not connecting to our inherent body wisdom.

Women frequently use food to anaesthetise emotional pain, and as a result clothe ourselves in a suit of armour of protective excess fat. Our bodies have become overly acidic from the way we eat and our stressful lifestyle, so the fat actually protects our vital organs from being eaten away by the acid.

As babies we always had something put in our mouths when we were unhappy – a nipple, a bottle or a dummy, and so as adults we often put food in our mouths to fill that emotional gap and to soothe our feelings. We need to eat when we're hungry physiologically rather than emotionally, and nurture our emotional side in other ways. Ask your body what it really wants; its innate intelligence will inform you whether you are really hungry, dehydrated or needing some love.

What's Draining You?

When do you feel tired and drained? If you feel an unnatural tiredness after you have eaten or drunk something, an absolute necessity to shut your eyes for few minutes, this is your response mechanism warning you that what you have just put into your body is not supporting your energy. I have studied nutrition and keep up with the latest scientific information, but am not a qualified nutritionist, so I ask you to consider what you put into your body very carefully, and find what works for you.

Your body gives you constant feedback. What we put into our bodies really matters. When we look at our body as a self-generating energy system, if we put garbage in, we get garbage out. When we give it live healthy foodstuffs, we will generate energy; if we give it dead foods (manufactured foods) we will feel half dead. Packet food has no life-force in it, and many pre-packaged and non-organic foods may contain additives, preservatives and hormones which can affect women adversely, while artificial sweeteners and low-fat products cause unbelievable health problems.

Instead of feeling deprived, you can choose instead to fill your body with healthy, alive, vibrant, natural foods which in themselves contain vital energy. That generally means whole foods, fruit, vegetables (preferably organic) and pure clean water free of chemicals.

Just as an acorn contains the energy to produce a mighty oak tree, nuts, seeds, fruit, vegetables and salad leaves still retain the energetic power to grow. I know that when I drink freshly-made vegetable and fruit juices, my whole body responds in an unprecedented way. My eyes start to shine, my skin glows, my body feels firmer and more vital, the fat just drops away, my cells tone up and energy levels increase. (www.juicemaster.com)

Coloured foods that gladden the eye also gladden the heart, so delicious salads of spinach and lettuce, tomatoes, red onions, avocados, celery, cucumber, peppers, mangoes and strawberries will make you smile. Or freshly sprouted seeds with nuts and salads and fruits, or whatever makes your heart sing. Try it and see. And there is nothing that surpasses food prepared and cooked with love; you can tell the difference in the taste and how your body feels afterwards.

However, being vegan or totally vegetarian does not suit me. My body needs organic meat, fish and eggs – without this protein, my energy levels are just not sustainable for working out, dancing or for digging in my vegetable garden. And after all, animals in the wild don't wash the green leaves to remove juicy protein-filled caterpillars and insects!

Our bodies have evolved very little since cave-man times and so we're unable to process much of what we put into our bodies nowadays. We have eighty times the amount of chemicals that our parents had twenty years ago, we use our bodies far less physically, and our immune system suffers from all the stress that our frenetic life-style puts upon us. This means our naturally resilient body has become very much more sensitive, and we need to treat it with extra loving care.

Our soil has been deprived of essential natural minerals over the last few decades, and while the best nutrition comes from well-farmed natural organic foods, there may be times when we need to supplement to make up for the shortfall. Tiredness and lack of energy usually signify insufficient nutrition. There are some excellent natural nutritional supplements on the market, but do see a qualified nutritionist.

Believe it or not, if you eat while watching horror films or the news or if you are having an argument, you will digest all that negativity with your food and it will affect your body at a cellular level. When you reconnect with your natural instincts, you feel this strongly.

So whenever you can, only eat foods which you can pick, dig for or catch. And before you ask, yes of course this includes 70% or 85% dark chocolate! It's particularly good for women you'll be pleased to know, and you may well spot me running around the supermarket with a chocolate-catching net!

Sugar and Spice and All things Nice

Sugar is now recognised as being as detrimental and addictive to the body as heroin. It causes enormous stress as the body has to work overtime to remove it from our system. As a result, diabetes is on the increase, aided and abetted by a massive rise in obesity, so help your wonderful body and wean it off the white stuff. Sugar over-stimulates our pancreas, can be a cause of depression with the dramatic swing of insulin levels, and keeps us awake when we should be resting. A low glycaemic regime can help regulate blood sugar levels far more effectively. Again I recommend you research this.

Indulge in strawberries, blackberries, raspberries, mangos, juicy apples, pears, melon, pineapple, passion fruit, pomegranates, grapes and other delicious juicy fruits. Far more sexy!

Water of Life

Often we eat when our body is really crying out for water. Water makes up the majority of our blood system so it makes sense to replenish what we lose in sweat. (Whoops! I was brought up with 'Pigs sweat, men perspire, ladies glow!') Plenty of live foods, raw fruits, salads and vegetables will give us much of the water we need, but to supplement with pure water will help us with our energy and clear skin, removing unwanted fat and detoxing, and keeping all our insides functioning well.

Women are now drinking almost as much alcohol as men. Alcohol and coffee are ageing and dehydrating and put extra stress on the body, while too many fruit juices send our blood sugar levels soaring. Bottled water contains many heavy minerals which, rather than being beneficial, may form deposits on our bones causing arthritis and joint problems. My understanding is that distilled water is the best but again suggest that you research this for yourself.

Time for Sleep, Perchance to Dream

This most precious commodity often seems to elude us as we extend our waking hours into the darkness with artificial lighting everywhere we look, confusing our internal recognition of day and night. Away from our natural rhythm, we are jolted into wakefulness by the rude intrusion of an alarm clock which shocks our system. It even says it in the name – ALARM! And often we then turn to stimulants to wake us at the beginning of the day and relaxants to help us unwind at the end.

Women need more sleep than men, and the old adage early to bed, early to rise is still a useful one. Hours before midnight are worth double their value, so we can actually sleep a shorter number of hours by sleeping at 10p.m. and rising at 5a.m. or 6 a.m. to create much more value in our day.

Sleep is the time our body and mind use for restoration and rejuvenation. I used to go to bed and think over all the things I had failed to get done during my day and worry about what had gone wrong. I would lie awake for hours, often not drifting off until the wee hours of the morning, staggering out of bed the next day feeling exhausted after a troubled night. Typical of a woman, I failed to unwind before going to bed.

Now realising how important sleep is, I design my next day on paper. Let me share how to do this. As opposed to a to-do list, set your intentions and outcomes for a great day. Decide what you want to happen and how you want to feel, write it in the present tense as if it is already achieved and hand it over to the Universe to deal with rather like a prayer.

Then in your head, unwind your day (you see, even the word tells you!) going backwards over what has happened from this present moment till when you got up in the morning, making peace with it all and feeling really grateful for all the amazing things that occurred. If anything has happened which wasn't as good as you would have liked, re-run it in your imagination the way you would have liked it to be. After all, your unconscious mind doesn't know the difference between what is real and what is imaginary, and so you can go to bed with an empty, peaceful mind and just drift off into sleep. Your unconscious mind then won't have to do all the unravelling and sorting out while you are asleep, so you open up the possibilities for beautiful dreams.

If you need more help with this, you will find a sleep relaxation CD on my web site www.essenceofwomanhood.com

Sunlight and Moonshine

With so many scare stories about too much sun on our skin, we are now in danger of not getting enough light. We need sunlight on our skin; so, taking whatever precautions you deem necessary and preferably natural ones, go outside and get as much light as your body needs. We need sunshine for healthy bones, healthy eyesight, for well-being and because it makes us smile. If it makes you feel good, then it's probably good for you. Your body will tell you the second it has had enough.

'Moonlight becomes you - it goes with your hair,' according to the song. But for women it's not very healthy for us to sleep in full moonlight. Remembering the influence and pull that the moon has over the tides and over our monthly cycles, and tales of loony women (the word 'lunatic' comes from the word meaning 'moonstruck') I would suggest that sleeping in the dark may be better for our optimal emotional and physical health.

Listen to the Rhythm

As women we seem to be more affected by the seasons than men as our body is so linked to nature's rhythms. When we listen to our body and allow its response to the fluctuations of the seasons, we will respond to the need to rest and almost hibernate in autumn and winter, snuggling up and resting until the rise of the sap in the spring time wakens us up again.

Listen to the rhythms and allow your body to tune in. You will keep healthier for it.

Creating Your Perfect Environment

Just as plants need a perfect environment in which to grow, so too we need the right nurturing physical and emotional environment to grow and blossom to our fullness. Look at how you are living and with whom. Who or what has influence on you, and does it support or drain you?

Interior décor has focussed on minimalism recently which, while it has clean lines and space, can also seem rather harsh, cold and unwelcoming. Now we are seeing a shift again to colour, texture and warmth with soft and luxurious fabrics where we can release the stresses of the day and sink into relaxation.

Make your home a refuge from the outside world and instil a sense of beauty and femininity. This doesn't have to mean frilly bits, just softness and gentleness. Create your own feminine space with a delicious embracing ambience which expresses who you are; warm, welcoming and homely to nurture your own spirit, a place filled with love, tenderness, sensuality and happiness.

Fill your space with plants and flowers and pretty things that make you feel nurtured. If you want some help, Feng Shui experts will help you clear unwanted energy in your home and create an environment where good energy flows.

Words of Wellness

When constantly in the presence of men at work, women tend to adopt a more male body language as well as verbal language and behaviour traits. Because they are so masculine, it pulls us away from our connection with who we really are, and as a result our self-esteem gets damaged. When we rescue our feminine and behave in a more feminine way, we will either move away or achieve our success in a different area.

A number of overweight business women have come to me recently, their bodies big and chunky with a wadding of protective fat. Their voices have dropped, hormones are scattered all over the place, their relationships have soured and they are drained from 'f—ing' and 'blinding' across the room at their male counterparts in their strategic and financial world, exhausted because they are no longer able to sustain the pretence of trying to keep up with the men.

Every time we criticise ourselves we are saying in effect, "I'm not ok. Women are not ok." Take great care with the words that you use both out loud and inside your head. Words carry a vibrational energy of their own, and a very specific meaning, not just the meaning you attach to it. Remember the WOW principle – Words of Wellness and Words of Wealth.

Your Life Listens to Every Word You Say

Like many people when I am truly relaxed and my mind clear, I can see auras. In childhood I assumed everyone was doing so, but rapidly realised that other people around me weren't, so I closed down. Now once again I have opened up and can see the beautiful dance of energy around people, plants, trees and animals and sparkling from the sea and rivers.

The most dramatic occurrence happened last year when for a few weeks following the Educo™ Mind Master course I attended with Dr. Tony Quinn, (www.educomindpower.com) I could actually see the vibration and colours of words as people spoke. I could see whether the words were loving, spiritual, useful in business, harmful or inspired, whether they were reaching other people and going in, or just dropping to the ground. I realised the magic and power in each word, the vibrational essence and the intention.

Be more sensitive to the words you use; swearing wounds the spirit inside of you, and with negative language your energy shifts and your essence loses its spark. Professor Emoto's wonderful books, 'Messages in Water,' demonstrate very clearly the effects of the vibrational energy of words and emotion on water and on plants. And as our bodies are 70% water …!!!

I find it fascinating that in the English dictionary of 31,460 words, only 1,680 are positive, strong, powerful and stimulating, while 5,890 are negative; so we are immersed in negativity a great deal of the time.

Your life really is listening. As soon as a word is said your life has heard and takes it on board as a program. In fact every word is like a prayer. Do you remember as a child being told, "Wants never gets?" It's because the word 'want' implies lack; it implies effortful yearning, a feeling of being unfulfilled. It's much more powerful to say, "I really would like …" or "I'm so grateful now I have …" even if you haven't got it yet. Many of the books on the power of attraction demonstrate this clearly.

With many words you will feel a response physiologically. For years we have been encouraged to follow our passion, but the word 'passion' goes back to the passion of Christ, literally like being nailed to the cross. It actually means 'suffering.' For me, depending on how I use it, the word 'passion' can tighten up my gut, as if all my internal organs have to metaphorically gird their loins and push forward with zeal and urgency, so I use it more carefully now, even though you will find it used many times in this book.

We use the word 'love' carelessly from appreciating ice-cream, a movie star, a car, your job or your lover. In fact we use many words carelessly and wonder why our life doesn't quite turn out the way we desire. ('Desire' comes from a Latin word which means 'to wish upon a star' or from the French 'de Sire' from God.) This is why it is said, "Be careful what you wish for," because our wealth, health and happiness are in our words!

'Bliss' creates a different feeling entirely, one of untroubled, joyful acceptance. How about being in a state of bliss in what you choose to do? If your life is not blissful, easy, elegant and effortless, perhaps Life would prefer you to do something else. I'm not suggesting you be lazy and idle because when you follow your bliss you may find you're busier than ever before, but because it is blissful, the pleasure you derive from it is so great that it doesn't seem like work. It becomes an elegant and effortless way of being. What else is possible?

Our language is so rich and descriptive, so poetic and meaningful - and when we really understand the relevance of that and choose more carefully those words which empower us and heal us, our words can create health and abundance.

As children we are taught to be magicians – we are taught to SPELL. Look at the word LIVE. Spelled backwards it means something else entirely. Look at the word CREATION. Using the same letters but in a different order it becomes REACTION. The word EARTH becomes HEART. Same letters, different meaning. Every word in whatever language carries its own vibrational weight. How do you feel when you see the word LAUGH, or SADNESS? The words AND or BUT? Words really do make a difference.

You too can become a creator or a reactor – you can become a magician with your words and weave spells to create beauty and peace and harmony, or not! Your body will give you feedback with the words you use, tension or relaxation, resistance or allowance. Buy yourself a toy magic wand or a crystal wand and create the magic in your life just for fun. Learn how to 'spell' with the magic of words.

Be your own fairy godmother and sprinkle fairy dust over what you do. Start to realise the magic all around you to create wonderful outcomes.

Use your spells wisely

For they create your life!

The Poetry of Life

The media exposes us to such violence, abuse, despair, brutality, hostility and bloodshed alongside pornography and offensive films nowadays, to the extent that we often fail to notice. And we call it entertainment! Our instinct and innate courtesy has become so deadened; it seems nothing is too much. When we participate in that, we become it, we condone it, we encourage it, not only for ourselves but for our children, and we fail to honour ourselves as women. Ask yourself, "Is this bringing out my femininity? Is this encouraging me to remember who I really am as a loving woman? Is this what I really truly desire in my life?" Remember, you become your choices.

Crude art, bad literature and discordant music can actually be very detrimental and damaging to your body. In contrast, beautiful art, literature and music affect the human spirit in a deep and meaningful way. In my dance classes, we always select music which affects emotional well-being at a cellular level, triggers the hormones and stimulates the body's healing potential, from classical to love songs, from drums to salsa, from choral to jazz, from pop to ethnic, but always working with the positive.

When I used to sing and play choral music and uplifting classical music, mushy romantic songs and relaxing music, the plants in my conservatory used to thrive - they flowered and showed off their glory, almost as if they were joining in the singing and celebration and

180

dance. On the odd occasion when my husband used to play hard rock and heavy metal, they would shield themselves against the onslaught, almost hiding away in an effort to preserve themselves. They literally must have responded to the atmosphere and the energy of the music. Don't take my word for it - test it and see for yourself.

There is a poetic language of love, of life, which is visceral, powerful, enchanting and delicious. Poets have the ability to touch us in the deepest recesses of the soul with such astute perception, with such force that sometimes we can barely breathe with the intensity and joy they inspire within us, their pathos and depths of emotion. Treat yourself to some delicious tender love poetry, and delight in the power of chivalrous love, sensuality and desire.

When you set a new standard for your life, one that you are proud to uphold, you will come away from the mediocre and become extra-ordinary. The feminine does not seek emptiness; she seeks fullness through surrender and openness. Treat yourself as if you are your own best friend. It's not being selfish – quite the opposite in fact. It means living the best we can be, behaving in the best way we can and thereby attracting the best into our lives.

Aligning Your Feminine Energy

Have you, like me, come across women who are so obsessed about looking perfect or having a perfect body that they limit all the things they enjoy doing? Your greatest personal health and happiness lies in discovering what you enjoy doing most that serves you well, and making it a simple daily habit. Rather than coming from a place of fear of illness and ageing, give yourself permission to go in pursuit of greater happiness and joy as your positive driving force on your journey, quite simply because happy people are naturally healthier and stay youthful longer.

You now have a stronger vision of what you want from the previous chapter, but until you align your vibration and your energy with those desires, you will not draw them into your life, and they will just remain a wish list, or you will squander them when they arrive. So you need to be congruent, once again aligning your head (your thoughts) with your heart (your feelings and emotions) with your sexual energy (your ability to take action) to put yourself in harmony with the eternal laws of life.

What Are Your Values? - exercise

Knowing that at the essential core of the feminine being is a tender, compassionate, nurturing heart, ask yourself, "What really matters to me? What kind of woman do I ultimately want to become in my lifetime? What do my values need to be in order to achieve my ultimate destiny?"

Values are the principles, the standards or ethics which we individually prize and consider vital to our well-being as we live our lives. No two people have the same hierarchy of values because they will mean different things to us. So nobody is right, nobody is wrong.

The hierarchy of our values, in other words the order in which we consider them to be important to our lives determines not only our health, vitality and success, but also our relationships and our money. The hierarchy of your values literally determines your destiny.

What is so interesting is that your values go into your unconscious and you then live by them. Goals on the other hand go into your conscious mind, so if your goal is not aligned to your values, you have a moral dilemma. Automatically you will be frustrated as any time your goals don't match your values, it creates a conflict between the conscious and unconscious. The unconscious will always win.

The list of forty-nine values which follows is not complete in itself; there may be other values you may feel are important to you as well. Beside each is a suggested interpretation of most of the words, but of course they may mean different things to you. Go through the list and pick out your top 10, those which are most important to you:

* ACHIEVEMENT – attaining goals, a sense of accomplishment

* ABUNDANCE (wealth in all areas of life)

* ACCEPTANCE (belonging and approval)

* ADVANCEMENT (progress and promotion in your career)

* ADVENTURE (taking risks; having new and exciting challenging experiences)

* AESTHETICS (appreciation for beautiful things)

* AFFECTION (understanding affectivity)

* ALIVENESS AND VITALITY (zest for living)

* AUTHENTICITY (being one's true genuine self)

* BALANCE (steadiness and stability)

* BEAUTY (appreciating the beauty of all around)

* COMPETITIVENESS (striving to win to be the best)

* CONTRIBUTION/SERVICE (contributing towards society)

* CO-OPERATION (teamwork, collaboration)

* CREATIVITY (being imaginative, artistic, inventive, original)

✳ ECONOMIC SECURITY (steady adequate income)

✳ FAME (being at the top, renowned, distinction)

✳ FAMILY HAPPINESS (close relationship with members of your family)

✳ FREEDOM (independence, liberty, autonomy)

✳ FRIENDSHIP (close relationship with others, rapport)

✳ FULFILLMENT (realisation of your dreams)

✳ HAPPINESS (absolute happiness from inner core)

✳ HEALTH (physical and mental well-being)

✳ HONESTY (telling the truth to yourself and others)

✳ HUMOUR (in a way that does not offend)

✳ INDEPENDENCE (being totally self-reliant)

✳ INNER HARMONY (balance within)

✳ INTEGRITY (being at one with the Divine within)

✳ INTIMACY (closeness and intimacy within relationship)

✳ JUSTICE (seeking fairness)

✳ KINDNESS (benevolence and compassion for humanity)

✳ LEADERSHIP (ability to be a leader)

✳ LOVE (whatever love means to you)

✳ MASTERY (in control of mind and emotions)

✳ PEACE OF MIND (serenity)

✳ RECOGNITION (acknowledgement and appreciation)

✳ RESPECT (being valued and esteemed)

✳ ROMANCE (whatever it means to you)

✳ SAFETY and SECURITY (protection and safe-keeping)

✳ SELF-RELIANCE (independence, self sufficiency, autonomy)

✳ SIMPLICITY (ease and unfussiness)

✳ SHARING (involvement and contribution)

✳ SPIRITUALITY (connected with spirit of self and others)

✳ STATUS (importance of standing, position, significance)

✳ SUCCESS (being a winner, triumph)

✳ TRUST (reliance, dependability, belief)

✳ UNIQUENESS (individuality, exclusivity, rareness)

✳ WEALTH (prosperity, affluence, material ownership)

✳ WISDOM (perception, understanding, knowingness)

Now take your top ten and whittle them down to seven and put them in order of importance to you. When you are clear about your values, it's so much easier to make life choices; it will help you keep out of your life what you don't want, and invite in what you do want. These seven now become the values through which you can live your life. Write out your values on sheets of paper in big letters, put them on the wall and look at them every day. Or choose one per day or one per week and live your day/week with that value uppermost in your mind both at work and in your personal life until each becomes so deeply ingrained in how you behave and who you become. When we do this, we take our life to a new level – we take it out of that dreary state of mediocrity.

If you find that something in your life is not working, look at your values and see how important that area is in your unconscious mind. You may then want to change its positioning. Your values are not set in stone - some may change as you progress through your journey of life, and that is absolutely fine.

Creating Incantations

When we affirm things in our lives, in other words say positive statements to ourselves over and over again when we are relaxed and open, after a while they slip into our unconscious mind and become a new program, eventually overwriting the old ones, like re-writing music on a CD. Always written in the present tense as if you are claiming them now, you can use affirmations to keep yourself encouraged, supported, inspired, motivated, on track.

Incantations are even more powerful, spoken or sung with intensity and belief while moving your body. So while you're cycling or swimming, walking or rebounding on a mini-trampoline, repeat your empowering phrases or words like a song so that they are recorded into every cell.

Let me give you some examples: "I am happy, healthy, radiant and joyful." "I am strong, courageous, confident, sensual and loving." "I love my life. I have wonderful friends who support me in all that I do." If you find your unconscious mind pops up and says, "You must be joking," and, "Who do you think you're kidding?" just use inspirational words like "Health, happiness, wealth, family, joy, success." Your unconscious mind will just accept them as it has nothing to fight against.

I know it feels weird at first as we are more used to beating ourselves up than saying nice things. So it doesn't matter if you don't believe it yet; just repeat it over and over again with energy and feelingful emotion in your voice. Before long, your unconscious mind will accept it as a program while you look on with awe and wonder. When you start your day with incantations, it sets the outcome for how your day will be, how your life will be; and it works, it really works.

Starting With the Woman in the Mirror - exercise

A woman who is not praised internally will wither, but as we are often our own worst critics, our own worst enemies, the most powerful form of praise comes from yourself. When you can praise yourself first, you will be amazed at how other people start to praise you too.

We see our face in the mirror every day, and the tendency is to be critical in some shape or form. Instead say wonderful life-affirming things to yourself. It just takes practice: look into your own eyes and find inspiring, motivating things to say. Tell yourself you're beautiful. Tell yourself you're amazing. Tell yourself you're special. Say, "Hello gorgeous. I love you."

The eyes truly are the window of the soul and when you can look deeply into your own eyes and feel your own love and compassion and appreciation, untold wonders will occur.

Every time you do something well, or do something you were scared about doing – clearing your clutter, writing a work proposal, making a difficult phone call, going for an interview, winning an award at work, doing something new and challenging, getting out of a difficult situation, cooking a fantastic meal, dealing with the children without losing your cool, look in the mirror as you pass by and say, "Well done. I'm really proud of you!"

Find other wonderful things to say about you. Look at different parts of your body and admire them out loud. "I love your breasts, I love your eyes, I love the way your eyes crinkle when you smile. I love your stretch marks that show you've given life. I love your smile. I love you."

I have done this with a small mirror for the last few years and it has been life-transforming, but a few months ago I did this exercise with a full-length mirror. Tears poured down my cheeks as I realised how much we condemn our beautiful selves and our precious life so often. It seemed as if I had been affirming more of my achievements rather than who I intrinsically am inside, so again I felt a big shift in my life. Soft encouraging words where we gentle ourselves, make such a difference.

Keep practising. This is vital work for us girls because when we are good to ourselves it nourishes something very deep inside. Don't think that you're going to get big-headed - this is never about vanity, it is about healing a part of us which has not been sufficiently acknowledged.

At a recent conference so many women came up to me and said that I just radiated joy, confidence, centredness and calmness all day. I had not realised the impact this has on other people, but it shows, and gives other women permission to do the same. That is when the diamond inside you shines.

It's about who you are, not just the packaging. When you start to become friendly with who you are, your eyes start to sparkle, your self-esteem rises and you take better care of yourself.

It all begins with loving and honouring ourselves

Doing it With Love - exercise

Whatever you are doing, do it with love – making the bed, driving the car, washing the dishes, cooking a meal, writing a report, making love, working, gardening, shopping. Love is the magic ingredient. Once you put your loving feminine essence at the top, making it a priority, it is hard to make mistakes. You need do nothing – just be in your full deep feminine essence and trust to life.

You must begin this process by giving more to yourself. Until we do that we cannot be loved, acknowledged, appreciated and honoured by others. You can have more when you are willing to give more. Give yourself more time; give yourself more attention; give yourself more love; give yourself more of what you desire. Then decide how to offer the more that you are and have to the world, and you will receive even more back in return.

Love the One You're With

We all have our own special gifts; when we acknowledge and appreciate who we are now and share that with others then we can move forward, for we are forever changing, forever growing. Instead of having to 'come to terms' with who you are, drop all that rubbish, enjoy who you are, be enchanted by yourself, love and adore you, find everything to praise in yourself.

Be patient – it took a lot of years for you to acquire those old disempowering habits, so it may take a little time to totally eradicate them, but you can understand this in a heartbeat. If you think it's going to be difficult, it will be. If you think instead this is easy and effortless, it will be, and I know which one I choose.

Gratitude to Your Body - exercise

Understand that there are as many different body shapes as there are women in the world – there is no norm. So no more thinking about how fat your thighs are or holding your tummy in. Men love to be surrounded by femininity – they do not want to go to bed with a bag of bones, I am reliably informed. They love to sink into womanly flesh – they were nurtured on that from birth.

Often men forget that they have grown inside the belly of a woman, and when we forget to remind them, we belittle our femininity. We are all are born from between the thighs of women and men spend their lives trying to get back there! Yet we beat ourselves up for our curves and our flesh. Our shapely curves and rounded hips are designed to carry a baby to full term; a flat hard stomach is great for an eighteen year-old boy, but no good for us; all our reproductive organs nestle inside so it is supposed to have a gentle curve.

The idea of women taking pleasure in their own bodies is almost taboo. It is supposed to be pleasing for others to look at and touch but not ourselves. We seldom caress our own skin apart from a cursory touch when bathing or slapping body lotion on. Often when we do feel pleasure, we then focus on the parts of it we don't like; we spoil our own pleasure before we can enjoy our own body because religion has taught us to ignore and even denigrate the body.

Women's bodies are sacrosanct – it is the beginning of life here. Every part of your body is pleasurable simply because it's part of you. When you are constantly criticising your body, that is all you will notice. When you love your body, so will everybody else and no one will abuse it.

Play some heart-warming music such as 'Fields of Gold' sung by Eva Cassidy, or 'Thank You for Loving Me' sung by Jon Bon Jovi. Starting with the top of your head gently and very, very slowly stroke and caress all the parts of your body: your face, eyes, nose, mouth, neck, chest, arms, stomach, sex, bottom, thighs, knees, calves, feet and toes. Allow a feeling of gratitude, awe and wonder at having such an amazing body to house your soul, a body which works day and night without us having to do anything. It breathes, pulsates, digests, makes babies, balances and eliminates, constantly adjusting to keep us alive. In this exercise, working from your toes to your head will energise you, while working from your head to your toes will relax you.

When in the bath or shower, as you wash each part of your body, send it messages of thanks through your words and your hands. Thank your feet for carrying you around all day, your legs for supporting you; thank your knees for giving you flexibility; your beautiful round bottom so you can sit and rest; your belly with its gentle curves; your anus and bladder for their hard work in eliminating everything you no longer need that's toxic to your system; to your sex for giving you pleasure; to your heart for pumping thousands of times a day. To every cell, every atom, every molecule, every muscle, every fibre, every tissue give gratitude. Know that we are not separated into different parts but that every area affects the whole. We are holistic beings; if one part is out of balance, the whole body is out of balance.

People laugh when they hear I thank my anus, but if it doesn't work properly, what are we full of???

Inner Smile - exercise

I cannot stress enough how much touch keeps us alive; it tunes our cells into connectedness, into a feeling of vitality and sensuality, so give yourself a massage or receive a massage as often as you can, and as you do so, imagine your blood cells beautifully formed, round and red and freely flowing. Imagine each cell with a happy smiling face full of love, passing that loving smile onto all the other cells as they course through your body taking vital oxygen and nutrients to all the organs, and spreading love and joy. Imagine all the happy cells cleaning out your organs like millions of tiny little bubbles all scrubbing away clearing out anything that is not wanted, and restoring and rejuvenating your body.

Smile to all your body organs – play 'You Are So Beautiful' sung by Joe Cocker. Feel your smile travelling down into your arms, into your hands. Smile as you hold your hands over your heart, your lungs, your liver, your kidneys, your pancreas, and see them as healed and whole. Put your hands over your sex, your anus, your belly. Smile into your uterus, your ovaries and smile to these precious parts of you. Smiling into your own body is like basking in the sunlight of your own love, a love that responds and regenerates.

Belly Dance - exercise

We store so much of our emotional baggage in our sexual area, and when you really move here, it releases stress in a powerful way, bathing your vital organs with fluid like an internal massage. Belly dancing was not designed to titillate men – that's a recent development. It was created by women for women when they were in the villages together or in the harem, to connect with one another, to keep fit, healthy and supple, and to have oodles of fun.

Find a pretty top or sexy bra and a long flowing skirt, tie a scarf tightly around your hips, play some exotic belly-dancing music or drumming music, and with bare feet, dance. I do this to Loreena McKennit's 'Marco Polo,' and to Egyptian, Greek and Turkish music.

With soft knees, slowly begin to move your hips, your thighs, your pelvis, your belly, your waist. No need to hold your bottom or tummy in; in fact stick them out and enjoy it. Imagine holding a pencil between your buttocks and draw out a figure eight with your hips. Smoothly and sensually revel in the feel of your female curves as your body expresses itself through the music. Now start to engage your chest, your shoulders, and your arms. Invite your breasts to join in. Surrender to the sensuality in the music; involve the whole of your body, gently, delicately, fluidly, or wildly, alluringly, erotically.

If you have wobbly bits, wobble them – they are highly praised in some parts of the world. Just enjoy. This is not about being a perfect dancer – this is pure freedom, pure enjoyment.

How Do You Treat Yourself When You Are Alone?

Often when I ask clients this I find to my sadness that they do not 'treat' themselves at all. So what makes you feel feminine? What do you do to nurture yourself, to nurture your spirit, your essence? What is it that makes you feel happy? What makes you feel beautiful? If you know what it is, go and do it. Happiness is found in the enjoyment of pursuits, not in the pursuit of happiness.

Make a list of 100 things that you enjoy, and any time that you forget your magnificence, any time you get side-tracked into not being at your best, any time you find your mood being less than joyful, go and look at your list and do something on it.

Do something to nurture your body every day. Ask it what it wants to eat, what would make it feel great. It may be having a massage, making love, putting on make-up, wearing beautiful clothes, doing your nails, dancing in the rain, swimming in the nude (utter bliss!) singing in the woods, listening to sensual music, reading poetry, eating delicious food, painting, making daisy chains, paddling in a stream, decorating a room, sewing, creating a masterpiece, writing a poem, cooking a new dish, playing the guitar, painting a picture, going for a scent-sational walk smelling all the flowers as you go. Blow bubbles, do jigsaws, rescue your inner child and go and play games.

Some of my clients now take one night a week and use it specially to nurture themselves, body, mind and spirit – they have a girly date with themselves to devote purely to pampering and relaxation, doing what they want in luxury and peace, restoring their equilibrium.

As well as the above, on my 100 list are:

- Bubble bath, candles, delicious perfume in the air, soft music

- Massage – I love Japanese face massage. Better than a face-lift, it rejuvenates and clears the whole body (www.tsuboki. co.uk)

- Wearing long dresses – I love dressing up into beautiful graceful elegant clothes and going to elegant dinners where I can dance (and yes I know the conversation can be boring, but you can change that can't you girls?)

- Dancing barefoot, on the sand, in the woods, on the grass, in my sitting room

- Curling up on the sofa and reading a good book

- Sitting in a field of buttercups

- Drinking champagne

- Walking along the seashore barefoot and jumping in the little waves

- Going to the hairdresser's - I love having my hair touched and stroked

- Indian head massage which helps you … let … go …

- Reflexology – my feet love to be touched and stroked and cared for

- Being enfolded in the arms of a big strong male friend

- Having my face made up at the make-up counters in big stores – I have done this all over the world and it makes me feel a million dollars

- Wearing beautiful lingerie next to my skin – the secret knowledge that I am looking after myself brings a glow of self-esteem and confidence

- Phoning someone I love

- Luxuriating in fresh clean crisp cotton sheets in a comfortable cosy bed

- Sleeping on a satin pillow-slip. It prevents wrinkles!

- Eating a delicious home-cooked meal with fresh ingredients fit for a Princess

- Watching a mushy movie and having a good cry

- Curling up on the sofa and having a well deserved nap during the day

- Being out in nature beside a bubbling stream

- Tending my garden – communing with my plants

- Being with animals

- Walking barefoot on grass

- Sprinkling rose petals on my bed

- Filling my home with flowers

- Going window shopping

- Doing a photo shoot

- Pampering myself

- Eating dark chocolate

- Swimming in the sea

- Having quiet time alone – relishing the silence

- Watching the rain

- Watching thunderstorms in the shelter and protection of a loving man

- Wearing a man's shirt

- Wearing beautiful jewellery

- Cleaning my home (yes, really!)

- Sneaking out to the cinema in the middle of the day - my local cinema is only 3 minutes walk away and is reputedly the most luxurious and best one in the UK. I love it there and am quite happy to go on my own as well as with friends

- Going to salsa classes

- Baking cakes

- Driving through the woods

- Walking through fields of gold - the wheat fields before harvest

- Dancing round the house in pure feminine energy

- Giggling at a funny film or book

- Singing when I walk, in the bath

- Getting together with girl friends and doing girly things

The only rules here are:

1 Whatever you are doing, do it with abandon, exuberance and with fire in your heart

2 Express all your energies and emotions. You can't have a rainbow without lightning, and sometimes there are dark storms in a woman. Just allow yourself to express them fully; not AT someone, but WITH someone.

3 Learn to be a goddess and smile

The Golden Rule - exercise

The Golden Rule is, 'Do unto others as you would have them do unto you.' So what would you like to hear other people say to you as you go through life? What has never been said or acknowledged about you? What would gladden your heart if you knew that people cared, really cared about you and appreciated you and loved you? So often, wonderful things are only said after a person has died – we fail to tell people how much we love them or care for them or appreciate them when they are alive.

We're not used to hearing nice things said about us. So in a group of five or so, have one person seated in the middle and sit down very close around her, on the floor or on chairs. All close your eyes, and now all at once bombard her with gentle whispers of encouragement for about three minutes. If you wish you can play some sweet gentle music in the background too.

Whisper in her ears, in her hair, on her skin:

"I'm so glad you're a girl. You are so beautiful. I love the way you move. Your eyes are beautiful. You are so clever and bright. We are so proud of you. Your work is amazing. You make such a difference to the world. Your body is delicious. You have lovely clear skin. Your smile makes everyone feel happy. You are a good friend. You are so pretty. You inspire me. I love your generous spirit. I am so grateful to have you in my life. You are so precious. We need you. We love you. Thank you for being you. All your dreams are coming true. You are so loved."

Keep telling her what she needs to hear, what we all need to hear. This may make you all cry but it is so delicious to be bathed in praise and adoration – something we have not had since we were babies when people used to coo over us in our pram – we have seldom heard it since. Somehow we have been made to feel that we are unimportant, unlovable unless we behave in a certain way, or unless we fulfil an outstanding achievement. That's just another of those myths – it's time to change those limited views. You are important, loved and lovable as you take your place rightfully in the world.

Now change places and give everyone a chance to be cherished and adored.

You may also like to do this with the person in the middle lying down on the floor with eyes gently closed. The people on the outside can lay their hands gently on her body so she feels the words entering into her body cells with your touch.

Caressing Your Hands - exercise

Take just a few minutes, close your eyes and very gently and very slowly stroke and caress your hands – these beautiful hands which do so much for us yet which are so often taken for granted. You can use the music 'The Scent of Love' by Michael Nyman to accompany you.

Your hands were not designed to hold a gun, to fight with or to do harm to anyone. Your hands are designed to create, cook, sew, work, touch, caress, stroke the face of a loved one, mould, shape, love, pass on tenderness, heal, form, express, communicate. Feel their utter perfection knowing that they too express to the outside world who you are at your deepest level.

Your Best Friend - exercise

When you have done all these exercises, I wonder if you realise just how far you've come.

If you were to make a list of the qualities of a lover or a best friend you would most want to accompany you through your life, what would they be? Perhaps they might include:

Attractive; healthy; successful; positive mental attitude; loving; supportive; humorous; sexy; warm; friendly; kind; patient; thoughtful; strong; funny; good company; sensual; adaptable; free-flowing; someone with integrity; trustworthy; honourable; happy; considerate of my desires and feelings; someone on my side; someone who will never let me down.

If this is your idea of a best friend or a lover, how about you being all of those things first? You can be your own best friend. Who is in a better position to offer you what you want in your life? And the more you live with these attributes, the more you will attract others into your life with similar ones.

Now go through your list again and see where you are on a scale of 1 - 10, with 1 being pretty poor and 10 being excellent.

Take a note of your answers.

Now close your eyes and picture or imagine what it would look like, feel like, sound like if you were a 9 or 10 in that area. Breathe into it – accept it in your body until it wells up in you so much that there is no separation between you and this attitude. Relax into it and visualise yourself being that - living fully in this area as a 9 or 10. Now reach up and squeeze your ear lobe.

Repeat the exercise and feel yourself being that. Imagine how you would look, sound, feel being that. When you really feel it as a 10 reach up and squeeze that same ear lobe.

Now do it again making the picture even larger, brighter, in glorious colour. And squeeze.

Any time you squeeze that ear lobe from now on it will act as a trigger or anchor and those wonderful feelings will flood through your body again.

Now ask yourself, "What would it take to get me to that 9 or 10?"

Take note of your answers and start living them. You cannot attract or keep the type of person you want in your life if you are not being that too, and cannot encourage a partner to behave towards you in that way unless you can show the way first. Make a contract with yourself to be a 9 or 10 in one area each day. No beating yourself up if you slip down the scale, just keep practising. But above all, enjoy it.

Now add to the list: loving, adorable, feminine and powerful and make a contract with yourself to give up what is interfering with your happiness, because a woman who is truly and fully alive doesn't limit herself. She has access to everything.

A Nurturing Daily Routine

First thing in the morning –

1   Drink hot water with a dash of lemon juice – this will cleanse
     and wake up your liver

2   Skin brush using a dry brush from the feet towards the heart
     (2 mins) which removes dead skin cells and also helps to get
     the lymph moving

3   Rebound on a mini-trampoline for a few minutes – you don't
     have to leave the mattress as the up and down movement
     forces the lymph around the body. As you rebound, repeat
     your incantations or say wonderful affirmations for the day
     e.g. "I love being alive, I enjoy exercise, I love being a
     woman. Today is the best day of my life."

4   In the bath or shower massage your body with loving hands
     and kind words

5   Massage your breasts (5 mins)

6   During the day, walk in nature or at least get twenty minutes
     of fresh air and light. In the winter months you may need to
     supplement with an artificial light box

So now you have nurtured yourself inside and outside, make it
an ongoing process for your life, because you deserve it, you really do. In

the next chapter we progress into what is traditionally known as labour as you continue on this process of giving birth to your feminine.

Your notes....

Labour of Love

There are times in our life when we have to work really, really hard, and most of us gain great pleasure from hard work and achievement; but you'll be please to know we've done most of the hard work in this book now. This next process of bringing your radiant feminine self out into the world will be short, sweet and effortless, playful and fun.

The Birthing Process

Uncomfortable though it may be, there's a reason for us having to journey through hardships and difficulty in our lives. It's the way we develop our strength and start to realise more of our potential. Nature demonstrates this in many ways – baby chicks will die if their passage out of the egg is made too easy; they have to peck and push through the shell to stimulate their muscles and internal organs. Butterflies have to wriggle and stretch their wings and push their way out of the cocoon in order to have the strength to fly. Baby hatchling turtles need to struggle unaided to the sea to activate their hormones and develop their strength for the long journey ahead, or they won't survive. Human babies too are designed to push through the birth canal. Nature's design is impeccable; she truly does know best.

Without challenges we remain weak and helpless, and without contrast to help us decide what we favour, life would be as boring as champagne on tap. So our life can be futile and dull if we dare not open up to unleash its potential. According to scientists we are only using 5% or maybe even as little as 1% of our mental capacity, so imagine what it is going to be like now you are opening more fully?

This chapter shows you how to tap into your fullest potential, and how to bring your dreams into reality. It encourages you to release anything else that the ego still wants to hold onto that may be preventing you from experiencing your beautiful life right here, right now. It's about giving up control, to surrender to what is, because paradoxically that's when we gain control. It's about stepping into our skin in a way we have forgotten since the innocence of childhood, to really inhabit our bodies fearlessly and passionately, to unite with our innermost being, to reconnect with that part of us which remembers how to relax. It's about reclaiming who we really are at a deep level, to joyfully surrender, and to allow the wisdom of our bodies and our spirit to direct our path.

I find it interesting that there's so much resistance to the word 'surrender.' It only implies weakness, powerlessness, submission or admitting defeat if you choose to think of it that way. For me, it is a willingness to listen to your inner wisdom, to stop the fight; a conscious choice to relax into beingness and let go with joy and pleasure to what is, relinquishing the struggle, a blissful capitulation. This then releases all that latent energy which previously was tied up maintaining the struggle and effort.

Through surrender to our feminine self, we can birth a whole new way of being. It is a process, and like the birthing process itself may take a while.

Stop Sweating the Hard Stuff

When I talk to other women about allowing men to do more for us so that we can bask in the freedom of our femininity, often their initial programmed reaction is one of outrage, indignation and disgust.

Then as the idea starts to sink in, they look relieved and abashed at the same time followed by the confessions of, "That's secretly how I feel too but I daren't say it out loud as we're not supposed to feel like that."

It's time to relinquish our masculinised behaviour and acquiesce gracefully to more of our feminine. I'm not suggesting that we become lazy or manipulative, not now, not ever. As we know, we are just as capable of doing virtually all that men do to a greater or lesser extent but just because we **can**, doesn't mean we **have** to.

Every man yearns for admiration for his masculinity, male-oriented skills, abilities, achievements, ideas, dreams and manly body. He longs for it, he hungers for it. He wants you to admire his manly qualities, not those same aspects that are available in women as well. He wants the contrast. He seeks the Yin to his Yang.

Relinquish those tasks that men are good at, and allow them to do it their way without your supervision. Make it easy on yourself. Make requests of them for the things that tax your feminine energy: ask them to move the furniture, take lids off jars, and mend your computer. Let them open doors, carry heavy loads, service the car, take the rubbish out, carry the shopping, carry your suitcase, climb the ladder, clear the gutters, paint the ceiling, do the heavy stuff. You've already proved yourself sufficiently!

Can you do it for yourself? Of course!

Can they do it for you? Of course!

Will they enjoy doing it for you? Absolutely!

And how much better will they feel about themselves if you request it of them in a sweet way? When we give men back their sense of self, we reclaim our sense of self too. Allow them to step up. Give them back their manhood.

And how much better will you feel when you relinquish the pain, suffering, defensiveness and martyrdom that you could win an Oscar for?

Labour Pains

Feelings aren't related just to pain and suffering, yet many of us only feel our body or remember moments of pleasure when we're in pain. Pain is a great motivator. We spend much of our life trying to avoid it or move away from it, physical, mental, emotional and spiritual pain.

Of course there may be labour pains as we have to use our Yang energy to push for who we really are, because any change can cause pain in some shape or form. Continuous pain means we are misdirecting energy that can be used elsewhere more constructively. It suggests we're off track, away from our centre because we're resisting instead of surrendering and going with our flow. But misery is always optional; it is always a choice. It doesn't have to be this way.

For many women, the word 'labour' immediately conjures up a picture of intense hard work with its accompanying painful pushing and shoving. We've all heard horror stories of maternal labour and some of us have been through difficult times ourselves when birthing our babies, but how would it be if we now choose a different way of looking at things?

Becoming Effortless

We don't have to suffer in order to give birth to what we truly desire. Passion and rage, fear and distress, disappointment and panic, depression, anger, anxiety and stress create strong focused tense feelings which rush through our bodies and our minds, bringing towards us the things we don't want. And then we push against them. We feel that whatever we ask for should be here right now, but when we fret about it, worry it like a dog worrying a bone, we vibrate at a different energy from our desired outcome – and of course we're not in our flow.

How would it be if you can now dissolve and relax away that feeling of needing to push against those unwanted things? It never actually does push it away; all it does is cause massive effort and create resistance that keeps you vibrationally apart from what you really want. When you can stop pushing against, opposing or trying to get rid of something, then you're no longer resonating with those negative thoughts and feelings, so you stop attracting them. Et voilà, life becomes truly magical!

So STOP PUSHING!

This is what effortless means. It doesn't mean that you don't take action. Effortlessness means *inspired action* when you do what you love and love what you do. Effortless means that you are fully engaged in doing what you are doing. It's rapt attention, where you are engrossed, fully absorbed, spellbound, unconsciously entranced because it's so enjoyable, that you are totally in your flow without your conscious awareness. It means that your focus, attention, love and enthusiasm are so absorbed and immersed in your outcome, that there's no room for distractions or interruptions, or any thoughts or feelings that could take you away from your path. It means that you wrap your entire mind around what it is you are doing so that no part of your mind is left over to contradict. This is what 'to concentrate' means – to align your centre, your inner self, your life force with what you are doing.

People who love what they do are fundamentally playing. How amazing it can be when you're totally immersed in what you love best, and someone else is paying you for it!

When you are being the best you, there's no stress or strain or effort – life just flows. That's how it becomes effortless living. Effort lies in trying to maintain the old programs of who you no longer are. Remember we are all perfect loving intelligent beings. Anything else is learned behaviour which takes such a lot of effort to maintain. It saps much more of your vital energy to be miserable and depressed than to be happy and content. It robs more of your energy to hold onto anger and grievances than it does to let go and enjoy life. It takes more energy to sustain bitterness and bad memories than it does to find something to appreciate in front of you and in your surroundings. And that stealing of energy makes you look old before your time!

In my class of self-hypnosis for pregnant women, we substitute the phrase 'birthing process' for labour, and the word 'surges' for contractions. The unconscious mind takes this on board as less laborious and painful as it responds to a new way of thinking. When your mind relinquishes its attachment to the idea of pain, struggle, determination and trying, and relaxes with the gentle rise and fall of the breath, embracing instead your desired outcome, you return once again to that wonderful flow where the wisdom of your body can take over. This is surrender time where you can gently relinquish your hold and open up to what is and what can be.

When you release with love and joy and when you give up resistance, when you stop focussing on pain and hardship, when you allow yourself to relax and ride the waves and flow gently with the current rather than paddling furiously upstream against the flow, when you are on your purpose, your outcome is going to be precious beyond belief. All that was previously hidden inside you will be revealed.

As always, I encourage you to breathe fully. It is just a reminder to you that you are indeed alive and allows you to gentle yourself into relaxation.

Breathe

The Breath of Life - exercise

In this labour of love, you need to learn how to breathe well. The moment we are born, the very first breath we take welcomes us to life, to our new beginning. Every breath is a new birth, a possibility of life, of new choices, a chance to start again.

When we breathe incorrectly, too fast or too shallow, we create great stress in our body; the exchange of oxygen and carbon-dioxide is disrupted, and we open ourselves up to dis-ease and illness. Stand in front of the mirror and watch what happens when you take a deep breath in. Most of us breathe only from the top part of our lungs so we are not using the full capacity of our lungs. We are operating at way below 50% of our potential. When you breathe in, if your shoulders rise up around your ears, allow them to rest and relax and stay still as you practice breathing from deep in your belly.

Ideally do this next exercise standing with your feet firmly planted on the floor about hip distance apart, with your knees soft and keeping your shoulders relaxed. If standing with your eyes shut creates a problem for you, then sit down for this exercise.

Accompanied by a gentle piece of music - 'Smaoint' sung by Enya or 'Scène D'Amour' from the film Bilitis (music by Francis Lai) with your eyes softly shut and your mouth half open, gently and slowly lift your arms in a soft flowing curve like the wings of a dove, up to shoulder level allowing your lungs to fill with air... then slowly lower your arms as you effortlessly exhale. Your arms act like soothing bellows releasing the air from your lungs as you lower them again; your hands tenderly caressing and stroking the air as they float down smooth and relaxed.

Keep breathing in this way, surrendering your slow, gentle movement to the music. Feel the breath of life entering and nourishing your body as you breathe in pure healing energy; breathe in joy, peace, light, love and all your heart desires. As you breathe out, release any stress or tension, any worries, fears, phobias, any negativity, all sorrow and pain and anger. Breathe love through your body in and out; breathe through every pore in your skin, every cell, leaving you clear and refreshed for the day, or calm and relaxed for the night.

As the music comes to a close, rest your hands on your chest to connect with your heartbeat and stay for a moment or two. Now slowly open your eyes and come back into the room.

Every Body Knows

Like breathing, nature births well - it has no problem with birthing. All the problems we have are based on fear, which by now I trust you are learning to let go moment by moment.

Our bodies have hundreds of thousands of years of history in them that allow us to birth with joy and ease. But we have come to distrust our abilities, our strength, our body and ourselves. Your body knows what to do when you let it, when you surrender, when you allow, when you nourish it, when you listen to it, when you relax.

Femininity surrenders only when in the presence of truth, when it's safe and when it's in touch with the Divine. As women, we make love to increase the depth of our feelings and only fully orgasm and experience total pleasure if and when we can surrender. If any part of us is holding back, we are not trusting and our female energy just will not flow.

That flow will happen the moment you no longer feel a need to push against anything that you don't like or that you disagree with. When you follow your natural intuition and the messages your

212

body gives you, your life will change beyond recognition. When you realise deep inside that you do indeed deserve and you give yourself permission, you give birth to your beautiful authentic self, naturally, healthily, easily and elegantly.

Opening To Receive

When you open up like this, you are getting ready to receive. When you can turn your attention and your focus now to your desire and live as though it is already accomplished somewhere in the great blue yonder in time and space, already achieved rather than effortfully striving towards it, life becomes easy and elegant. Never mind where you've been, what your 'her-story' is; it's no longer relevant. You don't need to spend any more time justifying or going over any of what has already been and gone.

Your Life inside you hears your requests, and so desperately wants you to live fully and abundantly and be fulfilled. Trust that your request is already granted. All you have to do is reach out and welcome it into your open arms.

Women are notoriously bad at receiving – we tend to give and give and give, and when we've exhausted our resources, we reach in yet a little deeper and squeeze out a bit more. It's as though we don't feel worthy enough to receive, as if we feel we have to earn everything, as if we don't deserve.

Many of us think it's selfish to receive, not realising that in fact the opposite is true. When we don't allow ourselves to receive, we deprive others the opportunity to give to us. When you give, it's interesting to note that it is you that is in control. Some people find it difficult to receive for this exact reason as it makes them feel powerless and vulnerable. It feels burdensome to them as they feel they always have to return the favour, always as if they owe.

Have you ever complimented someone about their dress and have them say, "Oh this old thing?" Or given someone a present you spent a lot of time and consideration buying for them, and then finding out that they haven't even used it months later? How does it make you feel?

When I was practising Buddhism, my Buddhist leader used to receive presents and pass them on to other people. It was a great lesson for us in learning not to be attached to the outcome. His pleasure in receiving was immense, his pleasure in passing on that pleasure equally immense so that more people would be made happy. To him a gift is pure energy. It is a lovely way to look at the things we own – as guardians for a time rather than possessors.

So how are you making someone else feel when you don't accept compliments from them? When you respond in a gracious way, you are giving back to the person who has complimented you. If not, you are saying in effect, "The compliment you've just offered me is worthless – I'm not going to accept it."

At a meeting last year, someone commented on how nice my suit was. I replied, "Thank you, how really nice of you to say so." And I meant it – I was delighted. It made me feel really good that someone had taken the time out to say such a nice thing. Later she took me aside and said how much pleasure it had given her to be appreciated for her compliment, and how rare it was for another woman to accept.

Accepting compliments and gifts is a gift in itself. It works both ways allowing others to give to us at the same time.

My niece Zoë took me out for a delicious lunch a couple of years ago, and when she popped out to the ladies room, I paid the bill. When she found out, her face fell because she had so wanted it to be her treat. Her beautiful generous heart was offering me such a gift so I had to give in. I confess at first it was a bit of a challenge because I'd got very used to being the giver. It felt lovely though to accept her gift to me and humbling to be on the receiving end. It taught me such a lot.

Give up your ideas about owing someone back when they give to you unconditionally. When we give unconditionally, the Universe generously gives back to us from other sources. It goes without saying that we need to be discerning, but when we are in our true essence and honour the pleasure of both giving and receiving without expectation, life becomes immensely joyful.

So am I saying to accept everything that is offered to you? No, no and no again. You don't have to accept unpleasant remarks or bad behaviour. So if someone is rude or offensive to you, remember it usually says more about them than it does about you and you can refuse it by gently saying, "Thank you for your opinion. I choose not to accept that and so you may keep it for yourself," or "Interesting point of view." This takes the wind out of their sails and scrambles their brain! And if someone says something particularly cutting, say, "Ouch!" rather than taking on board their remarks. It will stop them in their tracks. Try it and see.

Remember when you receive energy from another person in whatever form, it is not finite – it does not stop with you. It carries on and flows right through you out into the Universe. Giving and receiving is a continuous cycle of flow so keep it going. When you allow yourself to receive, you have more to give others; and when you are in a receiving mode, Life will deliver what you ask for. It is as simple as that!

The Language of Receiving – exercise

We've got into this horrible habit of saying: "No problem;" "No probs;" "Don't mention it;" "It was nothing;" "Not at all." Or when we are offered a gift we say, "You shouldn't have." It's like being slapped in the face with a wet flannel! Again we deprive the other person the opportunity to show their gratitude. Instead, say, "You're very welcome." Can you sense the difference? And enjoy their appreciation of you, because when you say, "It was nothing," that denigrates their expression of gratitude.

Read this next part aloud as you are walking around. Practise and allow the words to sink into your body. And turn your mouth up at the corners as you go!

Thank you.

  Thank you so much.

    It's a pleasure.

      That's really kind of you to say so.

I'm so pleased.

    How very nice of you.

        How very kind.

Thank you so much – I'm really pleased with it

      Thank you – I'm so glad you like it.

  How lovely of you.

      How delightful!

        Delighted to help.

How generous of you.

      Thank you. It's lovely.

  Oh I love it.

        I love it when you…

Oh! For me? Thank you.

      You're welcome.

You're very welcome.

      You're more than welcome!

If that hasn't made you smile, you're beyond redemption. No really, you need to practise this again and again. It is a gift you are giving other people when you receive graciously.

Ask and You Shall Receive

The more self-sufficient we become as women, the more we're afraid to ask others for their help, their advice, their support, their knowledge and their friendship. We seem to feel we might look a failure in their eyes, or that we're being a nuisance, that we'd be imposing or asking too much. We agonise, fret and stew in our problems, not realising that the antidote is often just a call away.

When we are appreciative and non-demanding, when we are genuine in our request and not attached to whether others will or won't help, most people are delighted and honoured to be asked and will go out of their way to offer their help, expertise and their support when possible. Your request is a tribute to their gifts, their abilities, their knowledge and expertise, and gives them the opportunity of sharing who they are. It expands us when we have the opportunity to give.

I have learned that when I am truly in need, all I have to do is ask. I receive such incredible support, love, friendship, advice and healing just by asking, and I know that those I ask also benefit for the time of their giving. Our asking and grateful receiving acknowledges the importance of the presence of others in our life. We can't do it all on our own. We are not supposed to, and we all love to be wanted and to know that we have contributed to the well-being of others.

A hormone releases in our brain when we contribute, when we feel we have done something good or helpful and it makes us want to give even more. Nature is so very intelligent. Back in the cave, we would have starved and died had we not looked out for each other.

217

Remember, we have survived as a species because of co-operation, not competition. We just have to rekindle that connection between us and keep it strong.

Awakening Instinct

Our reactions to the environment and technology are so fast and sophisticated these days that we sometimes forget we have a body with feelings. We've learned to anaesthetise our feelings by diminishing our sensations, by extinguishing the flame of instinct. Women in jungle tribes know every nuance of their body intimately without any self-obsession. In contrast we in 'civilised' society no longer really inhabit our bodies.

But do you realise that every indigenous people on this planet survived because they relied on their instincts? You are only here because of your ancestors' ability to trust their instinct. So when will you trust yours? Our gut tells us but we ignore it. It whispers to us through our senses and our feelings and is our greatest gift, our early warning system. We call it women's intuition while for men it is gut instinct.

For centuries in many cultures, the human body has been devalued and depreciated. Many religions have taught us over time to ignore our body as being something too base for the spirit, or to abuse it in the name of humbleness and humility. For too long, we've been led to believe that our bodies are somehow flawed, inadequate or deficient and destined to malfunction. Rubenesque women were plump and juicy, pear-shaped with alluring curves, which was probably not the most healthy, but now fashion has changed so dramatically to the extent that plastic surgery and body restructuring is almost the norm.

When you restore your faith and trust in your inner knowing and in the miracle of your body, you will restore a sense of balance that has been missing for many, many years. We have enough medical knowledge now to be naturally extraordinarily fit and healthy, but facts point to even greater lack of health and well-being. When you re-awaken your deepest instincts and re-connect with your body and feelings, you will make each day a most pleasurable and worthwhile experience. As women we have the capacity to do this to an amazing degree.

Living and working in big cities where we are disconnected with nature quenches our natural impulse; pollution from noise, light, electricity, micro-waves and constant exposure to visual stimuli and stress exhausts our adrenal glands and we forget how to restore our natural balance. We are still cave-women at heart, gatherers all. We need to reconnect with our natural energy, the life force that courses through our body when we release our stress.

Living Life as a Miracle

This energy inside you is the Divine energy which runs through all things, through the trees, through the rivers and waterfalls, through the oceans, through every blade of grass. Right now as I sit here in a friend's orchard on a sunny day in late May with the grass all around me higher than my shoulders, ducks are flying overhead and a small flock of beautiful green Paraqueets are gathering in the trees. Yes, we have Paraqueets in England breeding along the banks of the Thames. Divinity is in them, and it is in us too. When you feel and really connect with it, you will become more self-reliant – not through personality or ego, but through your essence. When you learn how to allow this energy to flow unobstructed, rather than blocking it the way we tend to, life becomes elegant, easy and effortless.

Elegant,

easy and effortless

These birds do not have to learn how to be beautiful; they just are. They exist in all their magnificence, as do the iris in the garden here, the honeysuckle whose scent is wafting on the breeze, and the fruits which are beginning to swell on the trees as the blossom fades. They don't hide away feeling not good enough. They 'do' bird fully. They 'do' flower fully. When will you 'do' woman fully?

Become a Flow-er

So how do we keep our feminine energy flowing?

Sitting here in nature's abundance, I realise that I too am a flower, a flow-er of energy. We are passing energy to each other all the time. When we feel our bountiful energy and transmit it to others, it will come back to us in turn. We will blossom like a rose in full bloom, like a peony opening its petals, like a lotus which comes into flower when its roots are embedded in the mud.

You know the expression, 'Go with the flow?' People often interpret that as meaning, 'Go with whatever shows up in your life,' but that's not what it means. It's about going with the place where the energy is flowing, where everything feels just right. You can feel it in your cells when your mind is sufficiently relaxed and clear.

If you are holding onto old programs, you can't get into the flow. If you are about to embark or get involved with a potentially damaging situation, the flow will stop and you will feel a slump or a slight queasiness. Habits always take us back to the past, into being like a tight flower bud instead of opening us up to bloom to our full beauty and magnificence. When the mind is so filled up with thoughts, judgments, your 'her-story' and victim-hood, worry and conditioning, it's impossible to feel this emerging flow of energy.

But when you can take time out to relax and really listen and connect to what is going on in the depths of your heart, you will find beauty and grace there. Spirit speaks if only you listen. Sometimes when you are in this place of quietude, it seems as if you are being guided by something outside of you. It seems somehow that the Universe conspires to assist you, and you feel truly alive, invigorated yet calm, on purpose and at peace. Life is giving you feedback to show you that you are in the flow, in your very own flow.

Give yourself permission to flower to your full potential and to be the very best you can be. Be a beautiful flow-er.

And Relax!

One of the greatest things we can do for ourselves is learn to relax and keep relaxing, not by watching endless drivel on the television, but something totally different. We've been taught to be really effortful as if it is a virtue. I feel as though I have a Ph.D. in effort - I don't know many people who have tried as hard as I have over the years – and it doesn't work, it just makes me unwell. Remembering those teenage years of school reports, "Must try harder; could do better!" I always thought it meant I wasn't trying hard enough. So I would double my efforts, as if we get Brownie points the more tired and exhausted we become.

My ex-husband and I used to compete as to who was the most tired, as if we were rewarded in some after-life for the greatest amount of energy and effort expended. Sound familiar? I still hear people boasting about how late they stay at the office, and how wiped out they feel, as if it is a competition.

But can you imagine how much more you can achieve in a shorter amount of time, now you have let go of so much of the baggage you have been carrying around? It releases you so you can spend more time flowing and having fun, the way life is supposed to be. What can we say to ourselves that's kinder? Instead how about saying, "I deserve to rest now, to put my feet up. I'm ready to relax."

I don't know about you, but I'm sure I wasn't put on this earth just to pay my mortgage and worry about the bills, to get overwhelmed and stressed, to worry and fret. At last I get it. If what we're doing doesn't work, we probably have to turn it round 180° and do the opposite. Unless we do that, our spirit shuts down and our guidance system turns off. We become so overwhelmed that the REAL us disappears. It cowers in the face of effort.

When you can learn how to relax, mentally as well as physically, you can let go of everything and you can completely surrender to Life. When you do this, when you let go of how you think you are supposed to be, completely let go of the bad memories of the past and be who you really are, the world reveals itself in such glorious splendour. Reality sparkles and shimmers, there is iridescence in all that you can see. There is joy in every moment. Every new breath is a miracle in the making, an opportunity to grow, to desire, to love and to truly LIVE.

Opening to Change – relaxation exercise

Birthing a new way of being cannot happen until you can learn to relax and open your heart, your mind and your body. Relaxation involves more than just the body. It is a letting go of stress, tension, worry, fears, phobias, limitations and any negative thoughts. In fact anything that is standing between you and how you want your life to be – just for this moment. Feminine courage is total faith and flow. Instead of trying harder, stay totally in your feminine energy and just feel and let go.

Read through the following exercise, then lie down somewhere really comfortable where you won't be disturbed just for five minutes or so and gently shut your eyes.

Just imagine the fibres in your muscles opening up and letting go of any stress or tension starting with your feet and moving up your body; imagine the tissues of your body releasing, just letting go like a puff of smoke going out of your body. Imagine all the cells in your body opening up and sharing their light with all the others.

Imagine with every out-breath any thoughts just drifting away on a fluffy white cloud – you can see them floating slowly by, but for now there is just no need to even take any notice of them at all. Just let them drift on by as you imagine your body sinking into the chair you are sitting on or the bed you are lying on. Letting go now ... and now ... as you allow yourself to relax deeper and deeper.

Imagine now your mind and body opening up like a rose bud, releasing gently fold by fold, petal by petal, slowly, delicately opening up to reveal the beauty and fragrance within. Allow love's openness to breathe you. Open so love can flow throughout your entire body, because you are made of love.

Imagine gold and white sunlight pouring down on that beautiful flower, and the petals and leaves basking in the sunlight absorbing all the warmth and the colours. And just rest there for a few minutes.

Now gently open your eyes and bring that shining light back into your day and into everything you do.

On a Clear Day

Imagine, what would happen if you woke up one day with no bad memories of the past, yet with all your instincts and intuition intact? How differently would you see the world? Imagine there is nothing to lose, if you just could not fail. You could just show up and be, live in the now, in the present moment enjoying every magical instant unfurling before you.

One beautiful early summer's day, I took my friend Mark down to the stream. The trees were full of blossom; the air was clear and fresh. We sat on the grass in the warmth of the sun and just opened our eyes to what was in front of us. I was teaching Mark how to connect with all his senses and with his instinct and intuition.

I completely emptied my mind, let go of all thought and was just there, completely relaxed in that beautiful setting. Within minutes, a heron dipped his long beak in the water, fish were jumping and splashing, a mare and her new foal lay down to roll in the hay. A fox appeared, rabbits popped out of their burrows, ducks and swans flew gracefully in, and a cygnet was playing roll-over in the water like a child and checking from time to time to gauge the reactions of its parents.

Dragon-flies skimmed across the water as it sparkled in the sunshine. The grass smelled delicious in the warmth of the sun, and the scent of blossom wafted its way across on the breeze. It was like a scene from a Disney movie, so utterly perfect and incredibly amusing, as all the animals seemed to be playing. I could see energy coming from the trees and shimmering on the water, and the colours were incredible. I felt totally at one.

Mark on the other hand was worrying and fretting about his work, so kept missing everything I could see. His head was crammed full of thought, and he was making lots of effort to try and see what I was seeing and share that oneness, but his mind was too full of chatter. What for me was paradise and total connection, for him was frustration and lack. And a total mystery.

When I was severely ill in my early 20's, I really thought I was doomed to spend my life in poor health. When I started to get better, I saw things in the most extraordinary light. Everything looked so beautiful, so exquisite, as if I was seeing for the very first time, and I appreciated every moment of being alive. I have heard this from other people who had near-death experiences. It is as if it wiped out the unnecessary. How wonderful if we could live like this from day to day!

Letting Go

Just let go, particularly of that old horned devil, fear. Fear is the opposite of love and it stops us in our tracks. How do we let go? Just stop thinking the thoughts that make you fearful because they literally cripple you, and put your attention instead on something that makes you feel good, right here right now. Thought means you can't feel, so **drop thought**, and just **be**.

The funny thing about letting go is that you don't have to do anything. You just have to stop doing whatever you were doing that kept you hanging on. Quite simple really. Get out of your own way. Get your personality out of the way with all its history, fears, and limitations, because when you recognise who you really are, then life becomes the greatest of adventures.

Nurture that vital force, that life energy. When you are in the flow, you can see energy all around you. Right now, there are two ring-necked doves billing and cooing at each other and a branch of honeysuckle has grown at least an inch as I have been sitting here today. Life in all its magnificence and delight is all around you if only you can stop and look.

Allowing

Birthing any of your desires into the world whether a book, a painting, a song or in fact any masterpiece, requires surrender to the pulsation of life. It requires a yielding to the inevitable waves of movement, a graceful acquiescence and obedience to what our body is telling us to do.

When we connect with the rhythms of nature, it awakens in us a primordial, archaic link with all that has ever been and all that will ever be through the ancient history of our growth and our development.

D.H. Lawrence expressed it so well as he talked about the civilising of love and relationship, by taking it away from our natural instincts.

> *"Oh what a catastrophe it was, what maiming of love when it was made personal, merely personal feeling, taken away from the rising and setting of the sun and cut off from the major connection of the solstice and Equinox! This is what is the matter with us, we are bleeding at the roots because we are cut off from the Earth and Sun and Stars, and love is a grinning mockery, because poor blossom, we plucked it from its stem on the tree of life and expected it to keep on blooming in our civilised vase on the table."*

DH Laurence – Phoenix 11

If your life isn't the way you want it, it's because you haven't allowed yourself to have it. With the right faith (and I don't mean religious faith here, but faith that you have everything within you that you will ever need) you really can allow yourself to believe in your dreams. It all depends on you from moment to moment. Each and every moment you have a choice as to how you're going to feel. If you can understand this and can just relax into it, you don't need to know anything else.

The Music in Me

The body is the vehicle everything else comes through. It has emotions locked into it in its cellular memory. Throughout all cultures in the world, music is the universal language. It connects with our feelings at a deep cellular level to unlock and heal. The body loves to move, yet most of us have forgotten how to experience joy in our movement unless it's formalised in choreographed steps. As young children we knew; you only have to watch little ones when music is playing as they move with the rhythm, free and easy with no self-consciousness at all.

Emotion comes through motion – energy in motion - to move, to sway, to flow, to curve. To express yourself through movement is to retrieve your feminine core at soul-level, and when your feminine essence is able to express itself, your life becomes a love-story filled with joy at every moment in even the simplest tasks. Our thoughts and emotions are expressed through our body and through our words. If you want to change the way you feel about yourself, your confidence, your possibilities, your relationships, your ability to communicate, your level of happiness, your health, even your direction in life, you can. You can learn to move in a different way, think in a different way, and use your language in a different way.

The exercises and dances here in this book inspired by my dancing training, allow you to over-write old unhelpful memories with new experiences of pleasure and joy just like a tape-recording as you reunite with your feminine essence. Express the exquisite beauty of who you are through the way you move. If for any reason you are unable to do these dances right now or if you are confined to a chair or reading in bed, your body will still respond as your imagination takes wings. Free your body and your mind and just be!

I invite you to allow your feminine energy to return to the safe, beautiful peaceful experience that Nature intended, to naturally unfold in its own rhythm. When you surrender to who you really are, life flows in a different way. Surrender to the Divine within you and allow it to shine through. Feel the fascination as you move, as your cells remember. Instead of dancing to the music, allow your body to be the instrument through which the music flows. Become the music.

As you go through the following exercises, take responsibility for your body and your energy here. Don't go beyond what your body is capable of. Listen to your breath and keep breathing; your body is giving you feedback all the time.

The Four Elements

Your body and your mind are deeply attuned to the four elements: earth, air, fire and water are instilled inside us. It is what we are made of. We are all composed of the same substance as planet earth, as the stars; our bones, our sinews, our blood. We are indeed stardust. When you allow the rawness of life to express itself through this connection with nature, you will start to wake up like Sleeping Beauty after a hundred years of deep sleep.

There is a Universal Eros, a natural feeling of love, which gives you the pleasure of breathing with everything and everyone, to walk in nature, to swim, to dance, to make love. The prescription here is to make the body more sensitive, and desensitize the mind of its constant activity, its constant chatter and judgment and to really feel through your senses. But you can only do it if you participate...

Allow yourself half an hour for these four dances with time between each to rest, drink water, and reflect. Feel the emotions stirring inside because you cannot help but be moved by them. Dance them over and over again whenever you feel inspired to do so. There is no right or wrong here, no judgment, no criticism – just you and your dance, your expression, your feelings.

Earth Dance - exercise.

In Vedic tradition, men were very rugged, swarthy and manly; they spent time chopping wood and digging and using their masculine strength, while the women basked in their own femininity.

Traditionally the women were also very physical, yet creative, nurturing and caring, very strong and very earthed. Female earthiness is a very appealing quality.

I use Helen Glavin's powerful inspiring music 'Earth Dance' from her CD 'To The Flame' for this dance (www.helenglavin.com). It will take you into a trance of earthiness that will astound you as you connect with that inner part of you.

Now take off your shoes and keeping your eyes gently shut and your mouth half open, allow the steady beat of the music to permeate your body and your soul with its rhythm and movement. Move like the ancient tribes treading softly on the earth thanking it for its gracious beneficent blessings of food and nurture, for shelter and nourishment, for strength and power, for the ancestors who lie beneath our feet. Imagine their energy and essence willing you on, these forerunners who have gone before us showing the way.

Feel the pulsating tribal rhythm as it connects deep within you. Feel the heartbeat of Mother Earth beneath your feet where we sow our seed and reap our harvest. We return our waste to the soil to nourish the plants; we make love on the earth, we give birth on the earth and at the end of our life we return to the earth. Everything is recycled - we become the flowers and the trees, the birds and the seed. Feel the earth's power and magnificence as you dance, allowing the pulsation of the music to take you into her entrancing energy. You may want to kneel or touch the ground as part of your dance, or even lie down to connect with the earth as the impulse pulls you.

Allow your body to become more sensitive to the rhythm and pulse of life, giving your mind permission to let go of its constant chatter and to have a well-earned rest.

The earth, like you, is feminine, breathing life into the planet. She creates, she engenders new life. In her fullness and voluptuousness she supports and holds us, feeds us, nourishes us, heals us. This earthiness that we have inside us connects us deeply to our sensuality, to our sexualness, to our deepest instincts.

Breathe

Air Dance - exercise

As little girls we used to dance around the room and the garden like fairies, alighting on flower petals and curling leaves, touching them like little dew-drops gently and delicately, lightly and softly flitting from bloom to bloom letting the breeze carry us. Like fireflies we would flit, blessing everything we touched with our magic wands, with our beauty, with our innocence, with our presence.

We have forgotten how to do this as we have taken on life with such heaviness, such urgency, such seriousness. But like angels, we need to fly lightly on the earth and not take ourselves so seriously, for this too shall pass. All things shall pass!

Pan-pipe music works well for this exercise. I use Gheorges Zamfir's 'Laryssa' to release my creative, playful, childlike sweet self, allowing my thoughts to take a well-earned rest.

When we rekindle this magic and innocence inside us, the little girl inside us is freed again to laugh, to giggle, to play, to dream magical dreams, to take flights of fancy, to be light and carefree. With bare feet, eyes open and mouth half open, and with no judgment whatsoever, release any thoughts and connect with that innocence as you dance around the room, in the woods, in the garden like a child at play, free and joyful, with a lightness of being.

Small children will delight in sharing this time with you. Let them take you by the hand and bring you into their world of enchantment.

Fire Dance - exercise

There is a richness and power and raw sensuality in those countries where dance is intrinsically part of the culture. In South America, India, Greece, Spain, Turkey, Russia, Egypt, Africa and many other countries, people dance the passion of their story, their ancestral energy. They dance their story of war, floods, savagery, triumphs, victories, losses, pride, sorrow, passion, lust, joy, desire, achievements, dignity and creativity. In their movements, they release all their pent up emotion and heal and transform themselves through the medium of dance.

In our softened western culture, our emotions tend to turn inwards and eat us up. So here we have a chance to connect with our ancestral past which is in each one of us, to creatively enter into the safety of expression through movement.

Astor Piazzola's music 'Libertango' reaches inside my guts and pulls me into a frenzy of feisty, fiery passion, peaking and subsiding, flickering and smouldering, creating and destroying to give room to the new like the flames of a fire. Yet there is anguish here too from some unforgotten ancient past which resides in the collective unconscious, both pain and triumph which is known deep in the hearts and bodies of women from South America, and to which we also can relate.

It feels so good to express it here, with your body, with your life. Enter into it fully with eyes open and release the passion. Throw off the shackles with your shoes; feel that power, that force, that vitality, the creativity that resides inside. Encourage the flame that is within you to burst forward. Let the music take you to places you have never been before and allow the phoenix to rise from the ashes, full, whole and new.

Keep breathing

Dance of Water – exercise

Sitting by the sea the other day on the south coast in glorious sunshine, I entered into the rhythm of the waves as they crashed onto the beach, and as they rolled back sucking ferociously at the pebbles gathering their energy before slamming back and releasing their plunder. Later as the wind died down, the waves calmed, rolling smoothly and gently in and retreating in a never ending flow.

Water can be violent and dangerous, or beautiful and peaceful. When you watch and listen to its rhythms, it will tell you what to do. It will tell you when to leave the harbour and when to return; it will direct your flow, it will guide you and steer you, yet if you fail to notice its warnings you do so at your own peril. It can be your friend or your foe.

Our bodies are 70% water and salty like the sea. Liquid flows through us, blood courses through our veins. When we learn to flow like water, it is as though all hard edges are soothed away. We can turn our lives away from the hard effort of continually paddling upstream against the current, and turn in the direction of the flow where we relax and are carried gently and harmoniously on course.

In this dance of fluidity, Jean-Michel Jarre's music 'Oxygène' will flow you slowly and gently as you melt into its hypnotic undulating rhythm. Keeping your eyes softly focussed and mouth half open, flow and float allowing your arms and body to curve and sway, to rise and fall like the waves on the ocean as you move in slow motion around the room.

Like a piece of sea-weed drifting on the water, there is no effort here; as the music swells and subsides, you too can move back and forth surrendering gracefully to where the current takes you, slowing down to the speed of life in the slow gentle lane. Let love's energy flow through the way you move and flow with love.

You may now start to notice more of a tingle in your body as your life force awakens to play. This is the Ki or Chi spoken about in Far Eastern traditions. It is your life force, your essence. It is calling you and urging you to reveal the real you.

Breathe and rest

You will by now have noticed changes in your body, in the way you move, in the way you think and in the way you feel. You will be nurturing yourself more. Your awareness will be heightened; you will have learned to breathe well, to relax, to dream a little and to let go. So now is the time to dare to believe in your dreams.

Creating a Pink Vision - exercise

You must have a vision for your life, or meaningless thoughts will take over. Your life is right now – it's not going to start when you have a new relationship, when you lose two stone, when you move into that house or get that job. It's here and now; heaven is where you are. And it will always be here and now, so when you start enjoying it you create your future.

As cave-women gatherers while our men were out hunting, we would go out into the wild meadows and pick nuts and berries and

233

gather roots and leaves while our eyes would roam wide, scanning the bigger scene keeping an eye on all that was happening with full awareness. We used all our senses seeing everything in the greatest of detail. We had to for our survival, but you can use that same capacity to its advantage now for your pleasure.

In my early twenties, I worked in the movie industry as a Production Assistant. The first time I visited the editing suite I found bits of film all over the floor. I was told they were 'miss-takes' – in other words bits that had been filmed incorrectly or in bad light, with inferior sound or poor performance, and later cut out from the film to leave the best bits in. They needed the 'miss-takes' in order to create an even better end product. Now you see how important our own mistakes have been in our lives so we can create the ultimate version.

For my fortieth birthday, I gave an Oscar winner's speech thanking my Producers (my parents) my Director (my husband) and my crew (my children) for their production of my life. It was great fun, but how fascinating to realise in all that, I had been so busy trying to please everyone else and forgetting about myself, my dreams, my heart's desires, my vision. I had forgotten that a happy mother meant happy children.

Now instead I have taken responsibility and have re-written my own life-script. So imagine this: pretend that you are the creative director of a scene in an Oscar-winning movie and the premier is coming up. You have the power to create anything you want in this scene, the mood, the characters and the scenery.

Create your movie using all your senses, see, hear, feel, smell and taste everything. We're very good at this – we already know how to do it, except we usually replay horrid old movies of our life's dramas that have made us upset, angry, frustrated and powerless. What I'm suggesting is that you edit those out and leave those miss-takes on the floor to be swept up.

Most of us are vibrating in response to what is happening around us instead of realising that what is happening now is as a result of thoughts and feelings we have had in the past, rather like a hangover. Very few of us are deliberately conjuring up images inside our head that cause us to feel fantastic now, in our full feminine flow.

You've already written out your life purpose – you have your incantations. So now write out in glorious detail in the present tense what you really would like in your life as if you already own it, as if you are already living it right here, right now. Write out the next ten years, the next twenty years, the next fifty years. I have even known people write out the next hundred years as they picture the legacy they want to leave. Be bigger, bolder and brighter than you would ever have dared before.

- visualise what it is you truly want

- wrap your mind totally around whatever it is you truly want so there is no room for anything else to come in

- attach desire to what it is you want

- believe that it will be so and let go of the outcome

- be grateful for its accomplishment even though it has not yet manifested

Picture yourself getting the results you desire, being thrilled at the outcome: your health, your relationships, your achievements, your home, your wealth, everything that matters to you as if it is already happening. See it, hear it, feel it, smell it, taste it as if it is accomplished. Suspend judgment and allow yourself to be really caught up emotionally with the end result as if it is already taking place. Write out every detail of your new life – everything you have ever wanted, all the people you want to meet, the things you want to accomplish, the talents you want to explore, the knowledge and skills you want to acquire. Imagine yourself living to be a hundred and twenty and doing everything you want. Go wild here, no holding back. Make your vision enormous, dynamic and boundless – and always include other people in it.

Some dear friends have given me permission to share some of their pink vision.

"I look down across the valley over the tops of the fever trees and flat crown acacias rising above the scrub and grass land which make up this magnificent landscape. The smell of the hot earth rises up as the cicadas shriek at the hot afternoon sun. The sights and sounds of my beloved land combined with the events of the day remind me how precious and blessed my life is.

Gratitude, humility, wonder, awe, massive respect and most of all love want to ooze out of every part of me. Love for life, love for my magnificent man, love for my beautiful children, love for my amazing and inspiring friends and family, love for our colleagues in our business; love for every soul I have been blessed to have connected with, and love for my beloved country on this precious earth. This land and its people that provide the fertile soul and open hearts for us to experience our greatest selves and be able to live every day knowing we are fulfilling our purpose." Annie – South Africa

"I travel all over the world and love to learn the ancient wisdom of these places and am forever in wonder of the diversity and the brotherhood of mankind. I love to take myself off to places where my contribution is needed. I only need to close my eyes and I can see their smiling faces, feel their

small hands in mine and hear the tinkle of their laughter and it fills me with happiness and great privilege. I teach overseas and also do community/conservation work. It especially touches me to be a part of creating something where children benefit – schools, orphanages, teaching, caring, wherever in the world that may be." Farah – England

"So, what had happened last night was the première of the film. I was so excited and proud as I sat in the front row with my husband by my side and all my family and friends around me. It was truly a magical feeling. At the end of the film as the lights started to go up I could hear all this noise and realised that it was all the audience applauding and crying as they were getting to their feet. I had never felt so much at peace knowing the effect this film was going to have on people who saw it and how it would change their lives.

After the film a party had been arranged and, unbeknown to me, Andrew Lloyd Webber was there. He approached me saying how much he had enjoyed the film and that he had also read my book. I was then taken aback when he asked if I would be willing for my story to be put into a musical."

Christina - England

No need to believe – just don't disbelieve, and keep honing it until it makes your eyes fill with tears because you've just touched the void inside and filled it. This may take a few hours, it may even take a few days as you continue to add to it, to enlarge it and make it your own.

When you are engrossed in this enough, your unconscious mind won't know whether or not you've actually had the experience as it becomes so real, almost second nature. You almost take it for granted that that is how it will be - the outcome is already established without any inner doubt whatsoever. And that's how it works.

Allow yourself to relax as you envision your desired outcome as if it already is, and feel the energy flowing throughout your body. Then let it go – don't worry about the how. That's not up to you - allow the Universe to handle the details. It is then, and only then, that our lives will become magnificent, that magnificence which we know is buried deep inside us.

Read your vision out loud as you wake up in the morning and just before you go to sleep at night, or make an audio recording and listen to it every day so it seeps into your unconscious mind. Just ten minutes a day is equal to a working week per year. Do this actively every day and watch the reality unfold.

Taking Inspired Action

Your inner quality, your inherent purpose is deeply touched when you follow your dream, so it's time to take the first step towards achieving it. Knowing what you want and having your vision in front of you will inspire you to take action, and inspired action feels effortless because your outcome is something you desire so much, something you love.

When you are passionate about something and you take action too, you change your mind-set and it takes you to a different level where miracles seem to happen, so take the first step no matter what it is towards your goals. Life will then unfold before you; it will guide you to the next step, and then the next step...

Your Life is Calling You

Life presents us with myriad opportunities at any given moment - there are so many possibilities, so many choices. The Buddha taught that there are three thousand possibilities in any given moment, so it is never a case of either/or.

When we let go of control, of having to have things the way we think they should be, Life in all its magnificence gives us a richness of experience way beyond the limitations of our imagination.

Learn now to relax, to trust, to let go, to let Life, knowing that all is well.

And it is so.

And so you flow inexorably onwards. Your new life is calling you, a place of joy and laughter, of freedom, of loving like you've never loved before.

And so you surrender now into the place we call Transition.

Your notes....

Transition

Do you ever get that feeling that if you can't be your real self you're going to burst? Clients come to me who are holding on to old relationships that aren't working in hope that 'one day' their partner will change; others are holding onto jobs that they hate until 'one day' they can afford to give it up; others to old reactive patterns of behaviour until 'one day' someone will give them permission to change; others in a state of depression until 'one day' it might go away.

Depression is simply a pressing down of the spirit, a crushing and squashing of one's inner essence; it means they are failing to listen to what their life is prompting them to do. Life gives you feedback moment by moment if you are not doing what makes your heart sing, what makes you dance with joy; and also incredible wonderful joyful feedback if you are.

These few pages in this small chapter hold a challenge – a challenge to you and your fragile ego. The decision to transform your life is not necessarily an easy one. Often it entails a crisis which brings us to that point of recognition that something has to change, but why wait until some drama forces you? What has to happen for you to be your true beautiful self?

Giving birth to the real you, is going to bring an abrupt ending to that safe secure period of stifling your old self, of keeping yourself small, of failing to open to and fulfil the enormous potential you have nestling inside you. It's going to bring an abrupt end to the way you are used to being in your present existence. When you make this decision now, you will emerge from your familiar limited world into a whole new series of experiences, like a butterfly emerging from her cocoon, and you will wonder why on earth you didn't allow yourself to let go earlier.

A butterfly never gets to see the beauty of her own wings. Maybe too we are like butterflies in embryo going through extraordinary transformation in order to emerge into the light. They actually go into melt-down during their transformation. But she has no choice, whereas you do!

Life is far too precious for you to not live it fully, to not live on purpose, to not live your purpose. Do you feel Life calling you? Do you dare you give birth to yourself, to that beautiful, inner, magnificent, feminine being who has struggled so long to hide away from Who You Really Are? Do you dare show your beautiful wings to the world?

The Universe is Waiting – Anticipating!

Transition is that extraordinary moment in the birthing process where time seems to stand still. It is like a parenthesis in creation - as if the Universe takes in a deep breath …

… and waits

… in anticipation.

It's like a girding of the loins, waiting for the final push into a new way of being. Yet it's at this point for many of us that we want to draw back, where we change our mind, where the old fears rear their ugly head and where we wish we hadn't started in the first place.

It's a letting-go of everything familiar - it heralds a jumping out into the unknown from which there is no return, and it can feel very scary. As women we want to be sure; we crave certainty.

At one stage when I did all the processes in this book together with my Mind Master training, I felt almost as if I was sliding down the steep, vertical sides of a fifty-storey glass building with nothing to hold on to, with no finger-holds to grasp, with nothing to cushion my fall. It was a combination of fear and excitement – the fear that if I let go of all my old patterns of behaviour, all the whinging and complaining, the excuses that I relied on, the justifications, my old victim habits, defensiveness, self-limiting beliefs and the ever-present fear of being wrong, maybe there would be nothing left. Maybe I wouldn't exist any more, maybe that's all I was. But that was just my poor old ego in its final death throes, tenaciously holding on in its last desperate attempt to pull me back from discovering my true essence.

The excitement lay in knowing that there really is more, that I really could change my hopes and dreams into something tangible, that I could allow myself to be the real me with no apologies, and I was willing to do whatever it took to claim it. I had seen miraculous transformation in other people, and I wanted what they had.

When I finally relinquished my hold, what I discovered in its place was extraordinary. I found a depth of calm, of happiness, inner joy, trust, groundedness, centredness, impeccability; a return to the well of femininity, a peace and absolute love together with incredible, gentle strength, power and youthful energy. As I let go, the stress in my face and body was released too. You see, a loving woman who has lost her ego is beautiful and fearless. I realised at last that fear is there to keep you safe only if there is danger, not if there's just an illusion of danger.

When we become aware of the automatic responses that we have taken on board, aware of our old continual reactive patterns of behaviour and the old trains of thought we used to run around our heads, this is such a gift. And you can choose moment by moment whether to run with them or not.

When you decide here and now that you can let go of resistance, let go of pain, let go of effort, you are going to reveal the most extraordinary masterpiece of your life - your amazingly beautiful, wonderful, creative, juicy, feminine self. Keep letting go; even let go of what you feel you need - then you will be free to have whatever you want.

Breathe

What's the worst that could happen? That you live out your days knowing there is more to love, more to life, more to being a woman, more to femininity, more to intimacy, more to relationship, more to your creativity, more possibilities to you, but not daring to show your face. How would it feel at your last dying breath if you said, "If only I had done such and such? If only I had been true to who I really am. If only I had dared to believe in my dreams."

Taking the Risk

The biggest risk you take is in not taking any risks at all – and of ending up with a colourless and unfulfilled life. I know many people who have been on dozens of seminars, read scores of books, taken endless courses to try and improve their life, but instead of taking inspired action and putting into practice what they've learned and pursuing their dreams, have taken yet another seminar, read yet another book – and never moved on. They have been trapped worshipping the tree of knowledge!

It's a tragic fact, but very few people are really happy and fulfilled at the end of their life – they feel they wasted so much time, so much life frittered away on inconsequential nonsense, never having done what they were capable of or what they really wanted. The happiest people live full out, expressing who they are in all their creativity, loving absolutely, making the most of life moment by moment. How would it be if you make the decision now to live fearlessly, without regret, to live the way you always dreamed about?

If You Don't Take Charge of Your Life, Someone Else Will!

Twisting ourselves into the shape of a pretzel to try and fit in to other peoples' ideas of how we should be, only pains us. We get afraid of being our authentic self for fear of being judged in the future.

When are you going to reveal the real you and start living full out, without all the 'stuff' we cover ourselves up with? That is what you are born to realise.

The immortal words from W.H.Murray say it all:

"Until one is committed

There is the chance to draw back"

Are you going to draw back into that old familiar shell, or allow yourself to be a passionate, loving, feminine, delicious, sensual extraordinary woman in all your glory, and step out into the world and make outstanding changes?

It's so much easier to stay put, to keep ourselves imprisoned in the old familiar ways of doing things, rather than jump out into the possibility of something more. And in order to compensate, we just decorate our prison and try and make it look nicer rather than escaping from behind the bars and going out in the world and really living. It's like staying in the womb and never really being born. And then we look for someone else to hold onto, to re-establish the umbilical cord that we can use as an excuse so we don't ever have to take that step.

There is a charming story of twins in the womb where one says to the other, "Very soon we're going to leave here and travel down a long tunnel into the light." The second twin replies, "I don't believe you. I'm warm and cosy and I'm used to being here. I'm not leaving."

So the first baby goes on to say, "It's true. We have to let go and just allow ourselves to flow with the waves. When you reach the light, you will be held and protected and loved in the arms of a beautiful mother."

Birth sounds like death sounds like birth – letting go, trusting and just being.

As babies, most of us as yell, scream and cry as we leave behind the warmth and comfort of a sheltered, warm uterus to be thrust out into the bright light of the world. But as grown-ups now, we can do it anew with joy and ease and elegance instead. As we make the decision to enter this new chapter of our life, to begin anew, how about smiling and cheering, laughing with glee and gratitude as we greet and celebrate a new way of living – of living our truth and doing what we are here to do? This is how we as women will change the world. This is how we will bring about a transformation.

A New Dimension

Do you know there's a whole world outside your old way of thinking that you've never seen, a dimension that is extraordinarily beautiful and truly magical, where you are the real you, where there is no pretence, no falsehood, no belittling? It's not intellectual; it's beyond intellect, it's beyond logic, it's beyond will-power. It's about letting go of intellect and coming back into intuition, guided by your inner essence, your authentic self. It's where you employ so much more of the untapped part of your mind and your energy, and use it to create your new life.

Now is the time to surrender and come out of the darkness of your old thoughts and limitations, like walking out into the sunshine after being in the gloomy shadow of a cave. When you tap into this amazing resource that is there inside you, that essence of your womanhood, you can create a life that is so glorious for you and everybody around you – a world of your making that is a much more rewarding place to be in. It's the way life should be – heaven on earth, paradise right here and now, a return to the Garden of Eden, happiness without measure as the ancient sages have always promised us.

Occasional cravings for those old limiting thoughts are going to occur to you because you are so proficient at them. However, when you can let go of these restrictions, stop reinforcing them and replace them with more empowering messages, the old neural pathways that created them in the brain will just frizzle out and die.

Feeling Fully Alive

Remember if it's a heavy uncomfortable thought that feels bad and oppressive, don't follow it. If it's a joyous thought that feels good and light, loving and life-enhancing, blissful and fulfilling, pursue it consciously and joyfully.

You need to be madly passionate about your life and pursue this feeling moment by moment as if it were your lover. The purpose of all life is to live fully in a loving way, feeling fully alive, using your gifts, your talents, fulfilling your dreams, so if you're not doing so, you are missing out in so many ways.

We are so blessed when we love but you need to make space for love to bloom in your life. If you spend your time thinking about your past, 75% of your attention will be focused there so you will be looking at the present moment through your 'her-story,' leaving only 25% of your time and energy for now. It's like driving a car continually looking through the rear-view mirror.

Life is not thought. Don't look through unhappy memories of your past at all. Don't look through the old aspects of your personality that were holding you back. Don't hold on to anything that is negative.

Where is your energy? How fully alive do you feel? How much energy is still tied up in the past and old programming that is no longer relevant to NOW? How much of your energy is available for now, to really live now?

Whatever you can do, or dream you can, begin it!

Boldness has genius, magic and power in it.

Begin it now!

Goethe

Your true loving nature, your real self emerges when you are no longer looking through any old limiting program; when you are who you actually are. And that is life - your life essence in it purest form.

Come with me now on this amazing journey and jump out from survival into life – you are not alone, for women around the world will be doing this with you. Together we will hold each other by the hand and emerge into the light of a new beginning in our true female essence.

Just one final push now and let go. Trust that you are safe, you are loved.

The unknown is where the greatest potential for creativity lies.

I invite you to join me there!

Your notes....

Giving Birth to Yourself

In this magical journey of giving birth to your authentic feminine, you have learned to let go of those thoughts that kept you trapped and that prevented you from experiencing the true beauty and flow of life on this miraculous planet. You have discovered your values, explored your vision and purpose, and learned how to nurture and nourish your feminine energy.

It takes effort to hold on to fear, pain and loneliness, but when we let go and flow with joy and love and just be who we really are, life takes on another dimension. We move from the intensely practical to an almost ethereal yet still grounded connection with our true self, a practical spirituality.

Most people are living in their thoughts instead of in life, but thoughts have a hugely strong hold over you, so much so that it seems unnatural to stop paying attention to them. But do you know, outside thought is another dimension which is all goodness. It embraces and enfolds you with such a feeling of security – almost like being in heaven, but we've never been taught to relax sufficiently to find it, because you can't take anything negative with you in there. It's what the wise ones have taught for aeons, the place that people who really are able to meditate manage to uncover. You know those times when you feel in utter bliss? There is no thought here, just the joyful simplicity of being, of feeling whole.

Now is the time to pursue your ultimate vision of how you want your life to be, and allow your potential full reign, to become a connoisseur of life with all its flavours, colours, feelings, smells, textures, tastes and sounds.

This chapter teaches you how to live in the present moment away from those old entrapping programs of thought. When we are truly living in the present moment, experiencing what **is**, rather than living in our heads and experiencing what we **think** is, life is truly miraculous, astounding, phenomenal, and I have to warn you, starts to become somewhat cosmic. When we are living fully in our loving feminine essence, life literally unfolds before us, and it guides and directs our path. When we trust, listen and obey, life will blossom and throw petals in our path full of fragrance and beauty and delight. Opportunities come out of nowhere – life flows in an extraordinary way, and although you may only dip in and out at first, the more you practice, the more you get to stay there.

When we fail to do what our essence tells us, we feel as if the clouds have obliterated the sun, knowing it is up there somewhere but inaccessible for the time being.

The world needs you – it needs me. It needs us to be in our rightful place, to awaken not only our own lives but to share this understanding with other women, with men and with other generations, allowing the true feminine spirit freedom to reveal itself, to allow the Goddess within to revel in the glory of who she is in full expression.

The recipe for successful living is when we live unfettered, uncluttered, using our intuition, expressing our true essence, our real self, the one we have hidden away for fear that we might overwhelm people with our passion and our emotion. I know in the past I have hidden the greater part of me away for fear of being judged, but when we reveal our true nature, other people come out of the woodwork to join you. It is as if our essence inside connects with theirs in a kaleidoscope of adventures.

The Genie Within

Do you know that the original meaning of the word genius is 'to give birth?' It relates to the word 'genesis,' while to be zestful and joyous is related to the word 'genial.' Essentially the word 'genius' means 'to give birth to the joy that is within each child.' So you are a genius, I am a genius. Every child is born with that capacity – every one of us comes into the world with wonder, curiosity, awe, spontaneity, vitality, flexibility, playfulness, sensuality, creativity and joy.

You know the genie in Aladdin's lamp who says in his booming voice, "Your wish is my command?" That genie lies in you, waiting for you to awaken it, to give it new instructions to fulfil your heart's desires, to grant you your wishes. This is no longer a fairy tale – it is real.

It is time for us to reawaken and reclaim our own natural genius, to acknowledge that capacity within us and learn to love it. Today has to be the day you start. If you carry on doing what you've always done and what everybody else does, then there will be no difference, no eve-olution.

Falling in Love with Your Essence

Have you ever fallen crazily in love, feeling your heart expanding in ways you hadn't even dreamed possible? That's what it feels like to give birth to your first baby, adopt your first child or welcome a child into your home. You change forever; you enter into a permanent state of falling crazily in love with this little being, this new life. Those of you who have children in your lives will know exactly what I'm talking about. The strongest emotion in all of human existence is the feeling between parent and child. This is connectedness at its absolute most powerful - so crazy in love that you are willing and eager to do anything, everything for this child.

Giving birth changes us. It connects us with that primordial thread which has linked womanhood together since the dawn of time, and it opens us to boundless love, a love we didn't know existed, a love we didn't know we had the capacity for. Whether you are giving birth to a baby, to a creation, to a book, to a business or to your true self the process is the same.

When you give birth to your authentic self, you can allow yourself to fall crazily in love with that too, with your feminine essence. And in turn be willing and eager to do anything, everything for that miracle that you are.

Today I am editing this chapter on my daughter Georgina's birthday. Is it a coincidence that this should be her birthday? There is no such thing in my world; instead I understand how life provides us with synchronous events which show us so clearly when we are in our flow. It makes me smile as I know this is what I am supposed to be doing, as I reconnect with those extraordinary moments of birthing her, and I see how connected this whole process is.

There has been a tendency to look with contempt at the beautiful and basic values of nurturing and caring and learning how to love. But this incredible gift we have, that spark of life, our true essence, is a sensitive substance like a small flame that needs protecting and coaxing into its greatness. When you can connect with it, it will give you the greatest things possible. Up till now you've not been allowing the wonder that is you to benefit the world. You have kept your essence trapped not allowing the world to see the extraordinary beauty of who you are inside.

When you connect with that inner flame and fan it with loving energy and encouragement, your world will change; the whole world will change, because when you shine your light with its unique talents and abilities, you light up the whole world. When you can just open to your own unlimited possibilities, your life and your spirit will work for you in such a magical way. Ask yourself: "What grand and glorious adventure can I have today?"

Being truly alive means living each moment of each day. Each day counts, each moment counts. Your life is a very precious commodity. You may feel it's selfish to think about yourself this way but there is so much misery and despair in this world because people are only half alive - they are not living their life on purpose. They just shuffle through and at the end ask, "What was all that about?"

When you are truly living your purpose, the reason you came to this planet, doing what you love and loving what you do, your power to affect the joy and well-being of other people will be immense, to motivate and inspire others out of their half-awake state. We've all been moved to tears watching movies where young down-and-outs are inspired into their greatness by teachers, musicians, sportsmen, coaches. This is the same – it's waking up that part of you that so longs to come out of hibernation. Our myths and legends have told us about this all the time, but we just read them as stories.

As we women change ourselves we don't lose our individuality or identity; we actually find it, and when we include others in our vision, the planet transforms.

You don't have to make effort to succeed here, because to be your natural self is effortless. The less effort you put in, the more you will discover this beautiful energy from within and the more you can use it. Stop tying up your energy by making mental effort and you will become more of who you are, your true nature. Think about what you really want, and allow yourself to have it. It is so simple.

You are the answer to yourself, to the world. Once you accept yourself, the effort stops. You're not striving to be confident or better; you don't have to try or to improve, so accept your beautiful self exactly as you are. Striving to be better becomes effort and blocks off the flow. When you stop, Life comes in and does it for you; then you are in present awareness, in contact with Universal Intelligence, with the knowing that whatever you hold in your mind will start to form. You don't have to make an effort to be yourself; you're either you or not you!

There's a lovely scene in 'Gone With The Wind' when Scarlett is holding onto the bedpost being laced up tight by her Mammy into her corset so she can hardly breathe. This process is like taking off that corset, being released from all those strictures, everything that stopped you from breathing out fully. Don't wait till you're fifty – do it now. Unleash that girdle!

You Are the Promise

Deep within, I always knew there was more to life than we are led to believe, and moment by moment it is revealing itself to me in ways I could not have possibly imagined, as if everything I have ever done has led to this moment. It is all about connection with your own essence you see. You are the promise … you are the world … you create your own reality … and when you can unlock the world from the grip that limited ways of thinking have on you, you can create a life that is beautiful and magical in every moment.

At a personal, societal and global level you have to be your own woman, in connection with your own spirit, with your own essence. To be one with Life you have to live in your authenticity, and let your light shine.

Be all you can be! We are so much bigger and better and brighter than we realise, and when you are really your true unabashed, exuberant, unlimited self, other people also start to shine in your presence. It's not even a question of faith, but just know it is so; have that certainty – just accept it as fact.

You have everything you've ever needed inside you. You have within you the history of 3.9 billion years of evolution encoded in your DNA; and you carry this around with you every moment of your existence. You can tap into the potential that you and every person on this planet holds any time you want. You literally carry the history of the Universe inside you.

When you have this extra awareness, and once you re-connect with it, your whole life will change and you will help create a different world. You are an extension of the energy that comes from Source, and the more you can allow the richness and abundance of that energy to flow through you, the more you and those you love will thrive into fulfilling their dreams, because when you are the real you,

you are the solution!

The Eternal Present

Living in the present, actually experiencing what you are experiencing moment by moment, is one of the greatest gifts you can give yourself and teach to others. The beauty of this, once it becomes an unconscious habit, is that it brings you into the eternal present, the NOW of life wherever you are. You really start to live, to notice, to participate in life rather than sitting on the sidelines and watching it go by, and the more you can do this the more you appreciate life itself, because life is just a series of moments of NOW.

It goes beyond conditioning because when you are here, right now, there is no thought, no conditioning, no comparison, no judgment. Your energy expands as it's not tied up in thought. You begin to see loving in a different light, see living in a different light and see opportunities you had not seen before. Your cells rejuvenate and heal as they let go of stress and tension. This is reality; this is life!

When you notice you're not doing it, that's when you're doing it – in other words when you notice that you are not being conscious, that's when you become conscious. So no beating yourself up – this is not about perfection. If you had already realized your perfection with nothing left to learn in this lifetime you would not be here – you would just be a spark of light floating around in the Universe.

Let me give you an example of how thought may still be controlling your life. Have you ever been for a walk in the country or by the sea or in a beautiful woodland and **just been there** with no thoughts at all going through your mind, just using all your senses and being fully aware, fully in the now?

We've all had flashes of what that feels like, but usually you are going over and over in your head what someone said to you, how you are going to deal with the problem, where the next amount of money is going to come from, all without breath and without puctuation. "Oh and I forgot to clean my blouse I need to get that stain off ouch I stubbed my toe did I leave the oven on must remember to phone the bank and pay that bill I need to wash my knickers tonight oh there's a squirrel what colour nail varnish shall I wear I need to wax my bikini line sort out that meeting with Jack mind the stinging nettle get hold of the financial director unblock the kitchen sink make sure the baby has her vaccination on Wednesday what lovely warm sun the car needs servicing I must start marketing my business."

All these thoughts interfere while you are walking through a beautiful, dapple-shaded wood with the river tinkling away beside you and the fish popping up out of the water. "Oh yes noticed them now what was Rory saying last night? and I hope Emma's exams are going well and what a pretty fern look at the way the sunlight is shining on that oh isn't it so warm and beautiful and the sky is so blue and I forgot to get the meat out of the freezer so what shall I cook for supper?"

This continual partial attention where our mind is being pulled in different directions causes us to go into overwhelm, so the primitive centre of the brain has to take over. Scientific research suggests that our IQ goes down 50 points when we are not immersed in what we are doing. It's particularly difficult now we have to deal with such overload in our modern day to day world.

If you find yourself constantly running thoughts through your mind and never switching off – STOP. Clap your hands, stamp your feet, bring yourself back to the present moment here and now and switch your attention to what you are doing. If you really manage to stay in the NOW, you are living life; and when you do, it becomes like a magic carpet ride – you see things unnoticed before in their purity, uncontaminated with thought.

Switching out of thought, into dealing with whatever is in front of you, helps you be much more fruitful in everything you do. It helps you focus, brings you into the zone that athletes experience, that flow of energy, and bestows upon you more satisfaction, more enjoyment, more happiness and more fulfillment. It is in these moments of absorption that your spirit, your intuition, your life, will pop up with ideas and magical creations for which your thinking mind would never allow space.

Practice being where you are and doing what you are doing – you will start to feel really well as your essence comes up to the surface. It will guide you and show you where to go next because you can't see heaven through loneliness and anger and negativity.

Being in the Now – exercise

This is a technique developed from Neuro-Linguistic Programming (NLP). This exercise is something you can do constantly to augment your happiness and keep you in the moment. The more you take this on as a way of being, the more you stay in the present and the more life rewards you. It is like a meditation where time seems to stand still and you open to infinite possibility and awareness.

The best place to do this is outside in nature, or at least looking outside. Deliberately for 15 seconds:

Look … Don't name anything because that's using your conscious mind. Just look and allow your eyes to absorb the sights and colours and textures. This is **Visual**, which we will call **V**. Keep looking for about 15 seconds. Then, if your mind starts to have a thought…

Listen … Again don't label anything just take in and absorb the sounds, feel them entering your body. This is **Auditory**, which we will call **A**. Keep listening for about 15 seconds. Then, if your mind starts to have a thought …

Feel … Don't label anything just feel whatever is there, the temperature on your skin, the feel of your clothes, you may feel your heartbeat, your emotions. This is **Kinaesthetic**, which we will call **K**. Then, if your mind starts to have a thought …

Taste … Don't label anything, just taste the air, the breeze, whatever is in your mouth; often the smells have tastes associated with them. This is **Gustatory**, which we will call **G**. Then if your mind starts to have a thought …

Smell… Don't label anything, just breathe in the air; smell the flowers, the breeze, the cooking smells, your skin. This is **Olfactory**, which we call **O**. Then, if your mind starts to have a thought …Go back to **V**.

Now keep recycling this series of **V A K G O** over and over again. Let me give you an example:

Right now as I'm writing this, it's February and I'm sitting in the sunshine on my friend's balcony overlooking the canal. For the purpose of this exercise, I will be labelling so you can understand what is happening and understand what is in my awareness.

So my **V** is taking in the sight of geese on the canal; the swans dipping their heads in their reflections in the water; ripples as fish bob up to the surface; narrow-boats moored on the side; ducks with head tucked under their wings, nestling together and basking in the sunshine; boys on the opposite side playing hockey in the school sports field; trees coming into bud; blue sky and small puffy clouds; frost on the rooftops; seagulls swooping and diving; church in the distance; castle walls behind me. Without labelling any of these, judging or going off into thought about them, I am just drinking in the sights, filling my senses with them.

Now my **A** is listening to the sounds. Pneumatic drill far away; belly-dancing music playing in the room behind me; the clunk of the balls on the hockey sticks; church bell chiming the hour; birds singing; plane flying in the distance; voices calling; fast speed-train whispering through the station; ducks quacking; seagulls squawking; chug chug of a little tractor. Again without labelling or analyzing any of these I am just absorbing the sounds, filling my senses with them.

Now my **K** is the warmth of the sun on my face; the chill of the breeze on my bare feet; the tremble in my stomach from drinking strong black coffee; feeling of being contented and loved; the desire to move and dance stirred by the rhythm of the music; enjoying the sensuality of being in nature; delight at being outside at the beginning of February; my mouth salivating; cool air making my nose tingle as I breathe in; goose bumps on my skin as the coldness penetrates my clothes. Without labelling any of these I am just feeling the feelings, letting them be; no thoughts of this morning, no thoughts of tonight, no judgment, no quantifying, just being in this moment.

Now my **G** is the taste of lunch still lingering in my mouth, coffee and the subtle taste on the breeze. Without labelling any of these, I am just tasting what is.

Now my **O** is the gentle aroma of the flowers below as they warm in the sunshine; the earthy fishy smells wafting up from the ducks and geese from the canal; smells of cooking from the kitchen; the pungent smell of coffee hanging in the air; perfume on my skin and smoke from a distant bonfire. Without labelling any of these, I am just breathing in the smells, filling my senses with them.

Now back to **V** and the puffy clouds going across the blue sky and the people walking their dog on the tow path ... and so on.

You need to practice and practice until you can come out of your fixed train of thoughts and really be here now. Switch out of thought to experience intensity and you will find yourself in reality. As the song goes, it's like 'Walking on sunshine.'

Imagine how uninspiring love-making would be if you were thinking about going to the supermarket to buy cheese, putting petrol in the car, your son's packed lunch tomorrow morning, whether the ironing is finished, your tax bill or your business meeting tomorrow – you'd miss out on the joy of intimacy, yet I bet most of us have done it. So next time you make love, do it the **V ~ A ~ K ~ G ~ O** way – really be present. Look, listen, feel, taste, smell – no comparison, no judgment, no self-consciousness; just be fully there and it will take you to a place you have never been before. Just relax your mind; when it clears, you will see what really is. You can step into it and you will experience life the way it is meant to be. Just accept yourself in your natural state with no judgment. Your love-making as you surrender to what is, will take you to a whole new level in your relationship, in your connection with your lover.

Letting go of thought releases an energy that will quiver through your body, making you feel alive and in touch again.

Asking Powerful Questions

We deplete our natural energy when we take anything into our bodies that is not life-enhancing – this means food, air, drink, environment, thought, belief and even people, particularly our sexual partner. Intrinsically, you know what is right for you. Your energy rises when you are on track, and gets depleted when you are off course. So you need to do things differently.

Remember, your mind only knows where it's been and what it's done before, and just replicates what it's done in the past. Every judgement you have eliminates the capacity to perceive anything that does not match it. Instead if you ask yourself an empowering question, it allows the Universe and your innate 'knowing' to step in to allow a much greater outcome.   Your intuition, which is the way your essence communicates with you, is never wrong, for it has no memory.

Ask instead, "What can I do differently? How can things be even better than this? What can I do to create a better outcome?" Any time you want an answer to a question about your life, you only have to ask. As you discovered in previous chapters, your body has such wisdom within in – you just have to tune into it and the answers will be revealed. Put your hand over your heart or over your solar plexus and ask yourself a 'Yes' or 'No' question. Then wait for the answer – it will come, maybe just a tiny, flickering feeling of knowing, but it will come. You just have to be alert to listen and to feel the subtle energy shift. You may either feel a sinking feeling (which signifies No), a strong excited nervous feeling (don't be fooled - this also may be a No), an encouraging uplifting upward tingly feeling (Yes) or one of complete calm (this is often a Yes). If there is any hesitation, the answer is No.

This is your spirit, your life force, the Greater part that is all loving, that knows best, and has incredible knowledge communicating with you. It is always there. It is the voice that says, "Go outside, drink water, exercise, phone your mother, have a bath, relax now, stop working, eat something, look out of the window, do your paperwork, tidy your desk, go to the village." How easy it is to ignore that guidance.

I used to go with the excited feeling, but after many false moves realised that my truth expresses itself as a calm knowingness, and when I am asking a question, my 'Yes' feels like a million little bubbles in my solar plexus gently fizzing and popping, or sometimes a whoosh rushes up my spine. And for something that really is important, something that really matters, the bridge of my nose prickles, like Samantha in Bewitched. My 'No' feels as if I've fallen down a lift-shaft! When I am truly in my flow, I feel relaxed yet energised, and am aware of a tingling feeling running through my legs, arms and hands, and I connect with the energy of everything around me.

> *I listened to that inner prompting last year when for some unknown reason I felt I had to go down to the village. I walked there not knowing my purpose, asked where I should go and found myself in the Italian Delicatessen. Not knowing why I was there, I browsed around and within a couple of minutes in walked an old friend whom I hadn't seen for months. He enquired after the sale of my house and when I told him it had fallen through that morning, he looked delighted, said he would call me and disappeared. Within the next hour, he had arranged for the purchase of my house by his boss at full asking price, after months of offers falling through.*

Tap into this energy – it is there all around and inside you. When you can understand this information, it will totally change your life – and when you share this knowledge with other people, you will totally change their life.

So to remind you what we have learned in this chapter:

Recipe for a wonderful life

1. Live in the now – in the present moment - for now is where our power lies. In order to do that we can use all of our senses **V ~ A ~ K ~ G ~ O**. No matter what we are doing it will bring us into the now. Stay with the moment – every moment has the future in it.

2. Let go of the past – bring only into the present the good learnings you had from the past so that even the bad times were not wasted.

3. Let go of negative thought – when we live through negative thinking it clouds our minds, and shows us we are off track. When we relax and breathe and just BE and allow life to flow through us, we can trust that we will know what to do next.

4. Listen to the small voice within. It might be intuition (your inner tuition), it might be a flow of energy to tell you that you are on your path; watch for the signposts in the external world that remind you.

5. Trust that you are being guided by your own inner wisdom. This is the information that has been passed down to us throughout the ages from wise men and prophets and creators. It is as true today as it ever was – we only have to listen.

6. This information is the biggest secret – share it, give it away to all your women friends. Let them in on it too so that between us we can make a difference.

7. Live from the tree of Life not the tree of knowledge – allow yourself to jump into the unknown as that is where the creative force lives.

8. Understand that it's harder to think thoughts that are painful and exhausting. In your natural state they don't exist; it only happens by putting energy and effort into them. Loneliness, inferiority and failure are learned behaviours.

9. Use your inner guidance of discernment to stay with the people whose energy is supporting life, well-being and harmony.

Birthing can be a messy process; a leaving behind of all that is no longer required, or the arrival of something miraculous – it all depends where you focus your attention. As we come kicking and screaming into this new world, there is a death of what went before simultaneously and sequentially all at the same time.

Here now is an opportunity now to dance with life, to love and share and enjoy and have fun and live, really live.

Play Time – Creating Dream-boards - exercise

Being playful is so important to our feminine energy, so we are going to combine play with creating something very profound that works. We're going to create dream-boards, vision-boards, treasure-maps, whatever you like to call them.

If you've never done this before, here is your chance to have a glorious, creative girly time. This can be done on your own but is so much more fun if you do it with other women as you inspire each other and glean ideas from each other; it opens up pathways in the annals of your mind which you may have closed off, entirely forgotten or given up on.

Now you know your values and understand so much more about your life purpose, it is time to create a vision of how you would your life to be in detail. So what is a dream-board? Well it's a pictorial representation of what you really would like in your wildest dreams. The mind processes in pictures far better than in words, but the combination of the two generates strong emotions that take your dreams and manifests them into reality as if by magic. And it works! It really works!

Time to day-dream! Most people live in the 'What Ifs' predicting and forecasting potential failure, so they miss most of life. A dream-board breaks through the barriers of your conscious mind and accesses the unconscious which does not judge. It employs that miraculous tool the Reticular Activating System which we talked about in the chapter on Pre-conception – it filters everything going on in your life to give you focus and clarity, and so guides you towards your desired outcome. It focuses your mind and stops your thoughts being scattered.

Your imagination is a wonderful tool that can transcend the limitations of past, present or future. Used wisely you will get a bigger and better outcome than you could ever possibly have envisaged. You will start to move towards your goal when you can picture it so vividly in your mind's eye that your unconscious mind takes a photograph of it, plays it back across the screen of your mind, and then life presents you with opportunities until reality tells you that you've achieved your outcome. But nothing will happen unless your dreams are really important to you.

What were you given as gifts or talents that you have done nothing with or have yet to discover? What have you always wanted to do but never dared? What dreams must you fulfil in this lifetime?

I used to get told off incessantly at school for staring out of the window day-dreaming. It was good practice for later on. Do you day-dream at all? Good - make it more intense more vivid. Every detail of how you want things to be is vitally important. (www.achievetoday. co.uk)

Remember thoughts on their own have no power to them, but thoughts accompanied by emotion is like a direct order to the Universe. At every stage of life whatever you have or don't have can be directly attributed to your pattern of thinking.

How to do it? You need a few hours, sheets of paper or card (this can be A4 or bigger if you prefer) lots of magazines, scissors, felt-tip pens, glue, an open mind, a willing heart and the intention to have lots of fun. If you want, you can even use search engines on the internet which have image sections to select pictures of things you'd like to do or have. (www.audible.co.uk Maggie Lawrie - 'The Secret Guide to Getting What You Want.')

What will you allow yourself to have? We restrict ourselves as to what we are prepared to accept in life – you can now allow yourself to have it all. Never place limitations and restrictions on your dreams and desires or you will have a life half-lived.

Your desires become like a prayer in pictures that gets broadcast out into the Universe. Find pictures of objects or experiences that you really like, that really get your juices flowing, maybe holiday destinations or a car, or books published, charities you want to start, or a new relationship, or children or a particular type of home. Balanced across all areas of your life, you can find pictures to represent health, wealth, relationships, family, hobbies, fun with friends, career, personal growth, spiritual growth, your legacy, making a difference, living in a peaceful abundant world, whatever you choose.

Find pictures with a wider meaning for you, not just material objects. In the middle you may want to put a picture that represents your life's purpose or your higher self such as a diamond representing the clear jewel of who you are, or a tree, a sunrise, blue sky or family, a heart, a flower, the central point from which your desire stems. Stick them all on the large piece of paper or card and make a collage which gladdens your heart and eyes.

Whatever it is you want be very specific because the Universe really does deliver. This is like a mail-order service. Nothing will happen unless your dreams are really important to you – the mind cannot work without a clear vivid picture so make them more intense, more vivid, and more detailed. Find things that really resonate with you, which you get emotional about in a good way. Bring out the dreams inside your heart. What is it that will make your heart sing?

You see, your life is the result of how you see it. If what you are doing doesn't satisfy you, then see yourself doing what your heart desires. Your image must be that of a strong, dynamic, healthy, sexy, sensual, loving, gorgeous, responsible, feminine woman. Success is not a matter of good luck or overwork; it is a mental attitude. Don't be boring – think what you want to achieve and make it 100 times bigger; then you wake up all your mind-cells to assist you, otherwise they carry on sunbathing, watching soaps, eating chocolate and getting fatter and lazier by the second!

Find pictures of really feminine women – watch movies and see who you most identify with. Look at their body language, the way they move and the way they dance. Move like them with grace and elegance; copy their sense of dress and make it your own.

Everything in your world is a manifestation of what's inside of you. Whatever you accomplish in the world shows up because you established it inside first. So every detail is vitally important. This is a very powerful tool so be careful what you put there – put on it exactly what you want, and then trust. Use it wisely. Acting as if you already have it now is a great aid to success.

If you want more money, you will as if by magic, suddenly find money appearing at your feet, but it may only be 2p pieces in the gutter, because the unconscious mind doesn't know what to make of 'more money.' It wants specific detail, colour, size, shape, amounts – it can't work with just any old thought.

You may be asking yourself, "But how am I going to achieve all this?" Forget the 'How.' It's not up to you; it's none of your business. But you do need to be ready and take action when things and opportunities come your way. And they will – believe me!!

It's good to write words which produce strong emotions and enthusiasm alongside your pictures, which help to attract into your life those things which resonate at similar frequency – this is the Law of Resonance. Look at your dream board every day – put it on the wall, on the fridge door. Miniaturise it and carry a copy in your handbag.

Never underestimate the power of this.

I had beside my bed a picture of a man and a woman dancing together. A year later I fell in love with a wonderful Dutchman, a few years younger than me. When we were dancing together engrossed in each other's presence, someone took a photo of us and it was almost identical to that picture – right down to the angle of my head and the tilt of his chin and the way he was holding me. It was uncanny.

Sylvia.

Let your unconscious mind guide you now, and start to take the first steps towards your dreams, trusting that it will come to pass. Like stepping stones one after the other, follow the path as it opens to you. Without action, it will just remain a dream.

With your commitment to your new life, which can start at any time you choose, your life will be worthwhile – a life well lived. Because an open mind can see forever.

Your notes....

Cutting the Cord

No way back now, for once you have tasted life the way it is supposed to be, you will not want to go back. But beware, because other people will want to drag you back to their old way of thinking. Just remember who you are now.

Navel Gazing

Everything we see is contaminated by thought – we will only know the nature of that thought itself, albeit unknowingly. When you keep replaying over and over again a situation where someone has hurt you in the past, it is **you** who keeps it stuck. You are not hurting them or paying them back, **you** are hurting **you** and keeping yourself trapped, and those around you who have to suffer the consequences. It actually affects everything you do as you look at the world through a program of betrayal and anger. Until you release it, you still have an energetic link or attachment to that person like an umbilical cord, which gets reinforced and strengthened each time you talk or think about them, and what 'they' have done to you.

The Forgiveness Process

Forgiveness is not about condoning what others have done, or letting them off the hook. The word 'forgive' literally means 'to give up.' It is about releasing **them** and **ourselves**. We 'for give' or release them so that **we** don't have to carry around the misery for the rest of our lives. We forgive them because **we** deserve it. We do it for ourselves; it gives us peace, joy and freedom because we let go - we **give for** ourselves.

When you really can understand this and are ready to forgive, you will find some really powerful forgiveness processes on the web (www.radicalforgiveness.com)

How Far Have You Travelled?

Now it is time to re-cap all we have learned on our journey – to see how far we've come.

In the chapter on Preconception, we learned about our preconceived ideas and where they came from. As a child we saw everything with a newness, with awe and wonder as we discovered more, but that vision became jaded as we learned from others. We learned that we are still cave-women at heart and that many of our responses are still primordial and primitive, an automatic response that is wired into our unconscious mind. We learned about the power of belief, the magical reticular activating system that shows you in your life what you believe rather than what is. We learned the importance of thought and how to change it in a heartbeat, the importance of ranting, to play full out, to express and let go of all that has been holding us back from revealing our glorious true feminine self. We learned how to say "No" and more importantly how to say "Yes" to what we really want in life, to change our way of thinking.

In the chapter on Conception, we learned about the importance of Yin and Yang. Yin the female side is intuition – the deepest wisest part of us, the receptive aspect through which the creative aspect of the Universe can flow. It is an inner prompting, a gut feeling which contacts us in dreams, in our emotions and in our physical body, and that if we pay attention to it, it will guide us perfectly. In contrast the male aspect is action which thinks, speaks and moves our body. When you put the feminine intuition in the guiding position and combine it with the clarity, directness, fearlessness and passionate strength of the masculine, creativity and harmony will ensue. We learned that the female nature is wisdom and love, a clear vision through feeling and desire, while the male nature is all-out risk-taking action. When the male protects and honours the sensitive energy of the intuitive, it creates a strong open channel with wisdom, peace and love flowing through.

In our culture we have used our male energy to suppress and control our feminine intuition rather than to support and express her. The male is somewhat fearful of feminine power as they don't want to surrender to the power of the Universe as they are afraid they will lose their individual identity. While the masculine holds on to individuality and separateness, the female is a force which moves towards union and oneness. Nowadays, woman has learned to use her male energy to deny and suppress her feminine power which leaves her helpless, dependent on men, emotionally unbalanced and unable to express herself individually. As a consequence she will attract men who mirror this male personality and will act it out by being chauvinistic and mentally and physically abusive, or she will attract weak and spineless men. Once she starts to love and trust herself more, the behaviour of men around her will change dramatically to be replaced by men who are supportive and appreciative of her. Woman is not only energetic and dynamic but also the base of family, the fundamental base of relationship.

We have learned that we live in a vibrational Universe, that quantum physics has proved that we are all vibrational beings, that everything vibrates and that we attract into our lives that which we focus on most. We learned about the power of the mind and how the unconscious mind dictates our every thought; and that until we give it new information, we will continue to attract what we always have done. We are creators – we can create what we truly desire in our lives once we know how, and you have learned how to do that, by savouring, appreciating and enjoying. You have discovered your purpose, how

275

to change your rules to create more happiness, and the importance of being the real you.

Gestation has taught you how to love and nurture that feminine essence deep inside you, the beautiful feminine being that you are, the importance of what you put in your body and how to express yourself in the world. It has shown you how to reconnect with your instincts and how your hierarchy of values dictates your destiny. When you look at a woman who knows she is loved and feels it deeply, you will see in her body and in her face a bloom like the bloom of wholesomeness in mid-pregnancy. You have learned how to bring that to yourself. We enhance the love of our men by devoting time and attention to them and by loving ourselves. Love improves our health and our emotions.

The chapter Labour of Love has shown you an effortless way to get into your flow, how to relax, how to receive, how to breathe in goodness and really enjoy being a woman. Deeply connected with nature and with the earth which so influences us women, you have also learned how to create your own vision of your life. Part of being a true woman is to retain her feelings of self-respect, an awareness of her true worth.

Transition has taken you into the waiting room, wondering whether you will jump out into the unknown and live your true abundant glorious self, vibrant and juicy, inviting you to lose yourself in order to gain yourself. It is an invitation to fly.

Giving Birth to Yourself is where you rescued your courage, gave full expression to who you really are and showed you how to create a treasure-map to guide you on your way. Here you learned how to live, really live in the present moment, so that every second becomes extraordinary, knowing that wherever you choose to place your focus that is what will happen. At any moment there are literally millions of possibilities all leading to a different way of life. We have myriad thoughts each day. Which will you focus on? Which will you let go of?

Which will you ignore? Just because you have a thought does not mean you have to give it any energy. It is just a thought until you focus on it and it manifests itself in a more solid form.

Do I live in the present all the time? No, but when I remind myself, I can come back here to reality any time and I see life the way it is supposed to be for all of us. I spend far more time living in the now than in the past. When I am just grateful for everything, good, bad or indifferent, the magic happens.

If all you did was to appreciate your life more than anyone else, life will be very magical indeed. The art of appreciation is the key to it all.

Cutting the Cords That Bind Us

Energetically, we have threads like umbilical cords which tie us to our past and to other people. It's time now to let go, to release them, to release you. When you can do this and cut the cord to the past, to negative thinking, to all that is not you, you will reclaim your power and your magnificent energy, and live life moment by moment filled with such a sense of peace and calm and relief.

So imagining a large pair of golden scissors in your hands, you can now lovingly cut through the myriad of cords to release your attachments to your past, to your old memories which have brought you to now, to those people whose lives have touched you but who you no longer need in your life, to old habits, old behaviours, old ways of being.

Imagine those thoughts attached and coming out from around your umbilical area. Picture the person to whom you still have this attachment and envisage the threads or cords that link you going from your body into theirs. Now send loving thoughts of well-being and gratitude along those cords, and when you feel calm and peaceful and caring, take your imaginary golden scissors and cut through the cords releasing them and you.

You may also be aware of some attachment around the area between your eyebrows called the third eye which also need cutting.

And let go! You will feel a whole shift in your energy when you do this as you reclaim that which is yours, and release that which is theirs.

A New Life, A New You.

So, welcome to the real world beautiful one. Kiss your life awake now as you emerge from the darkness into a new way of living, a new way of being, a new way of expressing yourself.

Relax … let go … and revel in your womanhood.

There is an orgasmic quality to life. It is the creative spark in everything that lives and breathes, and when you can remember that as you use all your senses to keep you flowing beautifully and gracefully in the present moment, then all will be well.

Never underestimate the transformation you have been through in these pages. If you want to experience it in the company of others, please come to my workshops and bring your friends with you.

You see it's all about gratitude – judgment kills all possibilities, it contracts you. But gratitude expands you. Be grateful for everything around you, for each new breath, for each precious moment.

Thank you for taking this journey with me. I honour your courage, your presence and your greatness.

And send you my deepest love and gratitude.

Your notes....

Music for the Exercises

Buy, beg, borrow or download the music for the exercises in this book. These pieces have been specially selected and when you are ready to share the experience with others, please do come to my workshops.

Dance of Transformation – 'End Titles' from the album Blade Runner – Vangelis

Yang Dance – last section of Prince Igor from the Polovtsian Dances by Borodin (National Philharmonic Orchestra Tjeknavorian.)

Yin Dance – 'String Quintet in C Major'- Schubert; 'Prelude' from the album Tribute - Yanni

Integration of Yin and Yang – 'Kiss from a Rose' - Seal

Gratitude to Your Body – 'Fields of Gold' – Eva Cassidy; 'Thank You for Loving Me' - Jon Bon Jovi.

Inner Smile - 'You Are So Beautiful' – Joe Cocker

Belly Dance - 'Marco Polo' - Loreena McKennit; Greek, Turkish or Egyptian belly- dance music

Caressing Your Hands – 'The Scent of Love' – Michael Nyman

The Breath of Life – 'Smaoint' – Enya; 'Scène D'Amour' from the film Bilitis – music by Francis Lai

Earth Dance - 'Earth Dance' from the CD 'To The Flame' - Helen Glavin

Air Dance – 'Laryssa' - Gheorghes Zamfir pan-pipes

Fire Dance - 'Libertango' - Astor Piazzola; 'Djobi Djoba' – Gyspy Kings

Dance of Water – 'Oxygène 1' - Jean-Michel Jarre

Recommended Reading

The Female Brain	Louann Brizendine MD
Women Who Run With the Wolves	Clarisa Pinkola Estes
A Return to Love	Marianne Williamson
Secrets About Life Every Woman Should Know	Barbara De Angelis
The Hidden Messages in Water	Masaru Emoto
The Heart of Love	Dr. John F. Demartini
Maps to Ecstasy	Gabrielle Roth
The Aladdin Factor	Jack Canfield & Mark Victor Hansen
The Mozart Effect	Don Campbell
Excuse Me, Your Life is Waiting	Lynn Grabhorn
The Power is Within You	Louise Hay
The Path to Love	Deepak Chopra
Awaken the Giant Within	Anthony Robbins
Molecules of Emotion	Candace B. Pert PhD.
The Biology of Belief	Bruce Lipton PhD
Your Body Speaks Your Mind	Debbie Shapiro
Take Yourself to the Top	Laura Berman Fortgang
The Rules of Life	Richard Templar
You Can Get What You Want	Michael Neill
Women's Bodies, Women's Wisdom	Dr. Christiane Northrup
Journey to Freedom	Lesley Kenton
The Tao of Music	John M. Ortiz
The Key	Dr. Joe Vitale
Manifesting Your Destiny	Dr. Wayne Dyer
The Field	Lynne McTaggart
Using Your Brain	Richard Bandler
Dear Lover	David Deida
Power vs. Force	David R. Hawkins MD, PhD

Resources

www.educogym.com – The educogym® Time Machine: This unique advanced resistance-based machine is designed to rejuvenate your body by replacing lost firm muscle tissue, reducing unsightly fat, making you look and feel years younger. Nutritional advice and mind training

www.educomindpower.com – Dr. Tony Quinn's 2 Week EDUCO™ Seminars. 'Why Not Live The Life Of Your Dreams?' The only scientifically proven 'success system' in the world today. Life-changing seminars in an exotic location.

www.moxi.co.il – Healing energy and the quantum paradigm – Trond Bjornstad demonstrates his 20 minute healing energy session on video

www.biodanza.co.uk and **www.biodanza.org** – Biodanza™ is a system of human integration and growth, stimulated by music, rhythm and emotion and aims to promote personal development and a richer enjoyment of life. It is based on universal laws which allow the conservation and evolution of life in a healthy way. A rigorous system of exercises and dance scientifically developed and organised with the aim of regaining a sense of well-being, the joy of life, a healthy self-esteem, and the pleasure of expressing emotions.

www.tophermorrison.com – Dr. Morrison - 'Topher', as his friends around the world call him, is dedicated to assisting you harness your mind-body health skills, power your life adventure - and achieve the results you set out for.

www.beyondchocolate.co.uk – Beyond Chocolate is run as a workshop or as an e-course, both with ongoing, follow-up support for women who are unhappy with their weight and their relationship with food.

www.alkalinebydesign.co.uk – Discover your true state of health with a Microscopy Blood Assessment

www.tonyandnickivee.com Relationship experts with wonderful spa retreat for workshops for singles and couples in Austria

www.helenglavin.com – music 'To the Flame' – a Shamanic journey of ecstatic singing and dance trance rhythms. Helen is a gifted singer, pianist, composer and lyricist. The uplifting power of the human voice are threads of gold in her music.

www.tsuboki.co.uk – TSUBOKI® Japanese Face Massage is a wonderfully relaxing yet energising treatment.Based in part on the principles of acupressure, it is a modern take on meridian theory, which goes back thousands of years in Japan and China.

www.aspirecompanies.com – Samantha Collins, Founder and CEO of Aspire coaching and development for women leaders

www.audible.com www.audible.co.uk – Maggie Lawrie - The Secret Guide to Getting What You Want – relaxation CD inspiring you as you create your dream-board.

www.achievetoday.co.uk – Naomi Johnson creates magazine articles about your life as if your dreams have already been achieved

www.changeintelligence.com – Lucie Hobson - NLP courses for women

www.damselsinsuccessonline.com – self development club for women

www.femininezone.com – the online solution for intelligent women

www.the-drawingroom.co.uk – cafe and restaurant in Chesham, Buckinghamshire is also the only Art Gallery in the UK to exclusively exhibit figurative, sensuous works, housing over 400 original works of fine art.

www.cliffwarner.co.uk – Artist with stunning portraits of women

www.noble-manhattan.com – coaching training courses and corporate coaching

www.juicemaster.com - Jason Vale's superb books and workshops on juicing to revitalise your life

www.drvoice.tv – Tony Wade also known as Dr Voice – voice coaching for singing and speaking

About the Author

Susie Heath has an extraordinary variety of working experience from being a French teacher, a fashion selector with a major high street store, a model, a marketing assistant with a major finance house, through to a production assistant with a film company. As a wife and mother of three children, she ran her own horticultural company for 14 years from home, writing, running workshops and lecturing for the Royal Horticultural Society. Trained as a TV presenter, she has been featured on several TV and radio programmes and has been a much sought-after specialist speaker and writer.

Later as a divorced single mother with two teenage boys to raise, juggling the tasks of motherhood, home and work, she qualified as a personal life coach and later as a Corporate, Executive and Business Coach, a Clinical Hypnotherapist with NLP, and a teacher of Biodanza™. In 2000 she started the journey of Life Mastery University with Tony Robbins, and later studied to become an Educo™ Mind Master with Dr. Tony Quinn. She is also a Relationship and Intimacy coach.

A great lover of life, Susie has been running personal development workshops since 1997, and is an inspirational speaker. She specialises in vision and purpose, Core Energy Dynamics™, relationship and intimacy coaching, how to use more of your mind, Understanding Men, Understanding Women, and Essence of Womanhood.

Although she lives in England, she has travelled extensively. She is in the process of writing the next book in this series for women in business.

For more details on her workshops and downloads from this book, please go to www.essenceofwomanhood.com

Susie Heath invites you to visit

www.essenceofwomanhood.com

Come and join us for Essence of Womanhood™ workshops and seminars; for transformational weekends for singles and couples at our beautiful manor house in the Cotswolds www.foxesmanor.com; for workshops and weekends of dance in exotic locations, both in the UK and abroad.

Sign up to our mailing list for our latest news, for opportunities for one-on-one coaching, special offers for "Essence of Womanhood" readers, and dates of workshops and talks, and to hire Susie Heath as a speaker at your event.

Be the first to know of the launch of Susie Heath's next books.

Written in the Rainbow

Discover the SECRET that hundreds of women around the world are using to build lasting confidence and self-esteem in 2 months or less

Tried and tested by women in business worldwide, our easy to follow activities and exercises give you all the tools you need to dramatically improve your personal, working and home life at the snap of your fingers.

Whenever you're short on time, feel over-stretched, or exhausted from a hard day at work, you can find **instant relief in its pages.**

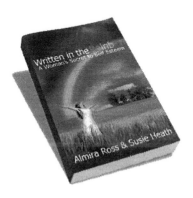

Whenever your boss is being impossible, when the kids are playing up, when you just can't cope any more, give your frazzled nerves a rest. **Discover tried and tested techniques to recover your calm and boost your energy.**

Whenever you find it hard to speak up for yourself for fear of being criticized, **discover how to handle criticism** and hurtful remarks with ease.

Whenever you feel fat, ugly or unattractive, learn how mirror work can **easily change your self-image and your shape.**

If you're successful, yet still feel there's something missing, learn how to **find your purpose and get into your flow.**

Discover the *secret to real self-esteem*. See how easily you can change, and how effortlessly your outside circumstances change as you do.

Order your copy of Written in the Rainbow: A Woman's Secret to Self-Esteem today

And rediscover the great woman that you are.

Call +44 20 8427 5894 or visit www.path-to-freedom.com to order your copy today

Made in the USA
Lexington, KY
01 March 2012